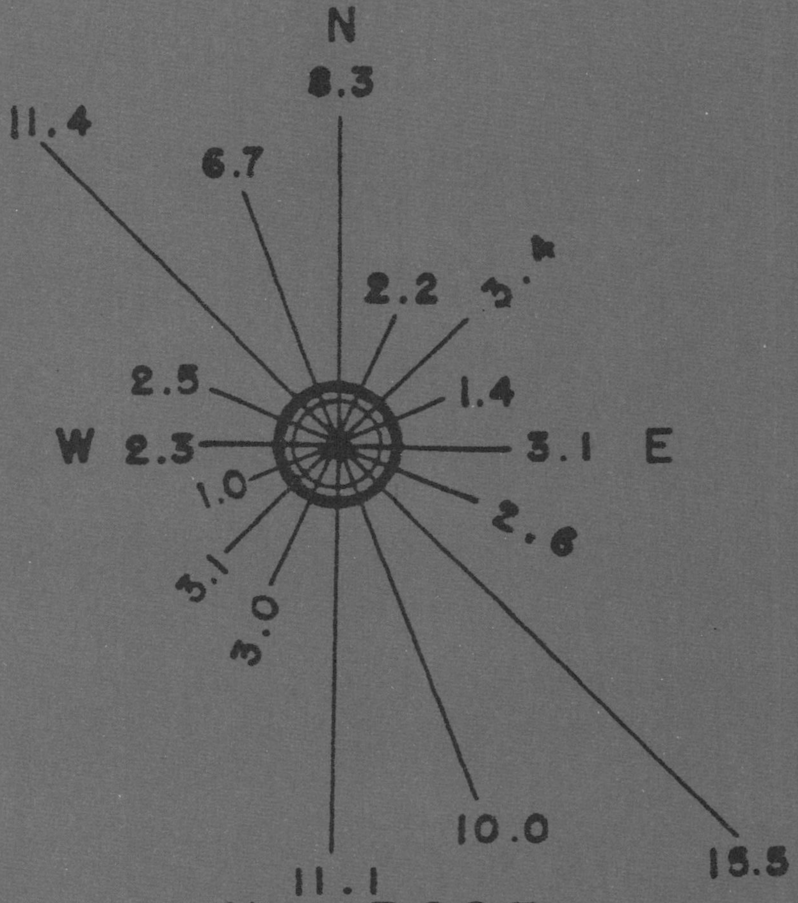

WIND ROSE

SCRIBNER AIRFIEL

DODGE COUNTY, NEBR.

VICINITY MAP

ALTITUDE 1320' MSL

Lieutenant Colonel George A. Larson, USAF (Ret).

GREAT PLAINS WARRIORS OF WORLD WAR II

AIR BASES and PLANTS Built for WAR

Schiffer Publishing Ltd®
4880 Lower Valley Road • Atglen, PA 19310

Library of Congress Control Number: 2014949129

Printed in China.
ISBN: 978-0-7643-4379-7
We are interested in hearing from authors with book ideas on related topics.

Published by Schiffer Publishing Ltd.
4880 Lower Valley Road
Atglen, PA 19310
Phone: (610) 593-1777
FAX: (610) 593-2002
E-mail: Info@schifferbooks.com.
Visit our web site at: www.schifferbooks.com
Please write for a free catalog.
This book may be purchased
from the publisher.
Try your bookstore first.

All maps are from the Directory of Airfields, Continental United States, Department of Commerce Civil Aeronautics Administration, September 7, 1945.

DEDICATION

With so many different people involved in winning WWII, the contributions that Nebraska contributed to winning the war are overlooked. I am dedicating this book to the citizens of Nebraska and to all the men and women who served during the war from the state or trained in the state for combat worldwide. Their stories are told in this book. Those who could not fight worked building the air bases and war production plants, were neighbors to POW camps, and worked in war industries, air bases, POW camps, and on farms and ranches. Their sacrifices made victory possible during the war, and as members of America's greatest generation, we owe them the freedom we all enjoy today.

PREFACE

From 1990 through 1991, my wife and I traveled throughout Nebraska, visiting WWII sites. Eleven of these were former Army Air Force air bases that trained airmen to fight the air war in Europe and the Pacific. This was prior to the restrictions imposed after the terrorist attacks on the United States on September 11, 2001. Many of the facilities and buildings are gone. We also visited former munitions production plants with no one stopping our investigations. Shortly after our visits, these sites were closed due to the Environment Protection Agency fencing them off and starting cleanup of hazardous chemicals from the production process necessary to fight a two-ocean war. The most exciting was visiting former POW camps in the state that housed German and Italian POWs whose labor in the agricultural and ranching sector was vital to maintaining the home front's food production. I was stationed at Offutt Air Force Base and my office was in the former Glen L. Martin-Omaha B-26/B-29 production plant. This plant produced the famous B-29s used by the 509th Composite Group to deliver the two atomic bombs on Japan, ending the war in the Pacific.

Keep us flying!
BUY WAR BONDS

CONTENTS

INTRODUCTION

World War II locations of United States Army Air Forces Bases (USAAF) and military installations supporting war preparations in Nebraska during World War II. (Author)

During WWII, the state of Nebraska, located in the heartland of the United States, was the site of eleven USAAF air bases, providing training facilities for fighter pilots; medium, heavy, and very heavy bomber aircrews; transport aircrews; glider pilots (glider infantry and paratroops); aviation mechanics; and armaments personnel. The state was the site of important war industries, agriculture and ranching, and farming to support U.S. troops and their allies operating around the world. These stories were documented during two years of research (1990-1992), as the war sites disappeared and members of the Greatest Generation pass away. This part of the war effort has been ignored, when looking at the battles and places U.S. personnel fought and died.

The open spaces of Nebraska's farm and ranch land were ideal to build large air bases with expansive concrete runways, taxiways, parking aprons, hangars, and various support buildings. Some of the hangars were immense, built to hold the Boeing B-29 Superfortress, which was larger than the B-17 and Consolidated B-24 Liberator. Nebraska's towns—Ainsworth, Alliance, Bruning, Fairmont, Bellevue/Omaha (Fort Crook), Grand Island, Harvard, Kearney, Lincoln, McCook, Scribner, and Scotts Bluff—prospered as AAF air bases and war plants were built and operated; war spending on these facilities pulled these towns out of the Great Depression. The bases and war industry construction, payrolls, and operating expenditures provided economic stimulus for a cash-short Nebraska and employment opportunities that included large numbers of women replacing men who were drafted and enlisting in the U.S. Armed Forces. The United States mobilized to fight a total war, with everyone involved on the home front. After WWII, some air bases closed and others changed roles or functions. Few Americans today know of the important roles these air bases and war plants played in training airmen and support personnel to fight the global war.

One squadron from the 504th Bomb Group (BG), assigned to Fairmont Army Air Field (AAF), became the core squadron for the 509th Composite Group (CG), referred to as the "Atomic Bomb Group." The 509th's B-29s were built at the Omaha-Martin B-29 plant at Fort Crook. The 509th dropped the only two atomic bombs in combat (6 August on Hiroshima and 9 August on Nagasaki, Japan). The two atomic bombs convinced the Emperor of Japan to force the military and cabinet to accept

Boeing B-17G Flying Fortress, *Sentimental Journey* (serial number N9323Z) flew combat missions in the Pacific during WWII. After the end of the war, it transferred to Eglin Air Base, Florida, as a sea-air rescue aircraft until 1959. The aircraft flew into the modern turbojet era of the United States Air Force (USAF) and went into storage at Davis Monthan Air Force Base (AFB), Arizona, until it was sold to a private company in California. The aircraft was converted to a Borate fire bomber and used in western United States forests. In January, 1978, the aircraft was donated to the Arizona Wing, Confederate Air Force (now called the Commemorative Air Force, CAF), Mesa, Arizona. A CAF crew flew the B-17G to Rapid City Regional Airport, South Dakota, for static display and rides for military veterans and aviation enthusiasts. (Author)

the Allied terms of unconditional surrender. This precluded the planned U.S. amphibious invasion of the Japanese home islands and deaths of hundreds of thousands of American service men, along with possibly millions of Japanese who were prepared by the military to fight to the end rather than surrender.

By early 1940, the United States began a slow economic recovery from the effects of the Great Depression, fueled by Lend Lease military shipments to England and China. The nation also began to meet demands of gradually increasing military expansion to be prepared for the dangers from Germany, Italy, and Japan. The U.S. military had a long climb to recovery from its years of neglect after WWI, yet was not prepared to fight a modern, two-ocean war. The Imperial Japanese Navy (IJN) carrier attack on the U.S. Navy (USN) and associated military installations at Pearl Harbor, Hawaii, the morning of December 7, 1941, forced the rapid expansion of America's air power to meet the urgent necessities of a two-ocean war. Air bases were needed to train thousands of pilots and aircrews and maintenance and support personnel. The AAF replaced the U.S. Army Air Corps (USAAC) on 20 June 1941, to better organize, equip, and train to meet the apparent military threats from Europe and Asia. After the United States entered WWII, there was not adequate time for an orderly transition from peace to wartime operations.

This Consolidated B-24J Liberator was restored to flying condition by the Collins Foundation, requiring over 97,000 hours to complete. The restored Liberator is named "All American," in honor of a WWII 15th AF bomber that was credited with shooting down fourteen German fighters over Germany in 1944. The Collins Foundation flew the Liberator to Rapid City Regional Airport, South Dakota, for static display and rides for veterans and aviation enthusiasts. (Author)

The only flying B-29 in the United States, "Fifi" is operated by the CAF, Midlands, Texas. It was flown to Epley Field, Omaha, Nebraska in 1990. Author is in the foreground. (Author)

Omaha-Martin B-29 plant at the northwest end of the runway at Fort Crook. After production ended on the B-26, the plant was expanded to produce the larger four-engine B-29. A B-29 is visible at the end of the production hall at the western end of the plant. Other B-29s are parked at the modification center to the upper right of the photograph. Courtesy of Strategic Air Command (SAC) Historian, SAC Headquarters (1990), Offutt AFB.

On Sunday morning, 7 December 1941, Americans learned of the Japanese attack on Pearl Harbor by breaking radio news broadcasts. This radio and home parlor display appeared in the Nebraska State Historical Society exhibit at Lincoln, Nebraska, "What did you do in the war?" The exhibit opened on December 7, 1991. (Author)

Two months after Pearl Harbor, the Second Air Force (2AF) was released from its responsibility of defending the U.S. North Pacific Coast against possible IJN carrier attacks on military installations and war industries. This was not a realistic threat, although the IJN did conduct limited submarine shelling of isolated areas. The Pearl Harbor attack wounds took time to drop off the front page and from the attention of the American public. For the first six months of the war in the Pacific, newspaper headlines printed one military reversal after another as the Japanese swept outward from Japan, occupying large areas. The 2AF assumed responsibility for AAF training of heavy bombardment aircrews and support personnel. The War Department modified aircrew training to spread functions over many bases, to prevent over-crowding and to use existing facilities without immediate construction updates. The AAF began a three-phase aircrew training program with a 30-day cycle at each base. This maximized training operations in a short period. To assist air base operations, base training units functioned as if overseas in a combat group.[1]

For Nebraska citizens, their first contact with WWII hardships was the implementation of rationing twenty essential items. In combination with price controls established to stop inflation and war profiteering, the federal government attempted to distribute scarce goods to both civilians supporting a growing military and Lend Lease to the Allied nations. The first ration was sugar, followed by coffee and shoes. Gasoline rationing had the greatest impact on American daily life, especially farmers and ranchers, whose distances used up large amounts of fuel, not including farm and ranching operations. Each car owner was issued a specific gas rationing sticker identifying that driver's purchase priority. Most Americans were issued the standard "A" sticker, the lowest allocation priority, that provided from three to five gallons of gasoline each week, allowing excess production to be used by the military. After the Japanese military victories in the Dutch East Indies cut off the supply of raw rubber, tires disappeared from service stations and wholesale houses. It would take the development of synthetic rubber to alleviate the rubber shortage, but this was still not enough to meet civilian and war demands. The U.S. used its crude oil production and refineries to fuel the war against the enemy. The complex program on domestic consumption control was meant to prevent hoarding, by evening out civilian distribution. Colored stamps were redeemed for a specific time. The program was administered by the Office of Price Administration (OPA), which permitted specific rationing of scarce commodities required to fight the global war.[2]

Primary AAF training bases functioned with the surrounding air bases to rapidly decentralize aircrew training and meet the War Department's escalating requirements for combat air groups.

During WWII, American women in war production were depicted as young, white, and middle class with glamorous looks. Good looking young women's photographs were used on recruiting posters to assure women they would not sacrifice their attractiveness working in war industries, replacing men serving in the U.S. Armed Forces. With so many men in the military, women filled essential positions in war factories and on military bases, farms, and ranches, performing jobs previously considered for men only. Company labor management committees created posters encouraging and empowering women as never before in their lives. This empowerment was narrowly defined. Women were encouraged to follow orders and work hard, but defer decision making to their male supervisors. The poster is from the WWII traveling exhibit, "Produce for Victory, Posters on the American home front, 1941-1945," sponsored by the Smithsonian Institution and State Humanities Council. The poster was displayed at the South Dakota Air and Space Museum, Ellsworth AFB. (Author)

Satellite training air bases performed all the training functions of larger training bases, but with reduced facilities. Aircrew training was maximized, temporarily bypassing time-consuming and expensive air base construction. Only those facilities directly related to training and support functions were initially built at satellite training bases.[3]

War construction programs began in earnest by June 1942, along with fierce lobbying from Nebraska's congressional delegation and citizens' committees from towns where bases and war industries might be located; there were thousands of others to be considered and authorized. Federal funding was no longer an obstacle, after the nation shifted from retarded Great Depression civilian production to all-out war production and mobilization. United States Senator George A. Norris, of McCook, Nebraska, believed his state was not being considered for its share of war construction projects, including AAF training bases. Senator Norris lobbied President Roosevelt to locate military bases in his state. Senator Norris pointed out that Nebraska's weather—although at times extreme in the winter—averaged favorably for yearly flight training operations. Nebraska's scattered population centers left most of the state open for construction of large military bases, training operations, gunnery and bombing ranges, and military support facilities. The open land provided ample space for low-level, hazardous flight training and construction of live-fire bombing ranges.[4]

Nebraska was also important to America's war effort in producing food. The United States had to feed its civilian population and military, along with its Allies. During WWII, rain fell in adequate levels in the central United States and western plains to end the Dust Bowl, allowing production of crops and fodder to feed exploding livestock numbers. Large numbers of men left farms and ranches to join the military or work in high paying war plants. It was part of the war effort to defeat common enemies. The acute labor shortage became so critical that the U.S. Congress passed the Tydings Amendment to the Selective Service and Training Act, to grant deferments to essential agriculture and ranch workers along with war plant workers, until replacements were found. This led to the use of thousands of immigrant (illegal) farm and ranch workers; women also worked on farms, ranches, and in war industries.[5]

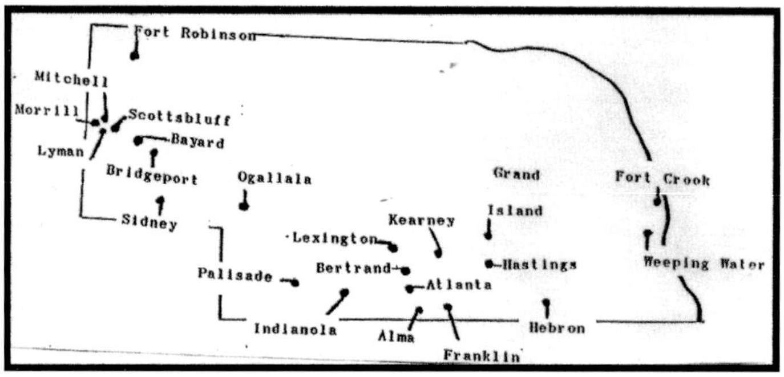

Approximately 12,000 POWs were held in camps in Nebraska. Main POW camps were built at Atlanta, Fort Robinson, and Scotts Bluff. Satellite POW camps were built at Alma, Bayard, Bertrand, Bridgeport, Elwood, Fort Crook, Franklin, Grand Island, Hastings, Hebron, Indianola, Kearney, Lexington, Lyman, Mitchell, Morrill, Ogallala, Palisade, Sidney, and Weeping Water. (Author)

German POWs under guard, marching into the main camp at Fort Robinson, in the northwestern panhandle of the state. They carried what possessions they had, retained after military weapons and items were removed by capturing and screening troops. Fort Robinson's camp consisted of three separate enclosures. Courtesy of Fort Robinson Museum, Crawford, Nebraska.

Prior to the IJN attack on Pearl Harbor, rumors were rampant that Nebraska would have sites authorized to build federal defense plants. Through the efforts of the state's congressional membership, war plants were built at Omaha (the Omaha-Martin B-26 plant, later converted to produce the larger B-29); Mead, Nebraska Ordnance Plant; Hastings, Naval Ammunition Depot; Grand Island, Cornhusker Ordnance Plant; and Sidney, Sioux Ordnance Plant. Each war plant would employ thousands of workers and pump millions of dollars into local economies starved for cash; it was their way out of the Great Depression. The influx of thousands of workers looking for employment created a severe housing shortage. Many farm and ranch families whose land hand been either condemned or purchased for these war plants argued this was an unfair process; at undervalued prices from the Great Depression they were displaced, with many forced to take jobs in war plants without housing.[6]

After the American and British invasion of North Africa, large numbers of POWs (Germans and Italians) were captured or surrendered. The United States started to receive small numbers of Japanese POWs and the numbers increased as fighting continued, although the majority of Japanese soldiers fought to the death, even when there was no hope of success. Enemy POWs were transported to Nebraska and other states into camps away from large cities, coastal areas, and borders.

Nebraska was ideal for the construction and operation of POW camps. The state's population was concentrated in large cities, with ample land for main and satellite camps. These camps pumped money into Nebraska's economy. More importantly, once POWs were screened for political doctrine they could be assigned to work in agriculture or ranching under acceptable use of POW labor as defined under the Geneva Convention on the Treatment of Prisoners. Nebraska was critically short of ranch and farm workers and POWs filled gaps in manpower in the production of food. POWs in America's wartime agricultural production became important as men and women moved into the military, war plants, and federal employment. Over three million Axis soldiers were captured before fighting ended in Europe. The United States took custody of 370,000 German and 50,000 Italian troops. England could no longer house more enemy troops, as empty areas were turned into troop encampments, military equipment parking areas, and storage depots for the planned English Channel invasion of France. Canada was over-stressed with existing numbers of Axis troops and had neither the troops nor resources to house additional POWs. Nebraska's location in the center of the United States was remote, away from coasts and population centers.

Satellite POW camps provided secure locations to house POWs so they could work on farms, in orchards, on ranches, and on other agriculture related projects, such as cleaning out irrigation ditches clogged by weeds or mud. The treatment of enemy POWs in Nebraska was considered very good by these Germans and Italians, except for hard-core Nazi POWs who were not allowed to work outside the main camps. The United States respected POW rights, as guaranteed under provisions of the Geneva Convention. POWs performed non-war related work and were paid a small hourly salary. When not working, they were allowed to play sports in their compounds, pursue hobbies, and take educational classes. When the war ended, many POWs remained in Nebraska because they were not allowed to go home until after the fall 1946 harvest. Nebraska was still short of farm and ranch workers, with military men not released from active duty, and even though war plants released workers, many decided not to return to their home counties, opting to remain in the large urban areas they became used to during the war.[7]

Many Nebraska farm and ranch owners suffered after the federal government initiated confiscation proceedings of their land for construction of war industries and air bases. Even though the federal government confiscated 129,000 acres in Nebraska valued at approximately five million dollars, the state had 128,000 farms and ranches operating. In 1942, during

Hastings, Nebraska was also the site of Harvard AB and within driving distance of Kearney, Grand Island, Fairmont, and Bruning ABs. The city was severely impacted by the need to find housing for construction workers staffing the air bases and war plants, including those working at the Hastings Naval Ammunition Depot. To ease the lack of housing, over seven hundred box-shaped trailers were moved into the city to establish a temporary workers' trailer park. Photograph from "What did you do in the war?" exhibit at the Nebraska State Historical Society at Lincoln, Nebraska, December 7, 1991. (Author)

increased war commitment as the U.S. shifted to mobilization, Nebraska ranked 12th in national farm income (approximately 496 million dollars), the highest in twenty years.[8]

By the middle of 1942 (in the midst of Pacific war news of Japanese ground, air, and naval victories, along with general war unpreparedness to fight an air war in Europe), the AAF had to manage thousands of war contracts worth seven billion dollars. Nebraska's share of these construction projects was administered and managed by the U.S. Army Corps of Engineers, Engineer Division VIII, Missouri River Division.[9]

Even as the massive military base construction program began in 1942, regardless of the urgency, it took six to nine months to complete the first group of AAF training bases and another seven and one-half months to graduate combat aircrews. Plans to fight an air war in Europe began prior to Pearl Harbor, in October 1941, with a growing realization of war involving the United States. To fight the global war, the AAF altered its training program to retain as many pilots and aircrew personnel as possible. Pilot candidates washing out of training transferred to bombardier, navigator, engineer, armament, communication, photographic, intelligence, or meteorology officer training. This enabled the AAF to meet officer requirements, especially bomb group production. No officers in the AAF visualized the high loss rates by the Eighth AF daylight bombing campaign over German-controlled territory. The concept was to fly unescorted at high altitude in tight formations, protected by each bomber's ten guns, dropping bombs using the Norden bombsight. The AAF was determined to validate the concept of high-altitude daylight bombing. It was not until North American P-51 Mustangs took on the Luftwaffe, clearing the skies over occupied Europe and Germany, that bomber loss rates were reduced. Improvements to P-47 Thunderbolts tore up the Luftwaffe and gained air superiority over Europe. These two fighters enabled the medium and heavy bombers to isolate the Normandy landing beaches and airdrop zones from German Army attack, keeping the skies above the invasion clear of enemy fighters.

On 24 May 1940, the Lincoln Airplane and Flying School, at Lincoln, Nebraska, was created. It was one of nine U.S. civilian USAAC pilot training schools under the War Preparedness and Expansion Training Program. Pressure to expand flight training after Pearl Harbor—before the AAF could expand its pilot training program—led to the creation of forty-one such schools throughout the United States. This was a short term, stopgap program until construction and military training facilities started turning out the numbers needed to fight the global war.[10]

Even in Nebraska, civil defense preparation against an enemy attack was required. Blackouts along the U.S. east and gulf coasts were essential, to stop offshore shipping lane sinkings by German U-boats. A small number of U-boats nearly halted the flow of vital war material—especially petroleum by tanker to England—desperately needed to fuel England's military equipment. Blackouts were part of the Battle of the Atlantic, which had to be won to build up troops, equipment, and supplies to invade Axis occupied areas. Russia desperately needed a second front to siphon German military forces and equipment off the Eastern Front.[11]

Lorena Smith, of Hastings, Nebraska, remembers: "I was twenty-seven after Pearl Harbor, when the first back out exercise was conducted. It was somewhat scary. It was held on Monday, 14 December 1942, from 10 to 10:20 p.m.; everybody was supposed to douse his or her lights completely. We hung

WACO CG-4A Hadrian glider. Glider crews trained in the powerless aircraft at Alliance AB. This glider was first used in limited numbers in combat in northern Burma in March 1944 during "Operation Thursday." Later it became better known during the large Allied airborne operation on 6 June 1944, the invasion of Nazi-occupied France, opening the second front. Selected airframes were saved from destruction after the end of the war, with many restored and on display in museums throughout the United States. Courtesy of WACO museum to author.

blankets over the windows. You had to turn off all the lights. You were not allowed to use the telephone. You could not light matches or use flashlights outside. All automobile traffic had to stop and turn off their lights and park, with the engine switched off. The blackout lasted until an all clear was sounded in each town. When the siren went off, it sounded one long blast and we would know the exercise was over and could go back to what we were doing. During the blackout and following air raid drills, volunteer wardens were permitted to patrol the neighborhoods. These exercises were taken seriously. Those who did not comply with posted regulations were fined. With civil defense awareness and the abundance of air traffic from AAF training bases, airplane spotting became a hobby in the state."[12]

The 2AF managed and implemented an accelerated training program designed to turn out the maximum number of heavy bomber aircrews, while meeting pilot quotas. AAF generals at the Pentagon believed existing air base runways and selected civilian airport runways could be used to support heavy bomber training. Unfortunately, these runways were built for lighter load pressure specifications. Repeated landings and take offs by heavy four-engine bombers rendered these runways useless within sixty days because of furrowing, requiring the runway surface to be dug up and resurfaced. U.S. Army Corps of Engineers tests indicated heavy four-engine bombers had to operate from thicker runways. It was recommended these runways only be used for emergencies. The alternative for maintaining levels of heavy bomber aircrew training if these airfields could not be used was to increase satellite training operations from squadron to the combat group organizational level.

AAF bases that supported training in Nebraska and those located in the state during WWII. (Author)

WWII fighter hangar at Sioux City Gateway Airport, Iowa. During the war, the air base functioned as headquarters for the 15th BW, supervising training operations at Scribner AB, Nebraska. The hangar, now modernized, was built of wood, quick to be erected, and was designed to last five to seven years. Many of these war structures continue to be used. A Federal Aviation Authority (FAA) control tower is visible behind the hangar. The area had many warehouses (1991) that have been replaced by newer buildings. (Author)

The Consolidated B-32 Dominator was designed as a very heavy, four-engine, long-range bomber as back up for the Boeing B-29 Superfortress. The AAF ordered 1,200 B-32s, but due to the B-29's success and production problems at Consolidated, only 114 B-32s were delivered to the AAF. Another ten production line B-32s were turned over to the AAF after the war. All B-32s were destroyed after the war, with none saved for museums. Photograph: Lockheed Historical Office, Fort Worth, Texas.

The use of satellite air bases allowed heavy bomber aircrew training to reach full capacity by September 1943, graduating six bomb groups (882 personnel) each month. The increase in training severely taxed satellite air base facilities, which were not eliminated until an additional Replacement Training Unit (RTU) cycle was added to the heavy bombardment training cycle.[13]

As the war continued, two new heavy bombers were developed, produced, and entered combat, although only one was in series production. The Consolidated B-32 Dominator was developed as a backup to the B-29, with limited production overshadowed by the Superfortress. The War Department issued large production orders for the B-29 while the bomber was still in engineering design and testing, creating post-production problems. These problems delayed the bomber's deployment to the CBI and the bombing of the Japanese home islands. B-29s were supposed to bomb Japan from four Chinese-built air bases, because the Marianas Islands (Saipan, Tinian, and Guam) were still under Japanese control. These islands became bases for large numbers of B-29s.

Consolidated also designed the very heavy, six-piston, pusher engined B-36, later named the Peacemaker. It had the range to fly from U.S. east coast air bases to bombing targets in England and Europe.

In 1940, during the Battle of Britain, the War Department feared the Luftwaffe was on the verge of defeating the RAF and an amphibious English Channel invasion was inevitable. The B-36 would be used to take back the British Isles and set up for an Allied cross-channel invasion of Nazi-fortified Europe. After the RAF defeated the Luftwaffe, the B-36's production priority dropped. Consolidated was heavily committed to building the B-24 and the B-32 took up remaining slack production line capacity at its Fort Worth, Texas production facility. The B-36 had to wait until the war ended, with production space eliminated for the B-24. The B-36 eventually provided the postwar United States Air Force (which became a separate service in 1947) with its first long-range, very heavy, strategic atomic bomber for the Strategic Air Command (SAC). SAC

After the end of WWII, Consolidated Aircraft Company became Convair. The Convair B-36 strategic bomber replaced the B-29 as the Air Force's heavy bomber, with the B-29 downgraded to a medium bomber. The B-36's design began before WWII, with series production only after the war. It equipped SAC with a long-range bomber able to reach targets deep inside the Soviet Union. The bomber was powered by six pusher engines, upgraded to the B-36D with the addition of four General Electric turbojet engines. This B-36D was assigned to the 28th BW, Ellsworth AFB, SD. Courtesy of 28th BW, Office of Historian, Ellsworth AFB, South Dakota.

had a bomber that could reach targets deep inside the Soviet Union without refueling.

AAF training for the B-29 had to be merged with the B-17 and B-24. This was made somewhat easier later in the war, as the number of training air bases for the B-17 and B-24 declined with the establishment of air superiority in Europe and reduced loss rates required less aircrews out of the training program. B-29s were built at three large production facilities: Boeing at Renton, Washington; Omaha-Martin at Bellevue/Fort Crook, Nebraska; and Bell Aircraft at Atlanta, Georgia. To meet increased bomber training while the air war raged in Europe, the AAF added an additional B-17, B-24, and B-29 training group each.

Second Air Force training bases in Nebraska were: Ainsworth, Bruning, Fairmont, Grand Island, Harvard, Kearney, McCook, Scribner, and Scotts Bluff. The Omaha-Martin plant played a significant role in bringing an end to the war in the Pacific. Lincoln was the site of the U.S. Army's Technical Training Command's Airplane Mechanics School. Alliance AB served as a training base for First Troop Carrier Command (C-47 aircrews, CG-4A pilots, and glider infantry and paratroop). Alliance came under Second Air Force control in September 1944.

Alliance personnel trained many of the C-47 aircrews, CG-4A pilots, glider infantry and paratroops who took part in airborne operations on D-Day, 6 June 1944. The Normandy operation opened the delayed Second Front demanded by Premier Joseph Stalin after the Germans invaded Russia. After German forces were stopped nineteen miles west of Moscow and forced to withdraw from Stalingrad and Leningrad, and were defeated during the large tank battle at Kursk, the urgency of a second front was reduced.

Second Air Force accelerated heavy bombardment aircrew training by increasing the number of aircrews at each base to 147. This met the current loss rates and provided for additional bomb groups to increase the number of bombers against Germany and Italy. With fifty aircraft on each base, squadron administrative and support facilities were increased to permit twelve aircraft per squadron. The AAF authorized only minimum facilities to be upgraded and new construction was limited. Base housing for officers and enlisted personnel was considered adequate, although over-crowded, but far better than expected in combat theaters of operation. This was war and time spent at a training base was short. The 2AF's goal for each training cycle was one B-29, one B-17, and four B-24 groups: Fifteenth Wing, Sioux City, Iowa, directed training at Scotts Bluff and Scribner ABs;

Seventeenth Wing, Rapid City, South Dakota directed training at Ainsworth; and the Twenty-First Wing, Salina, Kansas directed training at Bruning, Fairmont, Harvard, Kearney, and McCook.[14]

During WWII, many Nebraska communities organized canteens inside their railroad depots served by Union Pacific, which moved troops east or west to support the war in the Pacific or Europe. The North Platte Canteen was the most famous set up in Nebraska and possibly the United States. The canteen started because of a mix-up. Ten days after the Japanese attack on Pearl Harbor, North Platte residents were told their hometown Nebraska National Guard, Company "D," would be passing through, transiting on a troop train to the west coast before boarding a troop ship for an unknown location in the Pacific.

At the former Alliance AB (1991), the only remains of the large B-29 hangars are the tall brick chimneys at the rear of each hangar. These hangars once lined the edge of the base's aircraft parking aprons, with a squadron operations building between each hangar. This view looks west along the gravel service road behind the hangars. (Author)

North Platte's residents collected cookies, candy, gum, sandwiches, coffee, and cigarettes. They brought these items to the depot, setting up tables with all the goodies and waited for the train to stop. The train stopped, but as the troops disembarked they were Company "D" Kansas National Guard. They were fed and residents decided to meet all the subsequent troop trains, serving those onboard. On 25 December 1941, the North Platte Canteen was created. This was not a small undertaking given war rationing. The canteen was always full of food and refreshments and staffed by volunteers twenty-four hours a day. On average, the canteen served 3,000 to 5,000 servicemen and passengers each day. When available, magazines and entertainment were provided. Funds were raised by the citizens of North Platte and surrounding communities. The canteen closed operations in April 1946, after welcoming home thousands of service men and women.[15]

Nebraska's air bases slowly rose from empty fields, sprouting black and orange, checkerboard-patterned water towers; blue-green colored, glass-covered aircraft control tower windows; and arch-roof aircraft hangars of different sizes and construction. The bases were filled with temporary, wood frame buildings, most covered with tar paper siding or locally procured materials and set on concrete blocks for foundations, to speed construction and raise the wooden floors off the ground. It was determined these buildings only had to last five to seven years. These wooden structures were converted into squadron operations, headquarters, engineering, barracks, recreation, medical, chapel, mess hall, officer and enlisted clubs, and everything else requiring a building on each air base. The U.S. Army Corps of Engineers supervised construction activities at Bruning, Fairmont, and Harvard. Construction supervision for remaining Nebraska air bases was transferred from the Kansas City District Office to the Omaha District Office. This office supervised construction at Ainsworth, Grand Island, McCook, and Scribner.

During WWII, troop trains crossed the United States, stopping at various depots to drop off military personnel at training bases or pick them up. The majority were pulled by steam engines. Civilian passengers were also on these trains, but in fewer numbers. This is typical of the trains stopping at the North Platte Canteen operated by the Union Pacific Railroad. Courtesy of Union Pacific Railroad historian.

Training bases at Grand Island and McCook were initially built as satellite air bases, but were later expanded to main base configuration. Facilities at Scribner underwent an unusual experiment in testing airfield camouflage; U.S. Army Corps of Engineers personnel used large amounts of paint and locally procured texturing material to blend airfield structures into the surrounding terrain.

At Scribner AB, selected buildings were covered with chicken wire stuffed

Photograph of a surviving WWII aircraft hangar at McCook AB (1991). It was large enough to hold a B-29. At the top center, above the sliding doors a large square opening is visible, which when opened allowed the B-29's tail to stick out of the hangar when the bomber was towed inside for maintenance. The same method is used on hangars at Ellsworth AFB, allowing a North American B-1B lancer to be towed inside with the tail enclosed by the circular cutout above the door, sealed with fabric to keep out the elements. This hangar lasted longer than expected. The concrete apron in front of the hangar was used for outdoor maintenance of B-29s requiring minor repairs or servicing prior to the next training mission. The concrete remained in relatively good condition, although grass grew through the edges of the poured slabs. The concrete lasted longer than anticipated, supporting the heavy combat weights of the B-29. (Author)

At Scribner AB during WWII, as part of an unusual airfield concealment experiment, the base's aircraft hangar was painted to look like a farmer's barn. The barn outline is on the right side with trees painted on the left side. On the far right side of the hangar, where the doors retracted, an outline of a storage silo was painted. Other concealment experiments were conducted on selected buildings on the base. Eventually, it was determined none of these efforts would fool a detailed aerial reconnaissance by enemy aircraft. (Author)

with chicken feathers and were spray painted to blend into the background colors. Runways, taxiways, and parking aprons were covered with finely crushed corncobs in an attempt to determine if these flat surfaces could be hidden from aerial reconnaissance. This camouflage technique was time consuming, labor intensive, and expensive, changing colors as weather changed, in an effort to maintain background color compatibility. The experiment was dropped, but it makes another WWII story.

The Omaha District directed the upgrade of Grand Island AB. It required extensive grading, paving, and improved drainage for all-weather operations for heavy bomber training. Large aircraft hangars and support buildings for increased training operations were built. While all this work at Nebraska's air bases was in progress, construction work in the state was hard pressed to keep up with changing War Department, AAF, and Corps of Engineers requirements. It was necessary for Second Air Force planners to adjust officer and enlisted barracks' occupancies, to eliminate barracks construction. However, some construction could not be eliminated. Kearney AB was built to accommodate two training squadrons, then was expanded for four. Additional construction cost $240,000 and aircraft parking another $300,000.[16]

A surviving WWII hangar (1991) at Grand Island Airport. The hangar could accommodate a B-29 because of the tail opening above the sliding hangar doors. The large four-engine bomber could be towed inside with only the tail sticking out into the weather. The brick chimney is part of the hangar's heating plant. This is an excellent example of a large wooden hangar built to last for five to seven years and continuing on for many more years. The long one story building in the front of this photo, but actually along one side, was used as parts storage. Other similar buildings near hangars were used for squadron operations. This gives a rare, surviving view of a flight line at a WWII heavy bomber training base. Wood was easy to obtain and allowed rapid construction of training facilities. (Author)

There were not sufficient educational facilities to train officers to meet AAF aircrew production quotas for expanded flight training. A stopgap officer training program was implemented to meet officer requirements. Hastings College, in Nebraska, was selected for AAF officer training. The officer program consisted of six cadet officer classes, each of forty cadets, with a class starting every thirty days, commissioning the first group of Second Lieutenants in 180 days, then another group every thirty days. Officer candidates took selected college courses (academics) and physical conditioning. As AAF military training ramped up at newly constructed military air bases, the college officer program ended. Those cadets near the end of the program were no longer essential and were given the option to transfer to non-pilot aviation classifications. For those who just started the program, they were offered enlisted classifications, including gunner. This was not acceptable to those who wanted to be officers and enlisted—especially a gunner—was viewed as a death sentence on a combat aircrew.[17]

Nebraska's air bases served as staging bases for B-17 and B-24 aircrews prior to deployment overseas, primarily England and the Mediterranean. Grand Island AB began operations as a training base for aircrews headed to the Eighth Air Force in England. Harvard and Fairmont ABs later became retraining air bases for select aircrews transitioning to the B-29 for Pacific combat. Scotts Bluff and Alliance ABs also trained pilots to fly the P-51 and P-47. AAF personnel conducted a peaceful occupation of Nebraska.

Throughout the war, Nebraska residents were continually exposed to many types of propaganda supporting the war effort. "V" for victory was one of the most patriotic images. The story of AAF air bases built and operated in Nebraska during WWII is a seldom told and forgotten part of the war effort and the

WWII home front posters helped mobilize a nation faced with combat in Europe and the Pacific. They were inexpensive to produce and could be displayed anywhere; an ideal media to inform the civilian population on how to help the country and soldiers fighting far away. Federal agencies, war plants, and private companies created poster images linking the war "over there" to the home front, inspiring Americans of all ages to do their part. Poster from "What did you do in the war?" at exhibit at the Nebraska State Historical Society in Lincoln, Nebraska on December 7, 1991. (Author)

patriotism of those who served in the war. Wood frame buildings built to support training aircrews were only to last until the end of the war, but some survived long after the war. Most of the structures are gone. In 1990, the Nebraska State Historical Society researched the significance of the state's remaining WWII structures and installations to determine if a selective restoration was possible. Unfortunately, not much came of this effort. A few private organizations saved some structures. Even concrete runways, taxiways, and parking aprons have disappeared. I completed my own historical research, expanding my scope of this book to air bases, war plants, POW facilities and other war support areas. It is not possible to tell every story in complete detail, often not meeting expectations nor the memories of those who served during the war. The events of 1941-1945, viewed in 2010 as I write this book, are my part to retain a segment of WWII history for future generations. This is the story of Nebraska residents and service men and women and those who came to the state to help win the war.

Image courtesy of the U.S. Geological Survey

Satellite image from the U.S. Geological Survey of Ainsworth Airport. The airport is located six miles northwest of Ainsworth. The photograph gives a good view of the large area required during WWII to train combat aircrews.

CHAPTER ONE

AINSWORTH AIR BASE

Ainsworth, Nebraska, is the county seat of Brown County, located in the northwest panhandle, four hundred miles northeast of Denver, Colorado.[18] After the United States entered WWII, Ainsworth's residents began hearing rumors that the War Department was looking into the possibility of establishing a bombardier training school on an air base in the area. Ainsworth's mayor announced on 8 September 1943 that a Federal Employment Agency team would be in town to set up an office and take applications for workers to build a new air base near the town. On 27 August 1942, U.S. Army surveyors and Army Corps of Engineers personnel were seen at the proposed air base site, eight to ten miles northwest of town. The advanced survey and engineer teams set up temporary offices in the city auditorium. These engineering teams prepared drawings and specifications to allow contractors to submit construction bids.

Within two weeks, ninety percent of required construction contracts had been signed for work on the air base. Corps of Engineers personnel were impressed with the proposed air base site; surveys indicated only minimum grading would be required on a few sections of the air base. Workers began cutting corn on the site to prepare for runway grading and finishing. Consumer Power Company moved high voltage electric transmission lines away from the runway and flight operations. One of the down sides of construction was the U.S. Army's condemnation proceedings, beginning on 14 September 1942. Legal notices of federal condemnation seizure were sent to land owners to create the required air base acreage. The air base would consist of 2,480 acres and was designed to be a satellite training air base under the direction of Rapid City AB, South Dakota. The air base's primary mission was to prepare bomber aircrews for combat. The air base was classified a complete Second Air Force OTU.[19]

The Ainsworth (NE) *Star Journal* printed a good description of construction activities at the new air base. Interestingly, Army sensors did not block its publication, because it did not reveal secret information. "The development of the bomber field west of town has started in dead earnest. All week, workers have been pouring into town and the Government Employment Office on 3rd Street has been a busy place. Most of the workers come from other construction projects: Hastings, Alliance, etc., and they certainly seem to know their stuff, as far as construction work is concerned. One unnamed worker, talking to a reporter, indicated the work in progress is very important. 'We have a job today for you out there.' And we find, as we met them on the street, in their homes, that they are, just an average run of the mil tough, with a hard job to do and they are going to do it. Tough, you bet! Some of them got their toughness twenty-five years ago during World War I on the battlefields of France and from what was seared into the souls there; they know what this is all about. Others, of lesser years, got their toughness in the fields of Nebraska fighting the drought of the last ten years. All of them have sons, brothers, a few even perhaps fathers scattered all over the world and realize that if they are to win there, they must do the job here. They are just common Americans. The beautiful fields of corn are being cut down, temporary construction site buildings have been erected for engineers and construction contractors, with a mass of machinery of all sorts suddenly on the construction site from somewhere, along with trucks of lumber, sewer tile and building materials of all sorts are coming into the construction site and being unloaded, with everyone working there tearing into it and doing the job."[20]

As cornfields were cleared, construction of temporary site buildings began for contractor offices and on-site work sheds for storing equipment, with more added as the number of contractors on-site increased. An air base construction site is a mass of heavy and light construction equipment constantly shuttling from one area to the next, along with the arrival and departure of heavy trucks delivering lumber, bricks, cement, and all the material needed to turn an empty location into an

Main gate of the newly constructed Ainsworth AAFB, looking east towards the air base's parking apron. Barracks and warehouses are visible in the background. Courtesy of Nebraska State Historical Society (NSHS) to author.

AAF air base. The airfield was built in a triangular pattern with three runways (each 7,500 feet long and 150 feet wide), one parking ramp 250 feet long, thirteen 75-foot diameter aircraft parking hardstands, a control tower, hangar, and an underground fueling system. Theater of Operations type construction was used in the buildings, except for the hangar and dispensary, which were classified as mobilization type construction—wood and not deigned to last more than five years. There were many contractors involved in building Ainsworth Air Base: Nixon and Adams, Layne Weston Company, Anderson Construction Company, C.W. Roberts Engineering Company, and Clifton Engineering Company among them.

The air base was to be supported by the Chicago & Northwestern Railroad via a spur track, accommodating aviation gasoline tank car delivery directly into the base's petroleum storage area. To support ground access, six miles of

A hangar to the left, aircraft parking apron near the hangar, and a control tower in the far right of the photograph. Squadron operations buildings are to the left of the control tower. Courtesy of NSHS to author.

stabilized gravel road was built. To reduce cost, only limited paving was completed; under the plan, the air base was not to be a permanent military facility. As construction work progressed, the AAF made design changes to meet increased aircrew training requirements. These changes had to be balanced against planned facilities, so only minimum additional construction would have to be authorized. Contractors built sixty-four buildings to house 544 enlisted and 112 officers. The housing units were ready for occupancy within sixty days of the start of construction. Mess facilities consisted of one enlisted and two officer dining facilities. These mess halls fed construction workers on the site and arriving military personnel. A ten-bed dispensary was built to provide medical care. Provision was provided to set up a 1,400 square foot storage area to support training requirements. Water was supplied by two eighteen-inch, concrete-lined gravel wells dug to a depth of 63 feet, with a maximum capacity of 200 gallons per minute. This provided seventy gallons of water per person, per day, for the 2,400 assigned to the air base. To adequately distribute the water, a 100,000-gallon water tank provided adequate pressure and fire hydrant operations. Natural gas was not available. Coal was used as the primary heating and cooking source. The dispensary, hangar, armaments building, and warehouses were heated by warm air or hot water. Barracks, mess halls, and auxiliary buildings used space heaters. Electricity was purchased from Consumer Light and Power Company in Columbus. Sewage disposal was handled on base through an Inhofe tank and underground field dispersal system.

Because of problems in delivery of critical construction materials, the Office of the Area Engineer, U.S. Army Corps of Engineers provided pipes and fittings for the underground water distribution system from a nearby War Department defense project. Once the pipes and fittings arrived they were trucked to the defense project for installation, given that project's longer construction timetable. Even with the dispersion from this defense construction project, there was not enough pipe on site to complete the water distribution system. To make up for the lack of water pipe, engineers decided to use reclaimed A.P.I. steel pipe trucked in from Wyoming oil fields. This pipe comprised ninety percent of the water pipes buried for the distribution system. Most of the fittings came from the same source. All pipe and associated fittings were steam cleaned to remove scale and oil. This compromise allowed the air base to be completed on schedule. This action was typical of construction procedures during the war, when construction materials were hard to obtain due to the massive military infrastructure construction projects throughout the United States and around the world. Road grading and final surface application was a separate contract. It took coordination with the on-site supervisor to complete grading, installation of field drainage, and proper grade attainment prior to surfacing to remain on schedule.

Construction work in progress on the large aircraft parking apron. The hangar is to the far right, just off the edge of the photograph. The photograph was taken from the newly completed control tower. Again, sufficient room was provided to handle the B-29 after aircrews began training in the aircraft if required on the air base, with many transitioning from B-17s and B-24s. Courtesy of NSHS to author.

One significant slowdown in construction resulted from a scarcity of workers. The United States Employment Service made every attempt to locate and recruit available workers. The situation at Ainsworth was typical of other military construction projects in Nebraska and the United States. Many workers moved from one construction project to the next. These workers were valuable and it seemed there were never enough available to meet demand. As more Ainsworth AB contractors arrived on site and started work, labor shortages grew more severe. It became so bad that Ainsworth AB contractors ran advertisements in Omaha and Lincoln, Nebraska, as well as Sioux City, Iowa papers. This was not very productive, with only a small number of workers recruited and not nearly the number needed. Native American laborers were hired and brought to Ainsworth from Pine Ridge and Rose Bud Indian Reservations. Today, in Rapid City, one can go to a specific employment bureau and hire Native Americans as day laborers. They worked hard and did an excellent job today as during WWII. However, during the war three separate labor camps were built: two at Ainsworth—one for the Native Americans and one for the white workers—and the third camp in Ainsworth. As construction work progressed, finished barracks were temporarily used to house construction workers. It also became necessary to feed workers on site in temporary mess tents until the permanent mess hall was completed. The on-site mess facility saved time and allowed construction work to continue without hours wasted to feed so many workers. Sanitary conditions on the construction site fell under the responsibility of the Safety Department, Corps of Engineers Office. These temporary housing and feeding adjustments eliminated overcrowded sleeping accommodations in Ainsworth and the surrounding area. This was a positive factor in recruiting workers for Ainsworth AB. At peak construction,

View looking east along the main access road, with barracks to the left and a supply and maintenance area to the right. Courtesy of NSHS to author.

over 1,200 workers filled the base. These workers followed AAF modifications after start of construction to lengthen the primary runway to 10,000 feet to meet requirements for an operational 8,000-foot runway, plus one foot added length for every foot above sea level. No one knew why this change had been requested. When B-29s began training, AAF length requirements became evident. A combat-loaded B-29 required 8,000 to 8,500 feet of runway, plus 750-foot overruns to provide for safe operation. This is the length of the runways built in the Marianas Islands for combat-loaded B-29s to bomb the Japanese home islands.[21]

Corps of Engineers supervisors followed precise specifications for runway construction. Runway cross section for full-length paved runways and a 1,000-foot clear zone conformed to AAF grading criteria to improve flight operations. The cross section was essential for Second Air Force airfields; if an aircraft went off the concrete runway (pilot error, engine failure, unexpected high cross winds, etc.), the aircraft would not be damaged. The cross section eliminated sharp changes in grading, eliminating steep banks along the runway. Prior to this modification, many heavy aircraft were severely damaged when going off the edge of a runway.

Aircraft taxiway widths increased to 75 feet, with 12 1/2 foot stabilized shoulders. This allowed safe aircraft movement and passing clearance for heavy bombers, especially the larger B-29. Prior to this modification, inexperienced pilots had problems staying on 50-foot wide taxiways. If an aircraft ran off this taxiway width it took time to tow it back onto the taxiway and move out of the ground traffic flow. While this was in progress, following aircraft were blocked, creating a bottleneck and often stopping flight operations. If the aircraft was far enough off the taxiway, following pilots taxied at slow speed, referred to as "at a walk." The only alternative was to increase taxi operation distances to one and one half miles, reducing flight operations. This is why the modification was critical for current and future training operations (when the B-29 flight training commenced).[22]

Corps of Engineers directed an increase in aircraft hardstand parking diameter from 75 to 120 feet to accommodate larger aircraft without running of the pad. This was for B-17 and B-24 aircraft, without the larger B-29s on the scene at this time. Again, bomber pilots were running them off the hardstands while turning around. The time necessary to "right" these aircraft deprived aircrews of valuable training. With the planned introduction of the B-29 and its increased span between the main landing gear, the hardstands had to be bigger. If an aircraft did run off the larger hardstand with the stabilized edges, it could be rapidly repositioned on the hardstand.[23] The real reason for these modifications was to allow for safe training for the B-29. This was only known to a selected number of AAF officers and Corps of Engineers personnel.

All items of construction at Ainsworth AB were completed prior to 30 November 1942. The initial contingent of AAF personnel did not arrive until 11 December 1942. The first squadron (543rd BS, 383rd BG) trained in the B-17. At this time in the war, the majority of B-17 aircrews were assigned to the European Theater of Operations, especially to the Eighth Air Force. For the Eighth Air Force, it was a matter of numbers (aircrews and aircraft). Until the number of bomb groups increased, bombing raids were limited in number and effectiveness. The Eighth Air Force flew precision, high-altitude, daylight bombing raids, while the RAF flew less accurate night area bombing raids, primarily targeting German population centers. RAF Bomber Command's Arthur Harris believed that the morale of the German civilian population could be broken by the terror of night incendiary raids to destroy military production. This did not happen, even with AAF daylight and RAF night bombing raids. The destruction of German cities was tremendous, but the war continued. Many mistakes were made during the Allied bombing raids, such as not continually attacking ball bearing production, railroad yards, and petroleum production (especially the synthetic oil operations that fueled the German military). As more B-17s reached England, increased raid strengths were flown. However, initial losses almost forced a stop to daylight bombing. Aircraft production and aircrew training provided more crews than lost during the Battle of the Atlantic.

Training was credited with improved efficiency and survivability of bomber aircrews. Residents of Ainsworth and surrounding communities saw B-17s flying with P-47s at low and high altitudes, practicing fighter escort and bomber defensive tactics. Other fighter training aircraft from training bases were sent as hostile intercept forces and mock dogfights and bomber gunner training commenced. This provided B-17 aircrews realistic aerial combat. Fighter gun camera film was developed and analyzed for attacking and defending fighters. Gunner camera film was developed and analyzed to better train each gunner. This training increased aircrew defensive coordination. Pilots were taught to fly tight box formations, allowing a bomber's ten guns to be added to those in the combat box. If an aircrew fell out of formation due to combat damage, it had a very low percentage of making it back to home base.

The second training element to arrive at Ainsworth was a fighter group flying the Bell P-39 Airacobra. This fighter group trained at Ainsworth AB from 6 October to 10 November 1943. The AAF did not like this aircraft, although Russian pilots thought it a rugged aircraft, well suited for ground attack operations against the German Army on the Eastern Front. Many of this fighter type wore the painted Red Star in combat over German military forces. The final fighter group to train at the air base was the 53rd, flying the P-47. This group trained at the base from 23 November 1943 to 11 March 1944. The group lost three P-47s during training. The first was lost over Bock County, when the pilot parachuted from the aircraft because the cockpit filled with smoke. The pilot told debriefing officers he believed an electric malfunction created a fire and it was only a matter of time before the aircraft blew up. He was very fortunate, as the other two pilots did not survive. The two pilots were killed during a mid-air collision over the Cheery County Gunnery Range. The fighter group completed its required training and deployed to England.[24]

Ainsworth's bombing range was located in Tripp County, thirty miles west of the base, and consisted of 2,300 acres. Its size allowed ample combat training operations. The gunnery range was 7,680 acres. Each range had three pattern sections. However, as indicated by the mid-air collision of the two P-47s, ground safety officers worked constantly to clear each range for proper aircraft spacing and live fire operations. If one pilot or two pilots lost concentration while focusing on the ground target, a sudden appearance of another fighter or bomber left little time for evasive maneuvers. The AAF decided to enlarge the two training ranges. Once again, local landowners were unhappy with the federal confiscation procedures and money received for their land, equipment, houses, and crops at depressed prices. The bombing range added four square miles and the gunnery range twelve square miles.[25]

The AAF set up a camouflage school to teach personnel how to create trees from boards and tin cans to mask structures in the surrounding terrain. The camouflage building was ninety-six feet long and fifty feet wide. The 2AF's attempt to teach camouflage was a follow-up to the initial experiment at Scribner AB. Instructors demonstrated how to build what appeared to be a woodshed, but was actually canvas that could be collapsed in seconds, uncovering a manned anti-aircraft gun. This gave the anti-aircraft gun's crew 360 degrees of fire to protect the airfield from attacking enemy aircraft.[26]

On 30 November 1942—eighty-eight days from the start of construction—Ainsworth AB became operational. Unfortunately, an operational shortfall was identified. The base aviation fuel storage area, with a capacity of 75,000 gallons, could not support twelve aircraft flying an average of eighteen hours a day, which would consume 42,000 gallons. The already over-taxed railroad fuel tank car availability and movement from large petroleum storage areas could not be a daily occurrence. Storage capacity had to be increased to 105,000 gallons to allow at least two days of flight operations before off-loading railroad tank cars at the aviation storage area. It was difficult for railroad schedulers to meet the two-day supply operation, given the distance from the petroleum tank farm, lack of tank cars and locomotives, and heavy train track on the railroad system. As more AAF training bases became operational, the strain on the railroads increased.[27]

The single hangar on the air base was eighty feet wide, but only 20 feet deep. It was classified as a nose hangar, allowing B-17s to be towed in with engines inside and their tail sticking out the door for maintenance work out of the weather.

To decrease aircraft maintenance time, a petroleum oil and lubrication storage building was built near the aircraft parking ramp. It was built of concrete block to prevent fire. Courtesy of NSHS to author.

In combat zones a hangar might not be available, so maintenance was performed on the flight line. To meet combat maintenance operations, AAF engineers designed a temporary hangar. C-47s could airlift the hangar to a forward field, unload the hangar, and allowed for quick assembly. The air-transportable hangar was designed by Scott Tent & Awning Company of Omaha, Nebraska, and manufactured by the Butler Company of Kansas City, Missouri. The hangar had a steel framework with fabricated sections of fire-resistant canvas, creating an arched roof structure with walls. The canvas was opaque to let in light and waterproof. Canvas sections were erected and laced to the steel framing by a system of ropes hung from pulleys. The finished hangar was one hundred feet wide and sixty feet deep, with a center height of twelve to eighteen feet. The seventeen crates were numbered to reduce assembly time. Interestingly, the crates would magically disappear. Airmen took the wood to make furniture, improving their living areas and some for wooden barracks. The hangar could be used in all combat theaters of operations: not only for aircraft maintenance, but also for temporary barracks, warehouses, vehicle motor pool maintenance, hospitals, or as required. The hangar could be camouflaged to blend into the surrounding terrain. In cold weather operations, the roof and walls were strengthened to support snow and were insulated. Each sixteen-foot panel weighed 4 3/4 tons, and the total weight was 52 tons.[28]

The Norden bombsight vault storage building consisted of two concrete vaults, each secured by a combination security lock. The vault was guarded twenty-four hours a day, seven days a week. The Norden bombsight was considered so top secret that bombardiers were ordered to destroy it prior to bailing out of a damaged bomber so the Germans would not obtain the technology. It is rare this type of structure remained intact so long after the end of the war. (Author)

Ainsworth AB remained an active AAF training facility until 27 March 1944, then going into standby status. Assigned personnel were transferred to other Second Air Force training bases, leaving only a minimum servicing section on the base. After flight training ended, the runways were classified for emergency landing and aircraft reconstitution. On 30 March 1944, the airfield's medium power loop range navigation system was shut off and the equipment dismantled and shipped to another AAF installation.[29]

On 24 October 1946, the Ainsworth Municipal Airport Air Service began operations at the former air base. A serviceable license was granted to the City of Ainsworth by General Dick, Division Engineer, Missouri River Division, U.S. Army Corps of Engineers, under authority from the Secretary of War and signed by Ainsworth's mayor and city council. The license gave the city the right to use fourteen of the air base's buildings, control tower, sewer system, and light and power distribution to include the emergency/standby power plant, runways, a total of 2,396 acres, and any remaining equipment. The bulk of the buildings were controlled by the Resident Engineers Office, U.S. Army Corps of Engineers, until transferred to the War Assets Office for disposal. Nearby Thorley Field ceased civilian operations and was placed on standby status, as operations were transferred to the large airfield complex. The City of Ainsworth could begin flight operations as a civilian airport facility because the federal government approved their application of *Use of Surplus U.S. Property*.[30]

Even though the City of Ainsworth was responsible for the former air base's operations, upon receiving a request from the federal government during a declared national emergency, Ainsworth's airport would return to temporary military control and operation. The runways had to be operationally maintained

A surviving WWII bombardier training building. After the war, the building was re-sided and used to store aircraft equipment. (Author)

for all-weather use. To upgrade civilian flight operations, the control tower was managed by the Ainsworth Airport Authority. The Airport Authority built a new administration building and installed an aerial agricultural chemical loading apron to support commercial crop dusting. Crop dusting aircraft were fitted with dispersal storage tanks to support area ranching and farming operations.

The hangar's exterior was resided to provide a more modern appearance and allow for a more comfortable interior working environment. The Airport Authority installed new underground aviation fuel storage tanks to support light and commercial flight operations. Between 1984 and 1989, the Airport Authority spent $600,000 federal, state, and city funds to upgrade the airport for all-weather commercial and civil aviation operations.[31]

The Ainsworth Airport Authority tried to save a few of the former air base's WWII buildings in the early 1990s. The

A single brick chimney now sticking up out of an empty field. The chimney was used to heat one of the motor pool buildings on the former air base. (Author)

twenty-six by thirty-eight foot bombardier building was resided. A rare historic structure, the eleven by thirteen foot Norden bombsight storage vault was constructed out of concrete blocks with two heavy (thick) steel vault doors secured by dial bank locks. During training operations on the base, the Norden bombsights were constantly secured when not in the B-17s' nose compartments with the bombardier present. It was considered too dangerous to risk the Norden bombsight to theft or sabotage in a parked B-17. The fifty foot wide and one hundred eight foot long warehouse was upgraded with steel roofing, steel siding, and steel doors while retaining the WWII wood framework. The twenty by forty foot T-shaped photographic laboratory building processed bomb bay film to track bomb impacts and gunner film to evaluate defensive gunfire against attacking enemy aircraft. The restored and modernized former air base buildings provide a look back at WWII AAF training operations.[32]

Modernized WWII aircraft hangar and updated parking apron. (Author)

WWII photographic processing building. When I went inside the building (1991), I located photographic wash and processing tubes, wood tables for enlargement equipment, and a small chemical storage area, along with photographic film storage. The building had been abandoned and not destroyed. (Author)

Modernized WWII supply/warehouse building. The WWII wood buildings were built quickly and designed to last until the end of the war in 1946-1947. Military planners were getting ready to conduct a large scale amphibious invasion of the Japanese home islands because that country's military and political leadership showed no indication of agreeing to the Allied terms of unconditional surrender. (Author)

CHAPTER TWO
ALLIANCE AIR BASE

After Pearl Harbor, the U.S. Army started to develop new tactics, including the deployment of massed airborne paratroops and delivery of glider infantry, following German use of gliders and paratroops in Belgium and the airborne capture of Crete. It took time for tactics used by German airborne forces to be evaluated and incorporated into the U.S. military. With a need to deploy a large airborne force, AAF officers determined the panhandle of western Nebraska suitable for this type of training, with open spaces to construct a large airborne facility.[33]

In March 1942, a Base Site Board Advisory Group consisting of AAF officers, Corps of Engineers personnel, and one civilian glider expert traveled to Alliance, Nebraska, to evaluate if the area met criteria for an airborne and glider training facility. They spent two days reviewing the area as a possible air base site, listing advantages and disadvantages, geographic suitability, and estimated construction costs. As a group, they requested an Alliance City Council presentation on lease options and negotiations for a military base near their town. At the

WACO CG-4A gliders produced by the Northwest Aeronautical Corporation (NAC) parked outside the factory pending aircraft tow out of the factory airfield to stateside training bases. Other CG-4A gliders were crated for rail shipment to ports of embarkation to overseas combat zones. Photograph on display at the World War II Glider Symposium, World War II History Round table, Fort Snelling, Minnesota (twin cities of Minneapolis and St. Paul).

The open areas of the proposed airborne and glider training air base were ideal for large numbers of C-47s, CG-4As, and associated glider infantry and paratroops. The grass areas around the concrete runways allowed for simultaneous aircraft take-offs, landings, and grass landings of gliders and paratroops. The open areas also allowed for troop exercises and combat marches. (Author)

A clamshell crane drops dirt into a dump truck during construction in the warehouse area. The warehouse visible in the background has Army trucks unloading supplies into the building, supporting construction and later training operations. Courtesy of Knights Museum, Alliance, Nebraska.

conclusion of the on-site inspection and meetings with city officials the Base Site Board Advisory Group did not indicate if a base would be built.

It took until 10 June 1942 for the AAF to inform town officials a training base would be built east of Alliance at an estimated cost of three million dollars. The Alliance City Council believed the deciding factor that tipped the scales for an air base was the town's power plant's excess capacity of 2,500 kilowatts; power to the air base site only required construction of electric transmission lines to the base and a substation.[34]

The air base's construction was formally announced by United States Senators George Norris and Hugh Butler (Nebraska), along with United States Representative Harry Coffee (South Dakota), on 15 June 1942. The air base would become a primary AAF training facility located on 3,265 acres with a 1942 estimated land value of $100,000.[35]

The air base would be controlled by Troop Carrier Command, training paratroops, airborne infantry, CG-4A pilots, and C-47 pilots and aircrews on airborne tactics and combat operations, as well as providing ground crews experience with C-47s and gliders. Civilian architects and U.S. Army Corps of Engineers advance staff set up offices in an empty Alliance storefront to begin preparation of blue prints and estimation of construction costs (materials and labor). Costs escalated to fifteen million dollars to create a large airborne training base.[36]

As construction bids were received and accepted, the arrival of contractors created an immediate office and housing shortage. Empty storefronts immediately became occupied, with rents escalating as demand created an instant economic boom. Alliance residents rented every available room, garage, shed, attic, basement, and animal barn to workers. Businesses turned warehouses and storerooms into sleeping barracks—crowded, but inside out of the weather. Contractors hired all available men and women to work on the airfield, with others hired as cooks, clerks, secretaries, and other necessary skills. There were still not enough laborers available to meet government construction deadlines.

Engineering building at Alliance AB. Its wood framework is covered with tarpaper secured by vertical wood strips. The building was functional, but not designed to be a permanent structure. The base hired many civilians and some of their cars are parked around the building. Courtesy of Knights Museum, Alliance, Nebraska.

Empire Construction Company of Omaha, Nebraska was awarded the paving contract for the four 9,000-foot concrete runways, taxiways, and parking aprons, as well as installation of water and sewer systems to Alliance distribution and processing plants.[37] Empire Construction converted an empty ranch house into a temporary office until one of the first barracks was available. After Empire Construction moved its offices into the completed barracks, the ranch house was torn down to clear the area for airfield construction.[38]

A construction company of Boise, Idaho was awarded the grading contract, except for the rail bed spur line into the base. Northwestern Engineering Company of Rapid City, South Dakota built most of the wood barracks and support buildings. These were turned into lodging for temporary contractors and Corps of Engineers offices, workers' sleeping quarters, and a mess hall. These completed buildings eliminated overcrowding in Alliance, which reduced rent income for local residents. E.G. Gee Company of Shenandoah, Iowa built the primary and

Base motor pool. It took a considerable number of trucks to keep an air base operating, from fuel trucks to cargo trucks and everything in between. Most were parked outside. Courtesy of Knights Museum, Alliance, Nebraska.

Mannequin dressed as an AAF Second Lieutenant in his dress uniform, positioned along the right side fuselage of a CG-4A on display at the Silent Wings Museum's former location at Terrell, Texas, prior to moving to its current facility at Lubbock, Texas. (Author)

Mannequin dressed in a WWII enlisted glider infantry uniform. Most in the glider infantry were not volunteers as paratroops; they were assigned to Alliance to learn glider tactics and procedures. The first use of gliders in combat by the U.S. military was in Burma. In northern Burma, during Operation Thursday, prior to the large D-Day amphibious and airborne invasion of France, British, Chindit, and American troops were transported by CG-4A gliders into northern Burma. The mannequin is on display at the Knights Museum, Alliance Nebraska. (Author)

secondary road system on the base. The General Contracting Company of Rushville, Nebraska built the warehouses and hangars. G. Meredith, Murdock and Associates of Denver, Colorado provided on-site architecture and engineering support. U.S. Army Corps of Engineers on-site representatives' revised construction plans after the AAF increased the base by 1,442 acres for airborne training.[39]

Heavy earth moving equipment cut down hills to level ground for the runways. Earth scrapers and bulldozers moved large amounts of dirt to construct runways, taxiways, and parking aprons. Workers rapidly erected buildings throughout the large air base's administrative and support areas. Most impressive of the wood structures was the row of hangars, large enough to hold a B-29. An even larger hangar was built at the end of the west end of the hangar row and was referred to as the Base Engineering Maintenance Inspection (BEMI) facility. It was used for aircraft inspection, extensive maintenance, and AAF or manufacturer engineering modifications.[40]

In September 1942, the first group of AAF officers arrived, dressed in lightweight cotton uniforms not suitable for the cold weather of western Nebraska. After the first heavy snow, the base commander dispatched a C-47 to Lowry Field, Denver, Colorado, to pick up winter weight officer and enlisted uniforms. Eventually, U.S. Army Quartermaster Corps' supply of uniforms caught up with demand as war contracts shifted from civilian to clothing manufacturing to meet war requirements. There were civilian shortages and rationing by the middle of 1943.

At peak construction, contractors employed 5,000 workers in a massive effort. They built 755 buildings and laid 35,503 linear feet of concrete runways and 12,232 linear feet of concrete taxiways. The runways were built to a length calculated by AAF Troop Carrier Command Officers to meet minimum C-47 and glider take-off rolls and landing operations.

AAF officers estimated the distance required by one C-47 towing two combat-loaded CG-4As on take-off would require 7,000 feet. Once training operations started, actual take-off distance was 2,500 to 3,500 feet. The longer runway provided for a considerable margin of operational safety and would later allow for B-29 training operations.

By 1943, thousands of airborne glider infantry and paratroops, along with glider pilots and C-47 aircrews, filled the base. By January 1944, over 14,000 paratroops were at the base, most training for the planned English Channel airborne support operations of the large amphibious landings in Normandy, France on 6 June 1944. To prepare troops for expected house-to-house fighting to clear German troops from French towns and cities, U.S. Army engineers built a unique training complex out of scrap wood and salvaged material they called "Fuerherville."[41]

Fuerherville was built to resemble a European town, with a church, stores, homes, and city hall. These were false fronts with no depth, like those used on a Hollywood movie stage backlot. The structures permitted troops to practice urban warfare tactics: infiltration, house-to-house movement while under enemy fire, and defense against the inevitable enemy counterattack. These types of military operations were expected to be encountered with more frequency as U.S. troops advanced out of France and crossed into Germany. It was expected German troops would fight fiercely as Allied troops approached and crossed into German territory. Adolf Hitler ordered his troops to stand and fight with no retreat, as on the Eastern Front at Stalingrad.[42]

Not only was Alliance AB critical to training C-47 and CG-4A pilots in airborne operations, but Troop Carrier Command and Airborne Command officers worked together to develop combined tactics on the air base. Flight crews had to learn formation flying, experience loading and airborne paratroop

One of the few brick warehouses built on Alliance AB that survived long after the end of the war. (Author)

A mannequin dressed as a glider pilot with a Mae West life vest that could be inflated by a cartridge if necessary if his aircraft went down into the English Channel. The pilot is wearing earphones for communications from the C-47 tow aircraft through a wire wrapped around the nylon towrope. On display at the Silent Wings Museum's former location in Terrell, Texas, prior to moving to its current facility at Lubbock, Texas. (Author)

Alliance AB fire station, probably the best surviving WWII example of such. This example consisted of three bays, with two surviving wood doors and one metal overhead installed during an upgrade. The fire station crew lived in the wood frame building covered with tarpaper siding. (Author)

Due to the haste of wartime construction at Alliance AB, the majority of wood buildings (barracks, administrative, and support) were not built on permanent foundations. Concrete blocks were laid on the ground and leveled and wood floors laid on top, with the rest of the building erected as in the current modular home construction projects. The grounds of the former Alliance AB contain thousands of these concrete blocks. It is amazing these concrete blocks remain on the ground in the pattern set out during construction. (Author)

jumps, and towing one and two gliders with glider infantry and equipment. Teamwork was essential to a successful airborne operation and was lacking during the Allied airborne invasion of Sicily. The post operation Sicily airborne evaluation stated tow aircraft aircrews and glider pilots needed increased joint training and preparation for future airborne operations.

Because of the Sicily post action airborne report, Alliance AB became the prime location for advanced training for Troop Carrier Command and Airborne Command pilots. Even with this added training emphasis, time was running against precise plans for full operational training timetables. A shortage of aircraft and trained personnel and receipt of deployment orders to move units to England made it impossible to reach the desired goal of optimum preparation. Many C-47 and glider pilots and glider infantry and paratroop exposure to each other was during D-Day loading operations. The situation would have been worse without their training at Alliance AB. The rush to get troops and equipment to England as soon as possible before the D-Day operation had a speed of its own, constantly gaining momentum and urgency. What does not make sense is the lack of joint airborne training once in England. There was a sense of security over German intelligence piecing together separate training exercises and figuring out what the Allies were doing.

On 23 August 1943, Alliance AB held its dedication and open house. Paratroops jumped from C-47s flying over the large grass landing area, enacting what the announcer commented was a re-enactment of the Sicily airborne operation. Alliance AB was opened for a friendly invasion of an estimated 66,000 civilians able to enter the base before the air show, with thousands stuck in a massive traffic jam on the narrow, two-lane road to the base. Most of these people got out of their cars, sat down on the ground, and watched the air show in the distance. Once the aerial demonstrations were complete, they got back into their vehicles and started home, long before those on base could reach the two-lane road and drive home. Those on the base watched a formation of C-47s towing CG-4As, then cutting them loose from the nylon towropes as the gliders landed on the grass adjacent to the concrete runway and discharged glider infantry, jeeps, artillery trailers, and combat equipment.[43]

Officers' club at Alliance AB. A large warehouse structure was turned into the officers' club. Lights were installed along each side of a wide central aisle, with two rows of tables on each side covered with tablecloths, silverware, cloth napkins, and condiments. The wood floor was painted and waxed to give it a shine. The doorway to the left center of the photograph leads to another wood side structure containing the kitchen. Courtesy of Knights Museum, Alliance, Nebraska.

On 23 August 1943, Alliance AB held its dedication and open house. (Author)

Example of a surviving WWII squadron operations building located between the aircraft hangars. This building was turned into a warehouse after the war, its condition deteriorating. (Author)

The WACO CG-4A glider was an engine-less, wood and fabric covered tubular steel-framed towed troop and cargo transport. It was one of the most economically produced aircraft of WWII; its average cost, spread out among all glider producers, was $50,000 to $90,000. The large number of manufacturers was deemed necessary because of the Army's requirement for training and combat operations. The Army specified sufficient numbers for training operations, accident replacements, and combat Theater of Operation shipments, including possible losses on transports sunk by German U-boats, gliders damaged during transportation, damaged during assembly, pre-combat training losses, and combat losses.

The CG-4A was initially considered a one-use aircraft for assault landings inside enemy-held territory. The Ford Motor Company in Iron Mountain, Michigan produced the largest number of gliders. Ford converted its wood body station wagon and truck bed factory into glider production. By the end of the war, Ford built over 2,000 gliders out of the production total of 14,000. WACO glider producers were chosen because of their wood manufacturing experience. A furniture company in Grand Rapids, Michigan and Villaume Industries, Inc., of St. Paul, Minnesota supplied component sections to Northwestern Aircraft Company of St. Paul and Anheuser-Bush Brewing Companies' wood barrel factory in St. Louis, Missouri.

The CG-4A's floor was built exceptionally strong to support heavy load combinations: one jeep; a 75mm field artillery gun; a modified field artillery gun; jeep-towed cargo trailer; rocket launcher;

airborne bulldozer; airborne towed grader; three pack mules; thirteen glider infantry; and various combinations not to exceed the maximum cargo weight limitations of the aircraft. The glider's wings were wood box spar construction and wood ribs covered with 1/16-inch Honduran Mahogany. The glider was held together with glue and non-wood covered sections were encased by heavy linen fabric.[44]

During WWII, 6,000 gliders were built, with 3,600 CG-4As delivered into combat theaters of operation.[45] There were many glider crashes during training operations. Many gliders had to be written off during crashes because of a design flaw. Its nose compartment was hinged at the top so it could be raised during loading and unloading operations, especially important when carrying oversized equipment. The glider's design allowed assault landings into combat areas while under enemy fire, exposing pilots and glider infantry to ground fire. The glider's fabric skin provided no protection to enemy fire and was a dangerous mode of transportation into a combat zone, with losses expected during an aerial assault. The glider's nose compartment was fitted with a metal locking mechanism to keep it closed, secured until manually released. Unfortunately, the lock mechanism was too light and not stressed to withstand the pressure to keep it secure during hard landings and abrupt stops when obstacles were hit.

Glider pilots referred to combat landings as "controlled crashes." During a hard landing a jeep, artillery gun, or palletized cargo could be torn loose and violently hurled forward out the front of the glider when the locking mechanism broke. The immediate and sudden release of the nose compartment resulted in a violent upward lift, with the pilots badly injured or killed. This was not a good event for the pilots.[46]

Restored WACO CG-4A at the Silent Wings Museum in Lubbock, Texas. (Author)

Interior of a WACO CG-4A showing the tubular steel framework, with wooden benches on each side for the glider infantry and passengers. The wooden floor was strong enough to carry heavy equipment when the benches were hung up and secured to the aircraft's wall. The pilot's position is visible in the upper right portion of the photograph. One of the canvas doors is visible to the back of the parachutes. It should be pointed out parachutes were not standard issue equipment to the glider infantry; they were considered excessive weight and nonessential on a glider. (Author)

First Troop Carrier Command directed training at Alliance AB, supported by the 507th Parachute Infantry until spring 1944, prior to deployment to England.[47] Army personnel described Alliance AB as a desolate, colorless, level plain located in the midst of an area with brown sandy soil with little vegetation, except for twelve-inch prairie grasses. It was always windy, with sand and dust seeping through the smallest cracks in the hastily-built wood buildings, making training and living conditions miserable. Individual comfort was secondary to combat training.

C-47 on display at the Silent Wings Museum, Lubbock, Texas. (Author)

Army personnel working in the control tower directed multiple take-offs, landings, paratroop drops, and nylon two rope releases. One runway was designed for C-47 and CG-4A launches. During double tow missions, each glider carried one instructor and one student pilot while carrying glider infantry and "equipment" of ballast-filled wood cargo boxes to simulate war operations. The second runway handled C-47 landings. After a C-47 landed, it taxied to the first runway and was positioned by ground crew personnel in front of two loaded gliders for take-off and another training sortie. At 150mph the aircraft were airborne, with the gliders taking off first while the C-47 was still on the ground. While this was in progress, the retrieval crew in a jeep recovered the dropped nylon towrope, hauling it back to the flight line, where it was coiled and laid out for hook up to the next glider and C-47. This went on all day during training operations. As the C-47 pulled the glider, the nylon rope stretched, absorbing the shock of take-off, returning to its original length once airborne. The C-47 towed the gliders to the designated release point, letting the glider go, then flying back to the towrope release point in the grass along the runway. This was a technical and precise procedure of training at the base.[48]

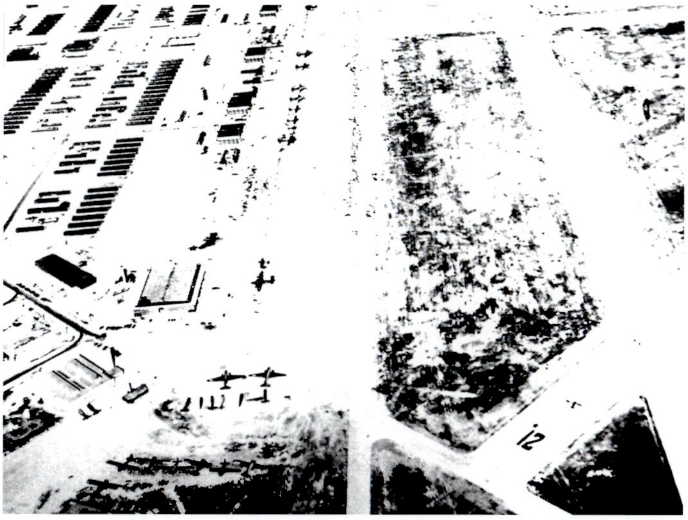

Aerial photograph of Alliance AB in 1943. A group of gliders is visible in the lower left corner and C-47s are parked along the edge of the parking apron, with gliders in the same area. The aircraft hangars and many of the wooden buildings are visible to the left side of the photograph. The base was very large, so this is only a small section of the air base facility. Courtesy of Knights Museum, Alliance, Nebraska.

Sometimes a glider instructor pilot took up a Second Lieutenant C-47 copilot on a training flight. Glider pilots would agree to create a demonstration of their empty gliders' capabilities, which did not happen very often because commanders did not want to damage a glider.

After the double tow launch, the left glider pilot released the tow rope at 1,000 feet, diving to increase speed to 135mph. The right glider pilot released the tow rope at 1,000 feet, climbing to 1,500 feet, then executing a 360-degree turn to give the left glider time to clear the flight area before diving to increase speed to 135mph. The left glider flew low over the ground, while the right glider approached rapidly from behind at 180mph—30mph above the glider's maximum tow speed and under recommended top speed. The left glider executed a near vertical left turn on the base leg, left wing low to the ground. The right glider, when approaching the same location, repeated the previous glider's maneuver, rapidly closing on the left glider. The left glider executed another vertical left climbing turn on the approach leg, rolling out and climbing to 100 feet. The glider pilot went into a nose high, maximum side-slip maneuver using full spoilers, dropping onto the grass landing area in a three point landing, rolling to a stop without brakes. The right glider pilot executed the same maneuver, except making a vertical 270-degree turn away from the grass landing area. The pilot rolled out, climbed to 100 feet, then completed a perfect landing. The young C-47 copilots usually froze during these maneuvers, not believing a 2,000-pound glider could perform or handle like a fighter.[49]

At Alliance AB, glider pilots practiced the ground snatch maneuver. They flew low over a glider, engaging a suspended towrope between two poles. The rope rapidly played out, pulling the glider airborne in two seconds. The nylon rope stretched to take the strain of the launch. Once in level flight, the C-47 aircrew winched in the trailing steel cable and hook until it neared the aircraft, with only the nylon town rope trailing behind. The rope appeared to hang below the aircraft before arching back up to the glider.[50]

The ground transportation route for many Alliance AB trainees (paratroops and glider infantry) was by train, with service provided by Burlington & Northern Railroad, stopping at its passenger and freight depot/terminal at Alliance. The wood depot building was typical of those built in the 1930s, with those surviving into the current time a remarkable piece of past history. The depot had a caged ticket booth—usually located in the center of the depot— wood benches around the inside walls, and sometimes the ticket booth.[51] After the trainees got off the train, they climbed into trucks for the drive to the base. Once on base they were processed and assigned to a squadron barracks.[52]

There was a special WACO Ferry Squadron assigned to tow gliders from the production factories to the glider training bases. With one experienced and one student pilot, glider training was also accomplished on these cross-country flights, with the C-47 aircrew learning how to do their job while towing a glider. Around Alliance AB, local residents became accustomed to seeing C-47s towing one or two gliders, some of these on cross-country tow missions to deliver gliders to Alliance and other training air bases.[53]

The grass area along the edge of the runway was used to drop the nylon towropes to the ground, where they were retrieved and hauled back to the flight line for another tow mission. The nylon tow ropes were pulled by jeeps and loaded into jeep wagons and trucks for movement to the flight line. A lot of towropes were cycled through this area during glider training. The nylon towropes were inspected for any damage before use on another tow mission. (Author)

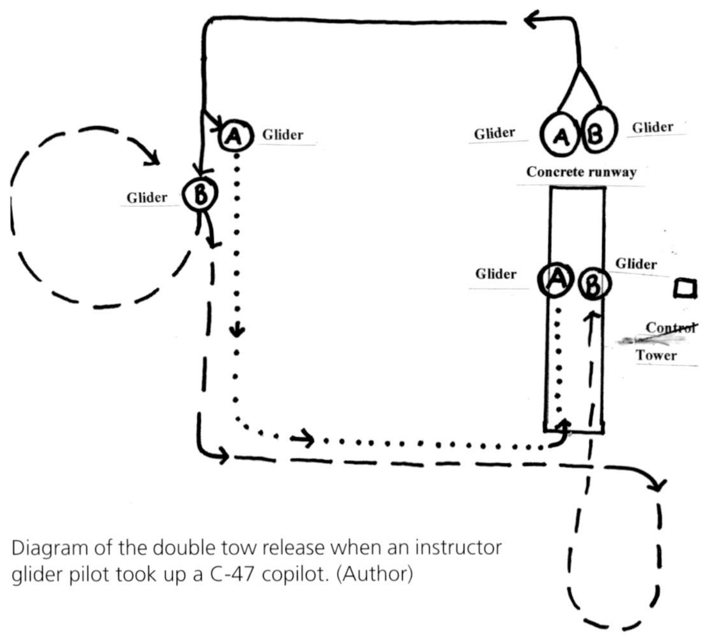

Diagram of the double tow release when an instructor glider pilot took up a C-47 copilot. (Author)

C-47 flying low over a CG-4A on the ground, with a steel hook below the aircraft to snag a rope suspended between two poles to complete a ground snatch, launching the glider rapidly into the air. Courtesy of Knights Museum, Alliance, Nebraska.

The standard U.S. Army jeep could be carried in the CG-4A. This was a display at the Silent Wings Museum's former Terrell, Texas location. (Author)

A link trainer at the Silent Wings Museum, Terrell, Texas. (Author)

At Alliance AB, there were more C-47 pilots than aircraft, making it difficult to meet their monthly flying hour requirements. Many C-47 and glider pilots spent hours in the Link Trainer to gain or maintain their instrument techniques, especially all weather and night flying skills.[54]

A. Link, Jr. designed the small looking trainer aircraft. It resembled a miniature toy, stubby-winged aircraft mounted on a pedestal base. The Link Trainer was capable of duplicating the entire range of an operational aircraft's flight maneuvers. The hooded trainer's cockpit was equipped with a stick, rudder controls, basic flight instrumentation, and interphone communications procedures to the instructor as if talking to a ground controller. Pilots were introduced to the Link Trainer during their basic flight training. Experienced instructor pilots flew the Link Trainer to maintain all-weather flying skills. Even the most experienced pilot sweated when the instructor threw one flight malfunction after another, requiring proper correction to prevent a simulated crash.[55]

Many Second Lieutenant pilots recently graduated from advanced flight school were not too pleased about being assigned to fly a C-47 as copilot. There often were problems for these pilots transitioning into the transport and acting as backup to the pilot in the left seat, who was in control of the aircraft. It was interesting for C-47 pilots to observe their copilots' reactions in the cockpit. Most of the C-47 copilots had the urge to grab their control wheel in front of them during landing, making for some interesting and intense cockpit conversations.

Cross-country C-47 flights without gliders took off at 8 a.m., landing at Sedalia, Missouri at 13:30 p.m. (Central Standard Time). The C-47 returned to Alliance AB after 6 p.m. The daily C-47 flight carried military personnel east and west on high priority orders, and carried mail and high priority cargo. Alliance AB pilots also flew glider maintenance personnel to

Field artillery, which could be carried in a CG-4A. On display at the Silent Wings Museum in Lubbock, Texas. (Author)

A CG-4A on a cross country tow to Alliance AB on 18 July 1943 broke loose from its C-47 and crashed into a field near Grand Island, Nebraska. Courtesy of Knights Museum, Alliance, Nebraska.

repair and retrieve gliders that crash landed during cross-country and training flights. Alliance AB gliders conducted mass training missions to Fort Robinson, Nebraska, west of the base. They were towed to Fort Robinson and cut loose by their C-47, landing on the short dirt runway or in the grass areas nearby. Many gliders were severely damaged or destroyed on landing, turning into piles of broken and mangled parts.[56]

C-47 pilots were not enthusiastic about pulling repaired gliders airborne from the short dirt runway. The pilots saw piles of wrecked gliders pushed together by an airborne bulldozer after spare parts were removed to repair damaged gliders. The gliders would be burned, with metal salvaged, trucked to a nearby railhead, then shipped to a metal reprocessing facility.[57]

On the ground at Fort Robinson, the C-47 aircrew unloaded a nylon towrope, hooking one end to a repaired glider and coiling the rope in front of the glider, with the remaining end attached to the back of the transport. During C-47 engine start and run up prior to take-off, so much dust was kicked up and onto the glider that the glider pilots had to use their instruments when taking off,

Air-transportable bulldozer used to create landing strips for C-47s and light aircraft after gliders landed. Improved runways were built and used to move air superiority forward and supply troops in the field. On display at the Silent Wings Museum, Lubbock, Texas. (Author)

Concrete block wall segments with three doors, steel doors removed, one wall gone, no roof, and concrete debris on the concrete floor. The building was used to store .50 caliber and small caliber ammunition for training flights. It was located in the grass area of the air base, away from aircraft and training areas. (Author)

since they were unable to see anything in front of them. Inside the C-47, the crew chief stood up in the navigator's dome on top of the aircraft, behind the pilots' compartment looking rearward to report when the glider appeared out of the dust cloud. For an aircraft to take off from Fort Robinson's runway, the slope was downhill, making it difficult for the C-47 and glider to reach lift off speed. Once airborne and across the valley off the end of the runway, the C-47 and its glider had barely gained sufficient altitude to clear the surrounding hills. Complicating the removal of repaired gliders from Fort Robinson was that if the C-47 was an early production model, its engines were not as powerful, thus requiring maximum throttle settings. The engines had to be firewalled in order to lift the glider with the tow rope and 100-to-200 pounds of dust on the glider's wings and fuselage that altered its aerodynamic characteristics.

Alliance AB C-47 pilots flew paratroop drop training missions. A normal paratroop stick consisted of sixteen fully equipped troops. C-47 pilots flew these drop missions at an altitude of 600 feet, releasing paratroops into an open field west of the runways. On other training flights, paratroops were dropped miles away from the main runways—sometimes up to 25 miles—requiring the paratroops to march back to base as if in combat, scattered beyond their designated landing area. This is what happened in the early hours of the airborne operation on 6 June 1944.

Paratroop mission profiles required C-47 pilots to maintain an air speed of 110 to 120mph at an altitude of 600 feet, flying straight and level into the drop zone. Four minutes prior to jump, the C-47's copilot turned on the red jump warning light. The jumpmaster told the paratroops to stand up and hook their parachute release straps to the aircraft's overhead wire, one side of the aircraft at a time. Each paratroop checked the other's equipment for correct hookup, then in a line they moved toward the open fuselage door on the left rear side of the aircraft. When the green light came on they jumped out of the aircraft. The C-47's radio operator held open the cockpit's door to allow the copilot to see when the last paratroop cleared the aircraft's door.

As paratroops shuffled to exit the aircraft, they looked like a moving caterpillar. As paratroops reached the open door the

At Alliance AB, the only part that remains of the aircraft hangars are the brick chimneys from the heating unit, with the service road running behind the WWII hangar row. (Author)

aircraft became tail heavy, only returning to level flight after it was empty. At this moment, the copilot tapped the pilot's right shoulder so he could add power to begin a climbing left turn out of the drop zone. The pilot was able to see the last paratroops reaching the ground in the drop zone. The copilot recorded the paratroop landing positions for the aircrew's post mission debriefing, and in this case, training evaluation. The pilot advanced the throttles and re-entered the air base's traffic pattern, landing as quickly as possible and clearing the runway for another C-47.

Mass paratroop drop training missions required a lot of planning and were difficult to conduct. Tactics called for C-47s to fly into the drop zone at low altitude, simulating entry into an area patrolled by enemy fighters. C-47s were unarmed and were considered by pilots as sitting ducks to anti-aircraft, machine gun, and small arms fire. Tactics specified a rapid climb from low-level approach to a minimum of 500 feet, which allowed paratroops to experience quick jumps that reduced their exposure to enemy fire. This altitude gave enough time for the main chutes to open, but not enough time to deploy the reserve chute if something went wrong. This jump tactic was used during the D-Day airborne invasion at night to screen the paratroops.[58]

The bomb storage building was located in the middle of an open field, away from the runways. (Author)

C-47 pilots flew day and night training missions at Alliance AB to learn and practice airborne delivery tactics and procedures: navigation, instrument and formation flying, glider towing, and ground jump zone identification. During night training missions, glider pilots had to locate their landing zones by moonlight or by oil-fired smudge pots set up by pathfinder troops. On these night training missions, many gliders were damaged or written off as irreparable wrecks. Glider training was made as realistic as possible to prepare glider pilots for airborne operations in Europe.[59]

As the invasion neared, C-47 production output for all combat theaters of operations barely met minimum requirements. This was a tremendous planning and acquisition problem, especially after D-Day, during Operation *Market Garden* in Belgium. Pilot training produced more pilots than needed to fill transport needs with selected officers transferred to gliders, which did not make them happy. This was a shock and disappointment to them, feeling demoted because through no fault of their own they had to fly gliders. Later in combat, these pilots earned the respect of glider infantry they delivered behind enemy lines. These pilots fought alongside the glider infantry and performed admirably during return to American lines.[60]

CG-4As on the ground in Normandy, France, the morning of 6 June 1944. Courtesy of Nebraska State Historical Society, Lincoln, Nebraska.

Airborne nine-tube rocket launcher on display at the Silent Wings Museum, Lubbock, Texas. (Author)

View along the service road behind the flight line (1991). To the left is a concrete slab of one of the hangars. In the distance is a surviving chimney, all that remains above ground of another hangar. Surviving wood buildings are visible. (Author)

By April 1944, training for C-47 aircrews, paratroops, glider infantry, and glider pilots at Alliance AB had rapidly decreased. Combat-qualified airborne troops, glider pilots, and C-47 aircrews were transferred to England. Troop Carrier Command transferred control of Alliance AB on 1 September to the Second Air Force to begin training B-29 aircrews.[61]

Alliance's long runways were ideal for safe operations of heavily loaded Superfortresses. As war priorities changed, the AAF reduced the number of B-29 training bases in November 1944; the AAF decided not to retain Alliance AB as an active training base. Alliance AB was deactivated on 1 December 1944. After Germany surrendered and plans for the invasion of the Japanese home islands were in final preparation, control of Alliance was returned to Troop Carrier Command on 25 June 1945. Allied invasion plans code named "Operation Olympic" would make the initial amphibious and airborne invasion of Japan. Japan's surrender on 15 August 1945 ended any further requirement for the AAF to retain Alliance AB, and Alliance was closed on 20 November and declared surplus federal property on 6 December 1945.

The former air base's return to local control was a slow process. It took a ruling by the U.S. Circuit Court affirming that the City of Alliance could take back ownership of the air base. On 16 July 1953, the Alliance City Council received the deed to the former air base, renaming it Alliance Municipal Airport. Many WWII buildings remained on the 3,500 acres owned by the city. The airport is served by commuter airlines to Denver, Colorado, with facilities for private and commercial aircraft.[62]

The large concrete parking apron survived long after the end of WWII, but was in need of repair. In 1992, the concrete remained intact, although showing stress from grass along the edges of the poured concrete, as well as effects of weather. (Author)

CHAPTER THREE

BRUNING AIR BASE

Bruning AB construction began in September 1942 on 1,480 acres of farmland. The federal government confiscated the land, paying twelve landowners a total of $73,400. As with other air base land purchases in Nebraska, land owners complained they were not adequately compensated. The field was activated on 18 March 1943. The base was expanded to 1,720 acres, with 234 buildings and three 6,800-foot long runways. By December 1943, the base was home to 500 civilians and 3,077 military personnel.[63]

A War Department press release showed how Bruning AB and other military installations were built. In the office of nearly every Area Engineer of the Missouri River Division of the Corps of Engineers there is cartoon depicting an Area Engineer receiving orders to build a war effort project on a piece of marshland while the orders from his superior are: "We are in no hurry for this major project, you can take your time, just so it is ready for occupancy in ten days. Under the fast pace set by Division Chief Colonel Lewis A. Pick, that order is not as far off as would seem at first. What should be an ordinary time of one year to build must be completed in one-sixth to one-twelfth the time. Speed, that all essential element in war, is the living symbol for the officers of the division. A close-knit organization supervised by the Division and directed by three districts (Kansas City, Missouri; Omaha, Nebraska; and Fort Peck, Montana) sends officers and men into the field to keep the Missouri Division ahead of schedule all the time. Men and materials are shifted just as a commanding officer shifts his men and material in battle.

"The construction program under the nine States of the Missouri River Division is in reality the background of the home forces. Huge maps are the working grounds for each chief of a division. Each hour will change the map when new installations are authorized and men and material must be shifted. Lines of communications and avenues of transportation open. An Area Engineer is placed in charge to direct the work.

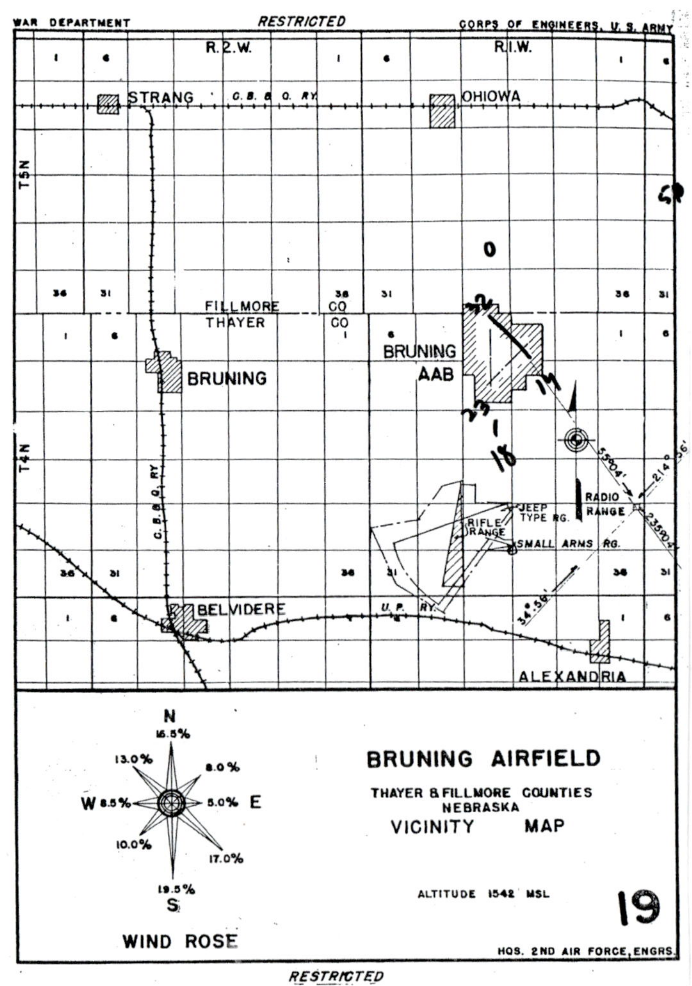

World War II airfield vicinity map of Bruning Airfield. (Author)

"It matters little whether the order is to build an air base, a satellite field, a containment, an ordnance plant, a depot, a warehouse, a hospital, a storage area, a relocation center or a dog kennel, it must be constructed at once. The site selected may be removed from railroads, bus travel or phone service. These must be installed and lines of communication, hundreds of telephone lines made available. The material sections must have all available material in use at the moment that the new war effort project is authorized. All of the big machines are working at top speed, but the new project must have attention. Material is pulled from several jobs as machines, taken from this place and that place, are either on the road or on a flat car bound for the new jobs almost before the area engineer arrives to hold on until something the Army forgotten is delivered.

"Real estate men set up their offices and began to buy the land. Surveyors, in many cases, are on the land almost simultaneously with the real estate men. They are laying out roads, runways, barracks, drainage systems while the real estate men purchased the land. Complete office forces must be recruited and set up by the Area Engineer, who in all probability has just finished building a large airport in 30-to-60 days ahead of schedule and has left his assistant in charge of mopping up the project while he takes over the new one.

"Equipment, material and manpower must be planned in advance and orders sent out. Trainloads of material must be arriving each day to keep the schedule and men busy. The average small airfield must have at least 150 train cars of material at one each day from the time they are paving concrete to keep the pavers busy. These must come in an uninterrupted flow either by train or truck.

"Sewage systems must be planned and installed if sufficient water is not available, then wells must be dug. This may mean that miles of pipe will have to be laid. The local power system is called upon for electrical service, but this is supplemented with an on-site power plant for the projects.

"Some idea of the magnitude of the job that confronts some of the area engineers may be realized when it is understood that runways are constructed in sixty days or less. That is, starting from the time the Area Engineer arrives, the plans, the surveying, the forms must be done before a yard of pavement can be laid. If a runway could be stretched out into a standard 20-foot wide highway, it would reach from Lincoln to Omaha, Nebraska.

"He still must build his barracks for the men, recreational halls, theater buildings, commissary, post exchanges and churches. Roads that will stand years of usage must be constructed along with the rest. Then, too, he must see that the roads into and away from the site are suitable for the usage to which the user will demand of them.

"Hangars for the air bases and shops, along with miscellaneous warehouses, are by no means a small part of this project. The Division Real Estate Section must work at top speed so that nothing is built on non-purchased land and that all available names are properly signed on the paper work. The Operating Division must know the exact status of the work of every project so as to be able to suggest changes of equipment. They must know the exact amount of material on hand so the surplus can be moved within the hour of necessary. The Engineering Division stands ready with available information as to cost and engineering problems. The Contracts and Labor Relations Division must stand ready to facilitate all contractors and assist in placing workers on the job."[64]

After construction work started, because of urgency in meeting requirements to train as many AAF aircrews as possible in the shortest time, work on the new base went to three eight-hour shifts, seven days a week. Workers' construction efforts had to alter former farm and ranch land into an operational air base.[65] The airfield consisted of three runways, each 8,600 feet long and 150 feet wide, and two concrete parking aprons (one 2,135 feet long and 600 feet wide, with the second 550 feet long and 425 feet wide). The runways were built thick enough to support heavy bomber (including the B-29) operations. Engineers set up the runways in a right-triangular pattern, which allowed take-offs and landings regardless of seasonal wind direction changes. Twelve bomber-capable parking aprons were built, as well as two large arch roof aircraft hangars to hold a B-17 or B-24. Once construction began, the air base looked like a small city, with 324 buildings (barracks, squadron offices, hospital, post exchange, theater, recreational, service club, mess halls, chapel, and other structures needed to operate a training facility). During the war, approximately 6,000 military personnel trained at the base, supported by a large civilian work force. The base began operations as a bomber training facility before transitioning to training fighter pilots.[66]

Bruning AB was activated on 18 March 1943 by written order, Headquarters, Second Air Force. Organizations on the base consisted of the following: 23rd Weather Squadron, 23rd Air Control Squadron, 46th Airdrome Squadron, and the 47th Airdrome Squadron.

By June 1943, the following units were operating on the base: 356th Squadron, 1186th Signal Company, Detachment 34 of the 902nd Quartermaster Company, a medical detachment, and the 449th Aviation Squadron. After air base activation, the 510th Headquarters and Air Base Squadron was organized to administer and service training operations on the base. As on any new training base, there were many problems, primarily because of the shortage of trained technical personnel and equipment needed to run a large training base. In the rush to begin training as quickly as possible, newly arrived personnel were simply assigned to the first empty barracks without maintaining squadron integrity. This hampered effective squadron training as a combat unit but was later corrected, so personnel in the same squadron lived in the same barracks.[67]

Bruning AB was dedicated on 28 August 1943. The 456th BG, consisting of the 744th, 745th, 746th, and 747th BS, was the first group assigned to the base, flying the B-24D. At the start of training, only four B-24Ds were available—one per squadron. At the dedication ceremony, these four aircraft flew low over the runways, accompanied by B-17s, one L-36, and one C-47 towing a CG-4A from Alliance AB.[68]

The air base's training facilities and buildings were opened to the public during an open house celebrating its dedication and beginning operations to prepare aircrews for combat. The

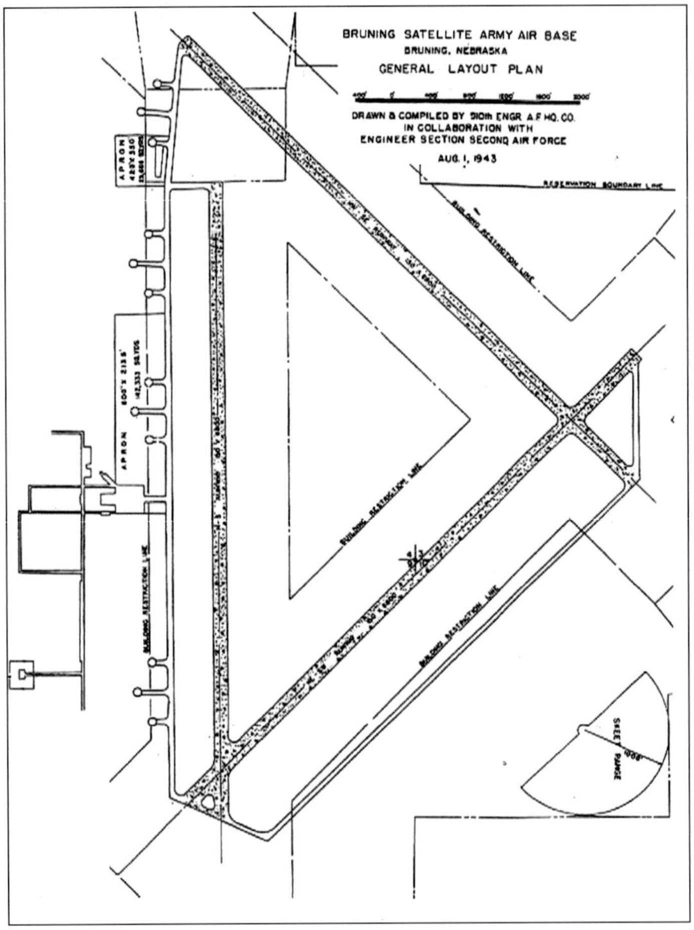

World War II airfield layout map of Bruning Airfield. (Author)

Link Trainer building was still under construction at the time of the open house, but its miniature planes were still a great hit with the children; these were planes just their size that they could sit in. After the Link Trainer building was finished, the six miniature planes sitting on their pedestals became operational, commencing 24-hour training to give pilots night and all weather instrument qualification, along with periodic retraining/certification.[69]

During training operations at Bruning AB, the following groups were assigned.

Group	Squadron	Date Operational at Bruning
456BG	744th	28 August to 9 September 1943
(B-24)	745th	
	746th	
	747th	
444BG	716th	12 September- 29 November 1943
(B-24)	717th	
	718th	
	719th	
487BG	837th	20 September to 24 December 1943
(B-24)	838th	
36FG	23rd	24 December 1943-14April 1944
(P-47)		3 March to 10 April 1944
507FG	463rd	20 October to 15 December 1944
(P-47)	464th	
	465th	
508FG	466th	15 November to 18 December 1944
(P-47)	467th	
	468th[70]	

After the 500-man Military Personnel Detachment arrived on base, administrative office space and barracks assignments were a problem. As military personnel formed into squadrons, they moved into barracks vacated by squadron personnel that had completed training. In November 1943, one squadron had to share its barracks with a newly-arrived squadron until finishing training and departing using the procedure "hot bunking." Training was at different times, allowing one squadron to sleep while the other trained, then giving up their beds to the other squadron for a specified sleeping period. The number of constructed barracks could only accommodate authorized training numbers, not allowance for overlapping! Personnel also gave a nickname to this over-scheduling, called "musical barracks"—not satisfactory for maintaining optimum training operations and results.[71] Bomber groups at Bruning flew the B-24D.[72]

Aerial view of Bruning AB. The main air base area is to the right of the runways and taxiways. Courtesy of NSHS to Author.

B-24 on display at Lackland Air Park, Lackland Air Force Base, San Antonio, Texas. (Author)

Photo of a P-47 Thunderbolt on display at Lackland AFB Air Park, San Antonio, Texas. (Author)

View in 1991 of the primary runway in its deteriorated condition. The other two runways had been dug up, the concrete crushed for highway fill material. The base complex had been turned into a cattle feed lot operation. (Author)

After Bruning AB transitioned from B-24Ds to P-47s in December 1943, training was hampered due to a lack of spare parts for the fighters. Overseas combat P-47 groups received the highest spare parts priority, with stateside training bases scrambling to keep their aircraft flying. Difficulties keeping aircraft flying slowed P-47 pilot training, stressing maintenance crews and disrupting pilot combat qualification. In addition, adding to P-47 maintenance backlogs was that because the air base previously operated B-24Ds, transition for maintenance personnel from four-engine B-24s to single-engine P-47s took training on the aircraft's technical specifications. Even when the P-47s were the primary, B-24Ds continued to be flown to the base for maintenance. B-24Ds clogged the air base's maintenance facilities, with parts flown into the air base by C-47s from active B-24 bases or scrounged from any available parts source.

Bruning AB's P-47 pilot training program was diversified. Pilots watched one orientation and three ground training films. Each pilot had daily physical fitness training to help prepare for the rigors of aerial combat. Ground maintenance personnel also went through daily physical training. To assist in retaining morale, dances were organized and held at the Bruning Service Club and USO entertainment troupes performed at the base theater. Mail was flown into the air base from Grand Island AB by one of Bruning AB's P-47s, fulfilling cross-country training flights, along with proficiency and navigation.[73]

There were many P-47 crashes during training operations at Bruning AB, reaching a point of serious concern for the fighter group commanders. The base's ground safety officers maintained a detailed log of all accidents, including six classified as pilot error, one ground wreck, and one mid-air collision of two P-47s (both pilots managed to land their damaged aircraft at Bruning AB). One P-47 nosed over during landing, one made a wheels-up belly landing, and two P-47s landed short of the runway. Fortunately, no pilots were killed during these crashes. Maintenance personnel worked long hours repairing damaged P-47s, often cannibalizing parts from P-47s written off as irreparable.[74] The P-47 was a large, single-seat fighter, the heaviest in the AAF.[75]

View of surviving buildings on the base, including one hangar, an operations building between the hangar and new storage building, and the water tower to the left of the hangars. The area between the runway and parking area was planted in soybeans in 1991. The building to the right was used as a warehouse for an agriculture fertilizer company (note the fertilizer wheel tank units in front of the hangar). The majority of the former air base was turned into a commercial feed lot operation. (Author)

Interestingly, at one time or another almost every type of AAF aircraft landed at Bruning AB, staging through the air base on delivery orders or training flights. On 18 December 1943, a CG-4A glider suddenly appeared on final approach at the end of one runway and completed a perfect landing. Control tower personnel were amazed to see a glider drop through the low cloud ceiling and land, rolling to a stop on the runway. The glider was only fitted with basic flight instruments, with no radio to communicate with nearby control towers. The glider pilots told Bruning AB ground crews their tow line broke while on a cross-country training flight. At that moment, the C-47 copilot called Bruning AB's control tower, asking if a glider had landed nearby. The glider pilot responded that when the tow rope broke, his aircraft was damaged by the whipping action of the towrope. The C-47 did not land, but continued on to Fairmont AB, where it refueled and flew back to Alliance AB, completing its cross training mission profile. Bruning AB maintenance personnel had to make many phone calls to Alliance AB concerning technical repairs on the glider. Once the glider was air worthy, an Alliance AB C-47 landed and positioned on the runway as the glider was towed from the taxiway to behind the transport; a nylon tow rope was unloaded from the C-47 and hooked onto the glider and the transport. The C-47 pilots gunned the aircraft's engines, rolling down the run with the glider airborne first, followed by the transport, then flying back to Alliance AB.

Another interesting incident took place on 18 December 1943 at noon, when another CG-4A made an emergency landing seven miles east of the air base, which was followed by control tower personnel using binoculars. Again, the cause was a broken tow line, with the glider pilot quickly releasing his section of the remaining tow rope so the weight of the rope would not cause the glider to crash. The glider pilots made an emergency landing in a wheat field, damaging the CG-4A's undercarriage. The C-47 tow aircraft circled the glider, calling Bruning AB's control tower and indicated what happened, and that the two pilots were out of the glider uninjured. The C-47 copilot asked and was granted permission to drop the remaining section of the tow rope alongside the runway prior to turning back to Alliance

AB. Personnel from the 404th Sub-depot were dispatched by truck, heavy haul truck with a flatbed trailer, and truck-mounted crane. The glider was loaded on the flatbed trailer for the trip back to Bruning AB for repair. After the glider was repaired, an Alliance AB C-47 landed, following the procures above, then took off and flew the glider home. The farm owner of the damaged wheat field filed an extensive claim against the AAF (loss of crop income, road damage from the heavy vehicles, and fence replacement). The federal government did not send a check to the farmer until late in 1944 and for only $200—nowhere near the bill of $2,500 submitted by the farmer.

Because of the frequency of P-47 crashes, Bruning AB maintenance personnel were continually short of spare parts to repair damaged fighters. There was a shortage of fully trained P-47 mechanics, as many were transferred to England. The shortage of aviation mechanics was complicated by the constant arrival of B-24Ds for maintenance. It was a difficult situation to perform B-24 and P-47 maintenance concurrently, along with unexpected repairs required by transiting aircraft or those on training missions from other air bases. This was an aircraft maintenance officer's worst possible scenario.[76]

P-47 pilot initial training at Bruning AB consisted of:

1. Basic gun training on the base's skeet range showing how to lead a fast moving aerial target so shot gun pellets and clay pigeon arrived at the same point, destroying the moving target. This assisted in learning aerial gunnery deflection techniques.
2. Aerial gunnery camera scoring of the aircraft's attack against various types of aerial targets, including mock dogfights with other P-47s, allowed the developed film after the mission to be reviewed.
3. Live air-to-air gunnery against towed target sleeves.
4. Ground attack gunnery with machine guns, rockets, and dive bombing to simulate ground support missions.

Advanced training consisted of:

1. Elementary flying
2. Tactical formation flying
3. Wingman responsibilities
4. High and low altitude flight operations
5. Navigation
6. Touch and go landings
7. Link Trainer time for instrument proficiency for all weather and night flying
8. Mission planning
9. Weather planning
10. Cross country-training missions
11. Day and night training missions

Ground training consisted of:

1. Ground school
2. Camp training
   Simulated gas attacks
   Experiencing dive bombing and strafing attacks
   Identification of mines and booby traps
   Camouflage techniques
3. Chemical warfare
4. Articles of war
5. Physical fitness
   Swimming and water survival

The 23rd FS suffered many P-47 losses while training:

1. Two P-47s crashed during a dual landing training mission. One P-47 carried too much speed after landing, over-taking and overshooting the lead P-47, then colliding with that aircraft, demolishing the lead aircraft's fuselage up to the cockpit. The second P-47 was badly damaged, with extensive engine and landing gear destruction.
2. A P-47 blew one of its main landing gear tires on take-off, swerving off the runway and flipping over in the soft dirt.
3. While at the gunnery range near Norfolk, Nebraska, a P-47 pilot concentrated so hard on hitting the cloth target suspended between two poles that he dove into the ground in front of the target in a fiery explosion, killing him and destroying the aircraft.

It was not unusual for farmers around Bruning to enter their field and find a P-47 that made a wheels up, forced belly landing into a soft field. The pilot was usually able to walk away from this type of crash if the aircraft did not burst into flames. These P-47 crashes kept base Recovery and Maintenance teams busy. P-47 training was conducted as close to combat conditions as possible, often resulting in accidents.

With the large numbers of P-47 accidents, it was only time before pilots were killed. Two P-47s collided in mid-air over the runway, killing the student pilot, with the instructor in the second aircraft bailing out and parachuting safely to the ground near the runway. Another P-47 pilot became disorientated while flying in heavy clouds, ignoring instrument training and using visual references. The pilot dove into the ground. The next morning, a Recovery and Maintenance team entered a farmer's field near the base and found the destroyed fighter with the dead pilot strapped in the cockpit.[77]

P-47 pilots had to learn the aircraft's strengths and weaknesses.[78]

A P-63 fighter unit arrived at Bruning AB in September 1944; most of the pilots assigned were combat veterans. The P-63 was an upgraded P-39 called the King Cobra. The P-63s were fitted with gun camera sights to record intercepts against B-17s and B-24s from area training bases. The developed film was shared with the bomber crews intercepted, flown to that base, and allowed evaluation of that crew's air defense coordination. This was as close to real aerial combat the bomber crews could achieve while firing live .50 caliber machine gun shells at friendly attacking AAF fighters. By reviewing the gun camera film, the bomber crews could determine proper enemy fighter acquisition, interplane communications to recognize the most serious enemy fighter threat, and determine if gunner coordination could be improved.[79]

It was determined specialized aircrew and ground personnel training using motivational films would be included in the training program. This would provide graphic visual incentives for why pilots needed to follow proper flight procedures and maintain cutting edge combat skills. These were made and

The hangar at Bruning AB was of standard construction, with an arch roof, wood framing, sliding doors, and a notch above the center of the doors to allow the tail of a B-17 or B-24 to protrude outside while maintenance work was conducted on the majority of the aircraft inside, out of the weather. The hangar (1991) survived long past its intended life span. (Author)

Former WWII hangar at Bruning AB converted into a grain storage facility to support the surrounding feed lot operation. (Author)

P-63 King Cobra on display at the Lackland AFB Air Park, San Antonio, Texas. (Author)

produced by Hollywood, California production companies under titles like "Why We Fight" to meet AAF specifications. Today, these are available as restored black and white DVDs and provide a look at the propaganda in the United States used to raise awareness on fighting a global, two ocean front war. At that time, the primary objective of the War Department was to present a vivid story of the U.S. serviceman's struggle to preserve and protect America's freedom and democracy.[80]

Initially, in order to obtain War Department base construction contracts, Nebraska's congressional members touted their state's supposedly ideal weather conditions, which would give the AAF maximum flying training time. In November 1944, bad weather forced the cancellation of forty percent of P-47 training sorties. In November, the 508th FG arrived with new P-47Ns.[81]

Dismantled aircraft hangar. Salvage crews removed the wood roof, framing, and siding for sale, leaving the concrete side shop area. In 1991, the former WWII base infrastructure was being torn down. The hangar's use had long since expired and what was built in haste to fight a war is now gone. (Author)

The P-47N was equipped with a more powerful engine, heavier armament, able to fly longer distances because of increased internal fuel capacity. It was ideal for Pacific combat, due to longer over water distances. The 508th trained 160 P-47N pilots. During 2,000 hours of flight training in this variant, there was not a single major mishap—very unusual given previous P-47 accident rates at Bruning AB. Most of the improved safety record was attributed to using new aircraft, higher pilot proficiency, and adequate preventive maintenance. Each P-47N pilot averaged twelve hours of transition flying before being assigned to an overseas combat unit.[82]

By December 1944, to make up for November's lost flying time, older Thunderbolts were flown to Bruning AB (P-47Bs, Cs, and Gs) to assist in transition training into the fighter. In January 1945, twenty-four P-47Ds were flown to the base to replace the older models, increase flight time availability, get the pilot training program back on schedule, and decrease down time due to maintenance required on the older model Thunderbolts.[83]

With the end of fighting in the Pacific, military training at Bruning AB completely stopped. By 1947, 174 buildings were torn down and the Pentagon offered the air base to the state for one dollar. The Nebraska Department of Acronautics was given clear title to the former air base by the federal government through the War Assets Administration by a Quit Claim Deed dated 15 January 1948, with provision for it be maintained as a civilian airport. The Nebraska Department of Aeronautics maintained the airfield as an active facility until August 1969, at which time the federal government granted the state a statement of release of maintenance. While the state operated the airport it was seldom if ever used; it was considered a day emergency runway, without lights or operational control tower. The runways, taxiways, and facilities deteriorated to the condition considered unsafe for any type of aircraft operations. In 1969, the Nebraska state legislature authorized Bruning airfield for sale at public auction as a surplus state property. In 1963, 285 acres were leased for a cattle feed lot operation. No land on the airport property was sold, but in 1977, the feedlot leased more land. In 1991, when I photographed the site, the former WWII air base was being dismantled, with only one hangar remaining and used as a feed storage facility for the feedlot. The concrete runways and taxiways were slowly being dug up, the concrete pulverized and used for high fill material. This is an excellent example of WWII history lost.[84]

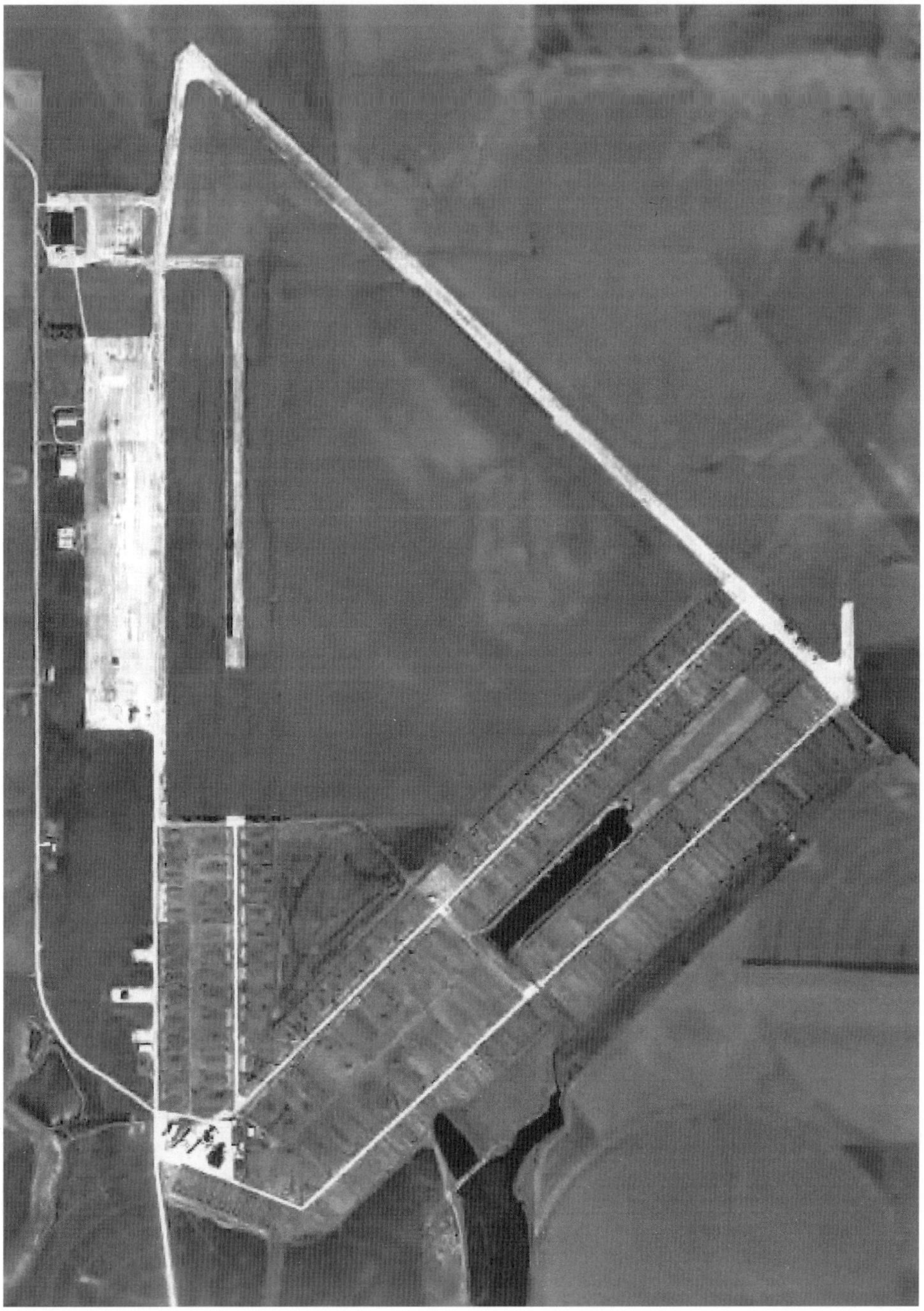

USGS photo of the former WWII Bruning AB in 1999. The feedlot operation is between the taxiways at the south end of the former air base.

CHAPTER FOUR

FAIRMONT AIR BASE

On 3 September 1942, Fairmont's local newspaper *The Nebraska Signal* stated: "The prospects of Filmore County having an Army airplane refueling base became more definite when several Army officers came to Geneva, Nebraska to set up a temporary office."[85] A few days later, U.S. Army Corps of Engineers surveyors were seen working at the proposed airfield site, taking soil samples and determining if sufficient ground water was available to support air base operation.[86] *The Nebraska Signal*, September 24, 1942: "Actual grading for the runways has begun at the air base north of Geneva and construction is expected to be in full swing by the end of this week. Work started Saturday on building a spur track of the Fairmont-Chester Railroad line into the air base. The spur rail line branches off the main track six miles north of Geneva and crosses the Bauman farm, owned by the Mutual Benefit Life Insurance Company. It will cross Highway 81. The contractor is to have the track removed by April 1, 1942. The spur will be used to haul cement and other bulky/heavy materials into the air base.

"Petition and condemnation under title of the United States against 1,840 acres of Filmore County land and interested parties was filed last Thursday in Federal Court in Lincoln, Nebraska, together with an order signed by Judge Donohoe gives petitioner immediate possession, subject to existing easements, owners and tenants to retain possession of houses and other buildings until September 26, 1942.

"The ground is to be used for a military airfield, petition reciting that it is for military and defense purposes. Twelve carloads of machinery to be used in construction work arrived at Fairmont last week and have been unloaded. The runways for the landing field are to be of concrete, eleven-inches thick, which sounds like some of those forty-ton bombers might be landing there sometime. This is thicker than is used at similar fields.

"The offices of Major W.H. Burgwin, Area Engineer, U.S. Army Air Forces, surveyors and draftsmen are at Fairmont.

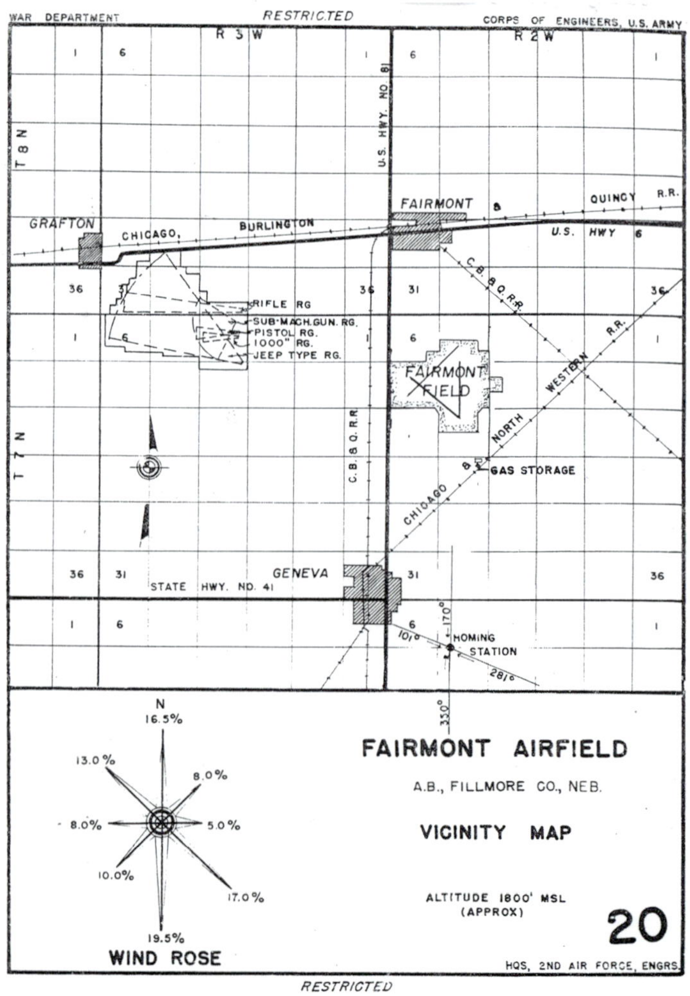

World War II airfield vicinity map of Fairmont Airfield. (Author)

Geneva County Court House in Geneva, Nebraska. (Author)

Historical marker, Fillmore County. (Author)

General offices for Kewit, Condon & Cunningham Contractors are located at Sutton. These contractors have worked at the Harvard, Fairmont and Bruning fields. About forty employees are working in that office. The telephone company installed a PBX exchange board for handling all local and long distance calls at the office and Western Union installed a new teletype machine for handling of all messages. The teletype prints the message as it is being transmitted over the wire and eliminates the necessity of having a telegrapher write it down."[87]

The federal government condemned 1,840 acres of land for the new air base, located two and one-half miles south of Fairmont.[88] When construction work started, it was a 24-hour, two-shift operation. To initially house workers and those who brought their families, temporary wood frame barracks were quickly built and occupied. Later, these barracks were used as married housing billets. A temporary trailer camp was set up at the Geneva Fair Grounds and empty buildings in town became sleeping quarters, along with every empty room in local homes rapidly being filled. Housing was always in short supply, not only because of workers at Fairmont, but due to construction around the area. Construction on bases within thirty miles of Fairmont consisted of Bruning and Harvard. Workers tried to find housing anywhere, with some shuttling from one construction site to the next depending on their skills, such as wood framers, concrete and brick masons, electrical and heating, etc. The new air base was initially called Fairmont Satellite Field, under control of Topeka Army Air Base. In 1943, it became Fairmont Army Air Field.

One of four large aircraft hangars at Fairmont AB able to accommodate a B-29. The base water tower is visible to the right. A wire fence separates the current taxiway from the old aircraft parking apron. (Author)

Second surviving hangar at Fairmont, located second from the southern hangar. (Author)

Construction workers built three large aircraft hangars to hold a B-17 or B-24, and later the B-29. Fairmont was classified as a final training base for heavy bomber aircrews. It had four concrete runways 11 1/2 inches thick. Many workers were local hires, building the base while still working on their own farms, ranches, and businesses. It was an opportunity for them to make good money and assist their families. The air base was completed in early November 1942, with the first group of military personnel arriving on 10 November; the U.S. Army Quartermaster Corps came first to sign contracts for food to support training operations on the base.[89]

By 1 December, the housing situation in Fairmont remained critical. The town built a new sewage disposal system north of Fairmont to handle the large temporary housing camp. The air base had its own sewage treatment facility and water and power distribution systems. The base consisted of eighty buildings to hold 1,000 military and civilian personnel. By May 1943, 600 military and 100 civilians were on the base.[90]

At this time, the 511th Base Headquarters and Air Base Squadron was created from personnel assigned to the 356th Base Headquarters and Air Base Squadron from Topeka Army AB and the 352nd Base Headquarters and AB Squadron detachment from Great Falls, Montana. From 22 February to 20 May 1943, there was no training at the air base. After 20 May, standardized military squadron level training started.

Basic Military Subjects:

Close order drill
Manual of arms
Military hygiene
Military courtesy and discipline
Safeguarding military information
Extended order drill
Care and cleaning of small arms
Chemical warfare
Technical Military Subjects
Identification of military aircraft
Individual protective covering
Camouflage[91]

Third surviving aircraft hangar on Fairmont AB. (Author)

The air base's hospital cost $500,000 to build and provided medical care for Fairmont, Bruning, and Harvard ABs. This allowed one facility to serve three training facilities, reducing costs and medical personnel requirements.[92] The base telephone system cost $50,000 and provided base-wide communications essential to maintaining on-time training schedules. As with other construction projects in Nebraska, federal dollars brought Fairmont economic prosperity.[93]

Construction continued at Fairmont AB with the building of a fourth aircraft hangar in 1943. Maintenance on the bombers during Nebraska's winters was difficult. The exterior metal surfaces became so cold that if a mechanic touched the metal surface with a bare hand it froze to that spot immediately. The first aircrew training commenced in August 1943, with a B-24 Standardization School. It only lasted until September 1943, then was replaced by B-24 bomb group training.[94]

Interior of the hangar in the previous photo. The concrete walls inside the hangar allow for grain storage. (Author)

A rare surviving example of a WWII era train (built in the 1930s) depot at Fairmont, where most of the airmen and support personnel arrived by rail to the air base. Most of the old train depots were torn down when passenger trains stopped running along the rail lines, except for the occasional Amtrak cross-country passenger train. Today, the majority of rail traffic is freight. (Author)

The following groups trained at Fairmont AB during WWII:

Bomb Group	Bomb Squadron	Date of operations
451st	724th	9 September 1943 to 26 November 1943
(B-24)	725th	15 September to 11 March 1944
	726th	
	727th	
	15th	15 August 1945 to 7 March 1945
(B-29)	16th	
	17th	
	21st	
467th	788th	25 July 1945 to 25 August 1945
(B-24)	789th	
	790th	
489th	844th	13 July to 23 August 1945
(B-29)	845th	
	846th	
	847th[95]	

On 8 September 1943, the 724th and 725th BS left Wendover Field, Utah for Fairmont AB. By 9 Septemer, the 451st BG had 600 personnel at the base. On 11 September, the 726th and 727th BS arrived with 627 men. The air echelon of 93 men and eleven aircraft arrived on the same day. On 17 September, thirty-four aircrews arrived on base to fill out the complement of flying personnel. Later in the month, the 451st BG received eighteen factory fresh B-24s, increasing aircraft availability to twenty-nine. Fairmont AB was the first base at which the 451st operated alone and was not paired with another training bomb group on the base—an unusual circumstance during WWII heavy bomber

crew training. Facilities on the base were new and a change from previously overcrowded bases with more than one group on the base at the same time.

Citizens of Fairmont, York, Geneva, and neighboring towns were solidly behind efforts to make the men of the 451st BG feel at home. The Service Club planned and conducted many activites (bingo, dances, and variety shows) with the cooperation of surrounding towns. Young girls were brought to the base for supervised dances at the Service Club. Many friendships were formed, as local residents invited members of the 351st BG to enjoy the luxury of a home-cooked meal and the serenity of an evening away from military life on the base. Available rooms, when found, were rented for spouses, who joined their husbands for a few months together before entering war. It was the merging of untried bomb group personnel and civilians into a deadly pursuit of aerial combat.[96]

The reunion of the 451st BG in September 1990 brought back bomb group memories of their war time training. John Suttler, WWII Supply Officer, recalled: "The runway held a B-24J flown in for the reunion, parked for us to view; it made it look like not much had changed." Bob Ackland, a Geneva, Nebraska farmer, stated: "I remember B-24s flying over my farm. I thought they were going to hit the barn, they were flying so low. Four radio towers were on the farm."[97]

By September 1943, there was an urgency to complete training to clear the base for the inbound 485th BG. There was no slack in training schedules, so any adverse events impacted training: maintenance, weather delays, and crews not qualifying on a training sortie. Any delay could result in more than one bomb group at the base at the same time, and this could become a scheduling nightmare, including assignment of quarters, transportation, and training operations.

The 451st BG Operations Officer noted: "to make matters worse, there was a high number of court martial cases. Many enlisted men who could neither read nor write were coming up to trial due to a low level of discipline and general diversion to authority. The low level of the personnel's education made it difficult to obtain the group's desired training objectives."[98]

There were mishaps during the bomb group's training at Fairmont AB. Lieutenant Robert Stone, 744th BS, remembered: "One B-24 on a training flight had a fuel line connection break, releasing about 250 gallons of fuel into the bomb bay that leaked out the bottom. The pilot called in an emergency, and after ten minutes of careful flying he landed the fuel-soaked B-24. Aircraft 41-29195 quickly earned the nickname 'gas house.'"

The 751st BG unit history reported the following aircraft losses:

1. A 762nd BS B-24 crashed near Wayne, Nebraska, in early October 1943.

2. On 25 October 1943, two 724th BS B-24s collided in mid-air, killing sixteen in the two aircraft.

By 15 November, the 451st BG had received its full allotment of sixty-two B-24s and was at full strength of 3,722 personnel.

The aircraft were distributed to the assigned bomb squadrons as follows:

Bomb Squadron	Number of Aircraft
724th	16
725th	16
726th	15
727th	15[99]

By 18 to 23 November 1943, all of the 451st BG were flown to Lincoln AB in preparation for overseas deployment. On 18 November, eleven B-24s assigned to the 724th BS took off for Italy. Over the next five days, ten to eleven B-24s took off each day for the European Theater of Operations (ETO).

A 451st BG Operations Officer marking training schedule/tracking sheets to follow training progression. Courtesy of USAF Historical Research Center, Montgomery, Alabama, Maxwell Air Force Base.

Fairmont AB bivouac training at Bruning AB. Courtesy of USAF Historical Research Center, Montgomery, Alabama, Maxwell AFB.

Photographic intelligence training and aircrew briefing at Fairmont AB. Courtesy of USAF Historical Research Center, Montgomery, Alabama, Maxwell AFB.

The bomb group's ground echelon boarded a train at Fairmont on 26 November bound for sea transports on the east coast and movement to Italy.[100]

The 485th BG arrived at Fairmont AB on 15 November 1943. As the bomb group occupied the base, another aspect of the war began. WWII had brought the fear that the enemy is listening, and U.S. Army intelligence officers prowled the base, attempting to detect and correct possible or actual security breaches. Intelligence officers reported incidents of AAF officers, enlisted men, and civilian employees talking when they should not. Operations Security (OPSEC) was serious business, with training and procedures set up to carry over into combat security to prevent combat missions from being compromised.

The 485th BG trained at Fairmont AB from 15 September 1943 to 11 March 1944. Even though it was the second bomb group to train on the base, there was still much work to do. Just to meet training goals, base neatness—the cleanup of construction debris—was not a high priority. It was not until December 1943 that a general cleanup began, picking up debris and stacks of lumber and construction materials. Salvageable wood was used to build 300 to 400 homes in Bruning. The 485th BG completed training on 11 March 1944 and deployed to Italy.[101]

The first B-29 group to train at Fairmont AB was the 504th BG, consisting of the 393rd, 398th, and 507th BS. The bomb group flew B-17s until B-29s were delivered from the Omaha Glen-Martin B-29 production plant at Fort Crook. Charles A. Harris remembers: "I started my military career as an aviation cadet. I lied about my age, I lied about my education, and I faked my physical. By the time my sins were discovered, I had become a washed out cadet. After leaving the hospital, I went to photo school at Lowry Field, Denver, Colorado, then on to to Fairmont Army Air Field to join the 504th BG. As a camera technician, I had no intention of remaining on the ground; therefore, I flew very frequently in B-17Gs to take pictures of the bombardiers' success or lack thereof at the bombing range. The bomb group, at the time having nowhere else to put me, assigned me to S-2

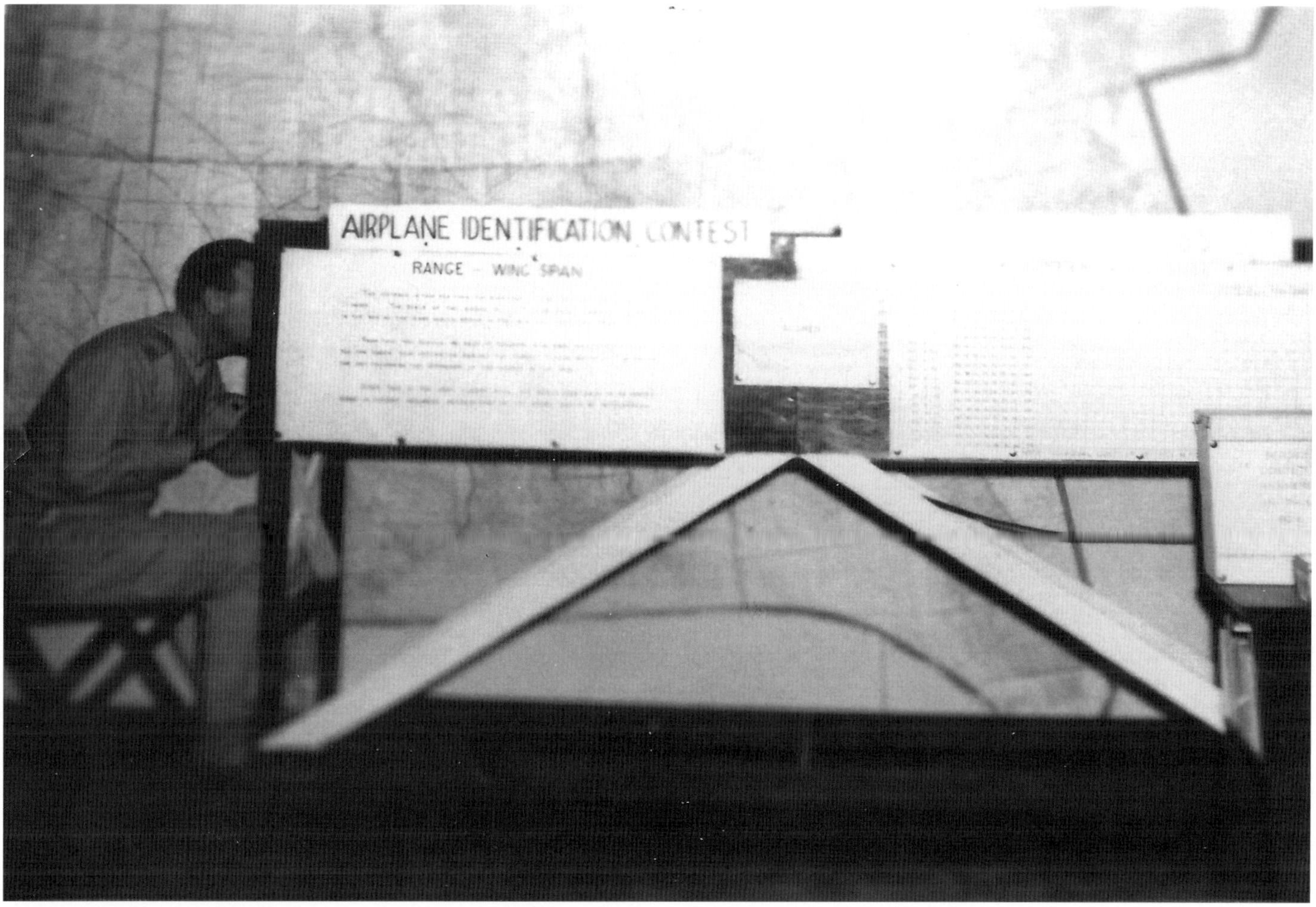

Aircraft recognition for aircrew members at Fairmont AB. Courtesy of USAF Historical Research Center, Montgomery, Alabama, Maxwell AFB.

Division. Beginning in July 1944, we started receiving our B-29s. I convinced our S-2 that I needed practice and flew even more."[102] Beaz A. Aldi, Navigator, 393rd BS, recalled: "I was transferred to Fairmont in January 1944 as an instructor in B-24s. I flew with every squadron navigator. In April 1944, when training was nearly complete, the 485th BG departed for Italy. I was assigned to the base—not to the 485th BG—and remained on base when the B-29s arrived. Because of a shortage of B-29s, we had to use B-17s to fill our training quota. My squadron that I was assigned to (the 393rd) was made up of Training Command personnel. Again, I flew with B-29 navigators and checked their performance. On one training evaluation flight, I indicated the navigator should use more than one navigational method."[103]

The B-29 was viewed as an elite combat program, with pilots assigned to a B-29 unit requiring considerable flying hours just to be considered for evaluation to be transferred to B-29s. To assist B-29 training, special mockups were built to provide radar familiarization, malfunction training, and repair. Spare

Ground equipment identification training at Fairmont AB. Courtesy of USAF Historical Research Center, Montgomery, Alabama, Maxwell AFB.

Side view of the south hangar at Fairmont AB. (Author)

buildings were converted for B-29 aircrew and ground crew training. Many enlisted aircrews' education was very low (a continuing problem, as noted in the previous B-24 training at the base, that was not corrected due to the need to bring in enough men to fight the war), and it impacted training, with 167 men reclassified and declared unsuitable for combat. Officers had to continue training regardless of manpower reductions: three-day bivouac, carbine, and .30 caliber machine gun qualification, chemical warfare training, close order drill formations, and platoon level drills.[104]

Until Boeing's production plants could reach maximum series production, thirty-three B-17s were used for squadron training, eleven allotted to each squadron. These substitute aircraft permitted eighteen training B-17 sorites per day, with others in maintenance, post, or pre-flight servicing. Maintenance crews did not have to contend with battle damage, but they worked long hours keeping the B-17s operational to meet training schedules.[105]

As each factory-fresh B-29 landed, it was guarded by military police, with its assigned crew required to show passes to work on or get into and fly the giant bomber. Harris noted: "Shortly before we left for what turned out to be Tinian, in the Marianas Islands, the 393rd BS was pulled out of the group. The story given to us was that a AAF team had come to the base called a Preparatory Overseas Movement (POM) team, and after evaluating the three squiadrons, the 393rd was classified as not combat qualified. Later, I found out Lieutenant Colonel Paul Tibbets, Commander 509th CG, selected this squadron as the CG's core personnel contingent because of their high training rate. This resulted in the 509th suddenly becoming a two squadron group until June or July 1945."[106]

Earlier in November 1943, the 20th Bomber Command was activated at Salina, Kansas. Lieutenant Colonel Paul Tibbetts selected fifteen highly qualified aircrews for a unique, top secret mission only known to a small number of military, scientists, engineers, Congress, and government officials, including President Roosevelt (later Vice President Harry Truman when he became president after the death of Roosevelt at Warm Springs, Arkansas, in 1945). The selected aircrews were flown to Wendover Field, Utah. Wendover was chosen for the 509th's

North hangar at Fairmont AB. (Author)

Fairmont's main runway as it appeared in 1991. (Author)

training location because of its isolation. The base was heavily guarded, with passes to get into separate internal secured areas and with OPSEC absolute. In September 1944, the 509th and its 390th Air Service Group broke away from the 393rd BS.

The Air Service Group consisted of:

603rd Air Engineering Squadron
1027th Material Squadron
320th Troop Carrier Squadron
1395th Military Police Company
1st Ordnance Squadron
1st Technical Detachment, War Department Miscellaneous Group[107]

Training was adjusted as base facilities were fully converted to accommodate B-29s, including crew position mockups and communication and radar proficiency. However, thirteen B-17 commanders had to train in B-17s, performing day, night, instrument, and formation flying. One of the biggest improvements was upgrading the gunnery building. Classrooms were equipped with a working B-29 gun turret, fire control system, machine gun laboratory, and gunner's mockup with interphone communications to simulate crew defensive fire coordination. Model airplanes hung down from the classroom's ceiling to teach gunners the clock system. A mockup of a waist gunner's position gave crewmen an idea of what attacking Japanese fighters looked like. The Gun Camera Training Section analyzed B-29 gunner procedures and operations and their capability to defend the bomber. Ground crews received armament training in a special facility with a mock bomb bay that allowed dummy bombs to be dropped out of the aircraft simulator while checking armament pin placements and release sequence. B-29 gunners used the radar mockup trainer to learn control and coordination against attacking Japanese fighters.[108]

At Fairmont AB, B-29s were equipped with the APQ-13; flyaway B-29s had the APQ-17 with an off-set bombing capability. The radar operator homed in on a prominent ground return built in the variation from the return to the target. For example, five miles out on a 349-degree radial from the return, the B-29 pilot would be directed to take a course to bomb the target. The APS-15 radar was installed on later model Superfortresses, providing the bombardier a more precise target definition and allowing all-weather bombing capability.[109]

Ralph Schell (19th BG) recalled: "The B-29 was a pretty good aircraft for maintenance. The engines, however, were another story. The early engines ran too hot and engine failures were common. The first time we had a B-29 land with all four engines operating, we got a day off. Cylinder baffles were inadequate, which contributed to overheating. The Boeing Aircraft Company's design was also a contributor to maintenance problems. The bomb bay doors were operated by Jack screws. Both of these systems took too long to complete the cycle. On take-off, the engines would overheat just waiting for the gear doors to close. The added drag only made the engine overheating problem more severe.

"Engine fires were also a problem. Other training bases were experiencing the problem more than Fairmont. We had very few. The ground crews were instructed to check the fuel system on 'high' boost. If we had no leaks on high, chances were good there would be no leaks on 'low' in flight. Carburetors often leaked around the mounting bolts. We found early in our training that the bolts would bottom out before they were snug enough to secure the carburetor. We added a washer to each bolt that solved the problem. We think this and ground checking the system on 'high' boost were contributing factors in eliminating engine fires. The design of the front collector ring on the 3350 engine was probably the worst any of us had ever seen.

"The collector ring was mounted inside the cowling and nine ball joint exhausts had to be slipped into the cylinder exhaust mount all at the same time, when the ring was installed. It took a lot of manpower and patience to get the job done. Cold weather maintenance was a problem on any aircraft and the B-29 was no exception. When the crews went to Puerto Rico to get their training, we were left short-handed at Fairmont. Many maintenance personnel worked two shifts, sometimes three shifts without sleep!"[110]

In January 1945, flight training moved to Puerto Rico to conduct long-distance, over-water navigation similar to what aircrews would encounter in the Pacific. Fairmont AB's mechanics identified a B-29 design flaw. One B-29 took off from Fairmont AB, and as it climbed to 500 feet a life raft door blew open. The large emergency life raft was sucked out of the bomber and became wrapped around the aircraft's tail, resulting in tremendous vibration and producing lateral control problems. The crew dumped their B-4 bags, oxygen bottles, and one half of their parachutes. By this time half of the crew had jumped from the aircraft.

After thirty minutes, the B-29's pilot eased the aircraft down to an altitude of 8,000 feet, at which time the life raft blew loose from the tail. Once on the ground, those who parachuted out of the aircraft before the life raft came loose were collected by a Fairmont AB truck and returned to base. The pilot landed safely back at Fairmont AB. This resulted in modifications to prevent a repeat occurrence: life raft doors were retrofitted with a metal grate to prevent crewmen from being sucked out of the aircraft if a malfunction occurred. A nylon web safety strap attached to each crewman's parachute at the nape of the neck between the shoulder blades was used to prevent ejection out of the aircraft.[111]

Taxiway looking south. Two new civilian aircraft hangars are to the left of the taxiway. (Author)

View of the new civilian aircraft hangars built on the old taxiway. (Author)

View of Fairmont's taxiway to the north. (Author)

View of Fairmont's runway (17 degrees). (Author)

The Southwest runway at Fairmont. (Author)

The Northeast runway at Fairmont. (Author)

Schell noted: "The B-29 engine was supposed to be started using just the primer. When it caught, you were supposed to slowly open the mixture and release the primer. At minus 20 degrees, this just did not work. We broke the rules and slowly opened the mixture. The big problem was if the engine caught and then quit, the spark plugs would ice up; then you would have 36 spark plugs to change. By using the mixture, we were able to get the engines started and keep them running and avoid a lot of maintenance and the loss of a mission. Hangar space was inadequate—one aircraft per hangar—and we only had three hangars. This was eased by the construction of a fourth hangar.

"Once an airplane came out of a hangar following major maintenance or periodic inspection, the remainder of the work was done outside. It took a while to do the engine run-up and make all the necessary adjustments and get it tested so it could go back to Puerto Rico. Almost everything that went wrong after it came out of the hangar had to be fixed outside, including engine changes. Snow also added to our misery. Many times when we had an airplane ready for test, we had to call and wait for a snowplow to clear the ramp to the taxiway and runway.

"When the fly away B-29s arrived, a lot of our maintenance problems were solved. The landing gear doors were modified to go up with the gear, eliminating the long time getting the aircraft clean on take-off. The bomb bay doors were modified from a Jackscrew to pneumatic system; it only took a second to open or close. The doors helped the flight crews. With this modification, flight crews would not be a sitting duck and not quite so long over an enemy target at reduced speed with opened bomb bay doors. Maintenance on the air-operated doors was almost nil. From a maintenance point of view, flyaway engines were a blessing. The engine baffles were modified to make the engines run cooler. We had gone to school on fuel injection while in Nebraska and thought we would have it on the fly away, but no such luck. We still had the old carbureator."[112]

Parallel taxiway north at Fairmont Air Base. (Author)

The Second Air Force required B-29 aircrews complete a rigorous training program:

High altitude formation flying
Five copilot landings
Four copilot instrument final approaches
Nine hundred mile navigation missions
Three thousand mile navigation missions
Twelve camera attack bombing missions
Four high altitude camera bombing missions
Four gun camera missions
Each gunner fires 1,400 rounds of ammuntion[113]

Beginning in November 1944, there was a problem with spare parts to keep the B-29s operational. Fairmont AB maintenance officers could only clear a back log of supply parts orders when Headquarters Second Air Force created the *Blue Streak* parts priority program. This gave the highest priority to filling critical spare parts, even higher than overseas staging bases.[114]

In December 1944, 16th BG training picked up intensity. Approximately thirty-four flying training hours had been lost to bad weather during the month and the maintenance index was 89 percent. By this time, sixty-two percent of the training missions required had been completed. On 12 December 1944, three B-17s—each with two crews from each squadron—took off for Batista Field, Cuba. The arrangement was to have one crew fly the aircraft to Cuba and the second crew fly it back. There was still a shortage of B-29s for training operations at Fairmont AB. The training mission to Batista Field was considered long-range navigation, but the primary purpose of the flight to Cuba was to arrange over-water flying missions from Batista Field. It was believed that this experience was vital for the aircrews. The aircraft did not perform well on the flight to Cuba, landing

B-24M on display at Castle Air Museum, on the former Castle AFB, Atwater, California. (Author)

at Mobile, Alabama. Crews still believed they gained valuable experience from the mission. Six crews returned to Fairmont AB on 20 December 1944.[115]

There was a dual burden for B-29 maintenance personnel at Fairmont AB to keep B-29s flying. This required 4.3 hours of ground maintenance per airborne training hour while making required follow-on, factory-directed modifications. One of these modifications authorized by Second Air Force Directive dated December 1944 reduced defensive armament. The Second Air Force provided an extensive list of modifications each B-29 had to undergo to meet Boeing Aircraft's modifications:

Removal of upper forward turret
Removal of AN/ARR-1 homing adapter
Removal of upper rear turret
Removal of SCR-729
Removal of lower forward turret
Removal of SCR-515
Removal of lower rear turret
Removal of SCR-718 radio-altimeter
Removal of Central Fire Control and crew equipment associated with gun positions
Removal of tail gunner's oxygen regulator
Removal of Bombardier's table
Removal of 20mm rear cannon, associated equipment, elimination of navigator's armor, except the glass on the forward and rear drift sight
Elimination of engine covers areas of the aircraft
Elimination of on-board storage boxes
Improved pressurization: turret walls remained with removed pressure signals and warning lights
Cover plates installed on the gunner's blisters
Powerplant controls for pilots' throttles eliminated

B-29 on display at the South Dakota Air and Space Museum, outside the main gate to Ellsworth AFB. (Author)

Because of extensive modifications required for each B-29, stripping out or removing these items did not begin at Fairmont AB until the arrival of supervisory maintenance personnel who assisted base personnel and 19th BG mechanics. While a B-29 was pulled out of training rotation, the remaining aircraft had to pick up that day's scheduled flying hours. Similar B-29 modifications were also made on B-29s assigned to McCook and Grand Island AB (these two air bases will be discussed later). Mechanics came to Fairmont AB to learn how to complete these modifications. A Second Air Force Directive (Confidential at that time) assured all commanders would take precautions not to release any announcements about these modifications.[116]

When over-water training was not available, cross country flights were flown the approximate distance from Guam to Japan.[117]

Later variant B-29s were equipped with APQ-15 radar, which provided target definition in bad weather (heavy cloud cover). This gave B-29 bombardiers the ability to bomb through the nearly constant cloud cover over the Japanese home islands. In early 1945, there were no ground-based trainers available to give bombardiers realistic simulation of releasing bombs during a simulated combat sortie. McCook AB was scheduled to have an APQ-15 bombardier trainer installed on the base, however, its acquisition was delayed until late February 1945.[118]

Radar set training, or the lack thereof, complicated bombardier qualifications. To test the capabilities of stripped down B-29s, the 16th BG flew training missions with the bomb bays loaded with 500 pound cement-filled inert training bombs, simulating a fully combat-loaded B-29. Maintenance crews modified B-29 guns to fire blank rounds so the gunners could have hot gun practice. Three 16th BG maintenance personnel flew to Laredo, Texas for instruction on APQ-15 radar.[119] In March 1945, 16th BG personnel constructed a B-29 flight engineer's mockup panel to assist training. This was the first training aid built for this crewman's position.[120]

The 16th BG departed Fairmont AB in March 1945, which impacted the air base's training program.[121] The bomb group's flyaway B-29s underwent extensive maintenance inspection. Each B-29 was flown for fifty-five hours, then corrective maintenance was completed and each bomber's exterior surfaces were cleaned. The 16th BG's B-29s were sent to Herrington Field for final inspection. About this time, the Second Air Force published new training guidelines that reduced high altitude training missions from 30,000 to 25,000 feet, reducing wear and tear on engines and maintenance.[122] The Second Air Force granted retroactive flight training credit for training missions flown at the lower altitude in B-17s. These training missions had been flown prior to the B-29s arriving and were not considered adequate for transition training credit. However, no delays could be allowed when it was necessary to get as many aircrews to the Marianas Islands as soon as possible.[123]

Airfield sign at Fairmont Airfield. (Author)

APT. MANAGER:	Tim Kreinert, Tele: 402-268-4521 Shop: 268-2591
FBO:	Ted Hedoen, Tele: 402-268-2241
WEATHER SERV.:	OLU FSS 800-992-7433
FUEL:	100 LL
HOURS ATTENDED:	0800-1700 (Mon-Fri)
TRAFFIC PATTERN ALT:	1000′ AGL

Overhead photo of Fairmont airfield. (Author)

By 7 March 1945, the 17th BG had departed Fairmont AB. The 467th BG was assigned to Fairmont AB from 25 July to 25 August 1945, along with the 489th BG from 13 July to 23 August 1945. They were designated B-29 units without aircraft. In June 1945, Headquarters Second Air Force announced Fairmont Army Air Field was to be deactivated, with remaining instructors transferred to active B-29 training bases. B-29 maintenance work continued at Fairmont AB, but at reduced levels. By August 1945, the remaining 2,760 military and 650 civilian personnel began a three-phase base closing cycle:

- Phase One: This lasted for one week, determining individual schedules and completing personnel out-processing.
- Phase Two: This lasted for two weeks: dismantling, packing, shipping or storage of supplies and equipment, and destruction of classified documents.
- Phase Three: This lasted for ten days and included completion of final reports, reduction of personnel, and final inspections.[124]

On 27 September 1945, the War Department announced that on 31 October, Fairmont Army Air Field would go into temporary inactive status. In 1946, the War Department changed the airfield's status to that of war surplus. Some of the air base's surplus equipment was transferred to area schools, while other equipment was sold at public option. Individual buildings were torn down, with salvaged lumber sold for one dollar per truckload. Other base buildings were moved or dismantled and rebuilt for civilian homes off base.[125] Hangars were used for various purposes, such as grain storage. In 1989, the airport came under control of Nebraska's Aeronautics Division. The runways are lighted at night if required for a night or emergency landing. Small steel aircraft hangars are available for light civil aircraft storage and various businesses operate from the airfield.[126]

CHAPTER FIVE

GLEN L. MARTIN-OMAHA, NEBRASKA AND FORT CROOK

The Glen L. Martin Company assembly plant and modification center, located in Bellevue, Nebraska (south of Omaha), was an important part of the state's contribution to America's WWII aircraft production effort. Over 1,500 Martin B-26 Marauders (twin-engine medium attack bombers) and over 500 Boeing B-29 Superfortresses (long-range, heavy strategic bombers) were built there. The B-26 production plant was authorized in September 1940, before America's entry into WWII, when the War Department directed new aircraft assembly plants to be located in the interior of the United States, at a minimum of 200 miles

B-26 on display at the Strategic Air Command Museum near Ashland, Nebraska. (Author)

A Martin company photograph showing the first shovel of dirt at the new B-26 production facility imposed over the final assembly building's exit at the west end of the facility. It is on display at the Strategic Air Command Museum. (Author)

from the coast line. The construction contract was signed on 14 February 1941 by the federal government with the Glen L. Martin Company. The Nebraska Aircraft Plant—owned by the War Department—operated under its supervision. This arrangement was necessary because Martin Company's production facility in Baltimore could not be expanded to meet the War Department's increased orders for B-26s.[127]

The prospective lack of skilled labor in the Omaha, Nebraska and Council Bluffs, Iowa area fortunately proved to be only a minor deterrent and inconvenience. The explosive growth of America's war aviation industries drained every available excess manpower pool in the United States of skilled aircraft industry workers.[128] The Martin Company created an intensive aviation worker training program, using its most experienced or core production plant workers as instructors to qualify new hires. Mass production techniques allowed workers to be trained on one specific aspect of the B-26 production assembly line and this allowed workers to be mated with the new production facility when completed at Fort Crook.[129]

Fort Crook was established in 1896, then in 1921, a flying field was set up on the Army post to be used by government aircraft. The flying field was named Offutt Field in 1924 to honor and in memory of a WWI Omaha aviator, Jarvis J. Offutt. Five hundred and three acres at Fort Crook were leased by the Martin Company early in 1941, with an additional ninety-six acres purchased to provide the necessary land area not included at Fort Crook.[130]

The economic impact of the B-26 production facility was important to the Nebraska Advisory Defense Committee, established in 1941 by the Nebraska State Legislature to coordinate state and local Defense Committees' efforts to bring war jobs to the state and their towns.[131] Committee members' primary responsibilities were to assist civilian defense activities and projects such as the Martin-Omaha Bomber Plant (one of the many names it was referred to during WWII) that were expected to increase the local area's population, creating an immediate housing shortage and rent inflation.

The city of Bellevue is located north of the confluence of the Platte and Missouri Rivers in eastern Nebraska. In 1941,

Omaha was the largest city in Nebraska and its downtown area was typical of the 1940s. The news that the Martin Company was to build an aviation production plant in America was a headline. Also, the Martin Company took out a full page ad in the *Omaha-World Herald* announcing jobs were available at the plant. The poster is on display at the Strategic Air Command Museum. (Author)

the city was the largest of five municipalities in Sarpy County. Its northern boundary was contiguous to Omaha. It had a population of only 1,184 in 306 dwellings prior to construction of the B-26 plant. Almost immediately with the letting of the construction conract, 3,000 workers and their families invaded the city, needing housing, school rooms, new streets, a larger sewer and treatment facility, water and electric distribution systems, police and fire protection, and public transportation. Property values skyrocketed after being depressed since the early 1930s. In September 1941, the average sale for a housing lot was fifteen dollars, but in January 1942, it was $825. Local builders sold simple cottages with three to four rooms for an average sale price of $3,000 to $4,500. Bellevue's budget expanded: $130,000 for sewer, $360,000 for water, and $37,000 for a new elementary school and an addition to the high school. The city requested assistance from the federal government under the Wartime Impact Assistance Program, which was approved to reduce the cost of locating a war plant or military base in or near the city effected. Bellevue's police and fire departments, recreational services, and streets were inadequate to meet the sudden demand.[132]

The proposed bomber plant created a zoning dispute over which local government entity had authority to control the development of the area surrounding the aviation production facility. Omaha Mayor Dan Butler insisted the city had zoning authority; however, Sarpy County and Bellevue government officials disagreed. Sarpy County Commissioners indicated they had government responsibility to protect arriving construction workers and their families, followed by plant production workers and their families, "from infiltration of gamblers, bootleggers, and women of shady occupation."[133] It finally took the Nebraska State Legislature to resolve the jurisdiction dispute. On 17 February 1941, the Nebraska Legislature passed L.B. 495, which gave zoning rights to the Nebraska Legislature Zoning Commission. The result was the extension of the State Legislature's authority to stop Omaha's desire to expand zoning and annexing power, especially to the south.[134]

East-to-west runway under construction at Offutt Field, Fort Crook, to support the Martin B-26 plant. (Author)

Runway at Offutt AFB, looking west from the road past the east overrun from the main base area to the base lake and recreation area. Building D of the former WWII Martin production plant is at the top right center of the photograph. (Author)

A zoning ordnance and subsequent building codes were successful in defining areas of future growth, establishing acceptable building standards, and resolving the problem of trailer units and meeting Federal Housing Authority requirements. Bellevue's housing boom was fueled by tax auctions held during 1941, allowing builders to purchase and acquire deed to properties at low prices. The land was then leveraged for short term bank construction loans. Most of the homes built were small with limited amenities but affordable ($100 down), making them within the reach of most Martin Plant workers.[135]

On 3 March 1941, Glen L. Martin shoveled the first dirt at the Fort Crook construction site.[136] Glen Martin was a pioneer American aviator and aircraft manufacturer.[137] Planning continued as preliminary construction work began on the bomber plant. Rail lines were organized to run commuter passenger train shuttles from Omaha's Union Pacific passenger terminal through South Omaha to Bellevue, making six to eight stops to transport construction workers. Street car service was available from Omaha to and back from Council Bluffs, Iowa. Bus service was added from Plattsmouth and surrounding towns to the west of Fort Crook to bring in and take home plant workers.[138] Additional Nebraska Highway Patrolmen were assigned to Fort Crook for traffic control to handle the increased volume of trucks and cars, estimated to average 1,600 per hour during peak traffic volumes into and out of the construction site.[139]

In 1941, the first divided two-lane highway—Highway 73/75, from Fort Crook to South Omaha—was built. It consisted of six miles of twin concrete roadway divided by a grass median with stabilized shoulders. Traffic activated control signs were installed at the entrance to the bomber plant. The northeast entrance to the bomber plant was connected to existing pavement on Highway 73/785 by 1.7 miles of twenty-two foot wide concrete pavement, relieving traffic congestion.[140]

Peter Kiewit Sons Company of Omaha, Nebraska and Paschen Construction of Chicago, Illinois (a Kiewitt Sons Company

B-26 at Ellsworth AFB, South Dakota open house. (Author)

Associate Company) won the construction bid to complete the major portion of construction work on the bomber plant. Two other companies completed grading work on the construction site and provided materials acquisition. The contract specified construction of nine buildings, one of which was a 600 by 900 foot final assembly building. Skilled construction workers were recruited and hired from Omaha trade unions with assistance from the Nebraska State Employment Service. The Employment Service met with local trade union representatives in January 1941, to discuss procedures for hiring skilled workers for the bomber plant's construction.[141] However, there were periodic complaints from job applicants who were told they had to join a specific trade union to be hired to work on the bomber plant. As complaints increased and to prevent federal involvement, Omaha trade unions slashed initiation (joining) dues so as not to come under federal wartime profiteering regulations.[142]

At the start of construction, a 70-foot elevation variation required filling or cutting down to proper level. Ground contours north and east of Fort Crook's parade ground changed as bulldozers and earth scrapers moved five million cubic yards of dirt. In the process, the fifty-year-old Fort Crook hospital, three brick duplex officer housing units, the post golf course, Non-commissioned Officers Club, and the headquarters building were torn down. Smaller wood frame buildings were moved to different locations at Fort Crook. The first concrete pouring on the final assembly building started on 7 April 1941. Structural steel work started on 18 June 1941. Construction crews worked on one of three shifts. The B-26 production plant consisted of 1,200,000 square feet. As construction work started, the War Department and the AAF gave the Martin Company a production order for 1,200 B-26Cs.[143]

It was classified as a "hot" or fast attack aircraft, then classified as a medium bomber.[144]

Construction crews completed ninety-five percent of the bomber plant's steel framework by September 1941. Finish work was immense: 250 miles of electric wiring, 47,000 cubic yards of concrete, 10,000,000 square feet of painted walls, five acres of glass, and ten miles of florescent tube lighting in the plant's lower level. The bomber plant's floors were covered with wood brick blocks soaked in creosote and oil. This flooring helped prevent back problems among assembly plant workers standing all day on their production shift. It also allowed comparatively easy movement of machinery to accommodate production changes.

Overhead photograph of Offutt AFB. The former WWII B-26 and B-29 final production facility is at the center of the photograph, off the northwest end of the main runway. The second runway is no longer operational. The WWII modification center is now hangar row of the air base. Highway 73/75 is visible running north off the west end of the runway. Today, a four-lane bypass provides a north-south highway to the west. Courtesy of Strategic Air Command, Historian Office.

Roll out of the first B-26C on 8 June 1942. One of the women working at the plant was imposed in front of the photograph to show the importance they played in building the aircraft. This poster is on display at the Strategic Air Command Museum. (Author)

By October 1941, construction work was ninety-eight percent complete.[145]

The bomber plant was scheduled to be operational on 1 January 1942. The majority of work had been completed prior to the Japanese attack on Pearl Harbor while the United States was officially at peace, although openly supporting England and China. Although the bomber plant was completed on schedule, the delivery of production equipment lagged. By 1 January 1942, only fifty percent of the plant's machine tools had been delivered and installed. This was because the plant's subcontractors were 750 miles away. The Burlington Railroad modified box and flat cars to deliver oversized aircraft components to the aircraft production plant.[146]

Great emphasis was placed on the B-26s' range, speed and altitude capabilities. The prototype flew on 25 November 1940. Quickly, aircrew confidence in the new bomber decreased because of the aircraft's hot performance, which required skilled pilots. Each B-26C required assembly of 25,000 parts, excluding the two engines and instruments. Approximately 50 percent of assembly work was completed in the final assembly building. After B-26 production ended and the facility was enlarged for the B-29, in house assembly work reduced to thirty-six percent.[147] On 8 June 1942, the first B-26C rolled out of the final production building. Thousands of plant workers collected outside, watching the bomber taxi to the end of the runway, turn onto the runway, increase power, and take-off. At this time, there were three concrete runways available:

Runway number one (NW/SE), 4,800 feet long

Runway number two (NE/SW), 5,100 feet long

Runway number three (N/S), 4,800 feet long

On 6 April 1943, President Roosevelt toured the B-26 plant in an open touring car with Nebraska governor Dwight Griswold, Glen L. Martin, and G.T. Willey (Vice President of the Glen L. Martin Company). They slowly drove through the final production plant and modification center for an hour.[148]

Diorama of the first B-26 produced at the Martin plant on display at the Strategic Air Command Museum. (Author)

Final B-26 produced at the Martin B-26 plant. (Author)

Early in 1943, controversy arose because of slow subcontractor deliveries of airframe components impacting production numbers. AAF Colonel George E. Strong, Internal Security Officer, AAF Central Procurement District indicated the production problem was not with the subcontractors. Production by subcontractors actually slowed because of the B-26 plant's slow assembly rate, creating bottlenecks. G.T. Willey vigorously denied Colonel Strong's comments. Plant workers reported the delivered wing sections were too large and they lacked tail sections to mate with on hand fuselages. Both problems were caused by design changes that decreased as parts were standardized and plant retooling caught up with these changes.[149]

The plant completed its 1,200th B-26 on 3 November 1943, meeting the War Department's contract. From 1 September to 1 December 1943, 349 "stripped" B-26s were assembled. Armament and other equipment were removed to modify the aircraft into trainers. By January 1944, B-26 production had slowly declined, ending in April 1944 with the delivery of the 1,585th Marauder.[150]

The Martin Plant operated a Modification Center beginning in October 1942, directed by Charles H. Day, former director of planning and layout at the Wellston Air Depot in Georgia. The Modification Center completed changes on the B-26 and other AAF aircraft. During its life span, the Modification Center worked on 1,593 B-26s, 893 B-24s, 12 P-40s, and later 188 Boeing Wichita and 236 Omaha-Martin produced B-29s.[151] After January 1945, only Omaha-Martin produced B-29s were processed.

Tragedy struck on 22 September 1943, when a North American B-25 crashed through the final assembly building's roof; three crewmen were killed and one critically injured. The B-25 lodged in the final assembly building's steel roof structure, tearing a 75-foot hole and not reaching the floor. However, after the B-25 caught fire its onboard ammunition exploded. One B-26 under the burning aircraft was destroyed. Fortunately, most of the plant's shift was outside eating lunch.[152]

There were two additional aircraft accidents involving Martin plant personnel, and one resulted in the death of two test pilots. It was a remarkable safety record at the Production and Modification Center in 108 million hours of work.[153]

A B-25 that crashed through the B-26's final assembly building and caught in the plant's steel roof structure. Courtesy of Strategic Air Command Museum.

By July 1943, the war was shifting direction, especially as American aviation production facilities reached maximum output for B-17s and B-24s. The Omaha-Martin plant was awarded a War Department and AAF contract to build a heavy, four-engine, long-range strategic bomber superior to anything flying, the Boeing B-29 Superfortress.[154] The War Department described the B-29 as a long-range bomber powered by four Wright-Cyclone 18-cylinder radial air-cooled engines each producing 2,200hp, equipped with four-blade Hamilton Standard propellers. The aircraft had heavy defensive armament in power-operated turrets.[155] Three production plants built the B-29 to meet the War Department's plans for an aggressive strategic air war against the Japanese home islands: Boeing at Renton, Washington; Martin-Omaha at Fort Crook; and Bell Aircraft at Marietta, Georgia.[156]

B-25 on display at the Strategic Air Command Museum. (Author)

As Omaha-Martin B-26 production neared completion, the B-29 *Over Run Project* began. On 6 August 1943, five B-29s were flown to Fort Crook to familiarize Martin Company mechanics with the large bomber. Training was completed on 2 February 1944, two months ahead of schedule while the production plant converted from B-26 to B-29 production.[157] On 27 August 1943, construction started on a 135,000 square foot addition to the former B-26 production plant costing $2,000,000. The shift from B-26 to B-29 production was a complicated procedure. Every square foot of the B-26 production line was dismantled, with salvageable equipment arranged to mate with B-29 production equipment to accommodate the larger airframe production line.[158] When the large frames for holding the B-29 sections arrived from Boeing's Renton, Washington production facility, the sections filled most of the bomber plant's floor space. Engineers manhandled these frames into place, maintaining perfect alignment. The B-29 assembly line weaved through the large floor area.[159] Each Superfortress was identical, built and delivered in complete sections by subcontractors and assembled in one of the three production facilities. This was to speed construction and produce the bomber in great numbers.

B-29 Subcontractors were:

Cessna Aircraft in Wichita, Kansas
Chrysler in Detroit, Michigan
Fisher Body in Cleveland, Ohio; Lansing and Goodyear in Akron, Ohio
McDonnell in St. Louis, Missouri
Republic Aircraft in Farmingdale, New York[160]

B-29 production began at the Omaha-Martin plant on 6 April 1944. Specially designed railroad cars delivered components for final assembly. The first Nebraska-assembled B-29, later named *Satan's Angels* by its crew, rolled out the west end of the production plant on 24 May 1944. The B-29 was assigned to the 444th BG, India (CBI), and was lost during a mid-air collision over the Bay of Bengal on 25 March 1945. Quality was final consideration in production and if a mistake was identified, corrections

To increase production in factories and on the home front, posters were everywhere, indicating what Americans could do to assist in winning the war. Poster from "What did you do in the war?" at an exhibit at the Nebraska State Historical Society in Lincoln, Nebraska on December 7, 1991. (Author)

Another poster from the "What did you do in the war?" exhibit at the Nebraska State Historical Society in Lincoln, Nebraska on December 7, 1991. (Author)

followed immediately. For example, one day a bolt was dropped into a wing fuel tank, and if not retrieved, it could eventually plug the fuel line where it exited the fuel tank. A woman plant worker from a small group of specially hired midget workers squeezed through the small fuel tank vent opening. She used a flashlight to locate the bolt, inserting it into the correct hole outside the tank. This was the only way to retrieve dropped parts inside a complicated aircraft.[161]

Each assembled B-29 was an engineering marvel. Its large four-blade propellers were precisely balanced. One worker folded a matchbook over a horizontally positioned blade, and it would slowly turn downward from the weight until the match book.[162] A *crab crew* corrected defects or production problems identified by inspectors, developing follow-up procedures to eliminate repeat mistakes.[163] Each B-29 was flown on a three-hour checkout local flight before it was handed over to a combat aircrew.

By 15 June 1945, the Omaha-Martin B-29 plant produced 402 B-29s, averaging 55 per month. Because of the plant's high quality production record, it was selected to modify fifteen B-29s to equip a special unit (the 509th CG). Later, plant workers were told after the dropping of the first atomic bomb on Hiroshima, Japan, that they had built these B-29s. The 509th CG's commander, Lieutenant Colonel Paul Tibbets, Jr., traveled to the bomber plant to select his own B-29 from the production line as they built the bombers for the group. Tibbets stated: "I looked upon this airplane as one of the best B-29s ever produced. I remember picking it out of the Martin facility production line and the Martin factory in Omaha with the help of a couple of foreman."[164]

509th CG Aircraft

Block Number	Serial Number	Squadron Number	Aircraft Name
B-29-35-MO	44-27296	84	(did not deploy)
B-29-35-MO	44-27297	77	Bockscar
B-29-35-MO	44-27298	83	Full House
B-29-35-MO	44-27299	86	Next Objective
B-29-35-MO	44-27300	73	Strange Cargo
B-29-35-MO	44-27301	85	Straight Flush
B-29-35-MO	44-27302	72	Top Secret
B-29-35-MO	44-27303	71	Jabbitt II
B-29-35-MO	44-27304	88	Up An' Atom*
B-29-40-MO	44-27353	89	The Great Artiste

B-29-40-MO	44-27354	90	Big Stinks**
B-29-45-MO	44-86291	91	Necessary Evil
B-29-45-MO	44-86292	82	Enola Gay
B-29-50-MO	44-86346	94	Spook***
B-29-50-MO	44-86347	95	Laggin Dragon

*Renamed after V-J Day to Up An' Atom. Aircraft carried different squadron numbers so Japanese intelligence could not figure out these B-29s belonged to the 509th CG[165]
**Renamed after V-J Day to Daves Dream
***Renamed after V-J Day to Spover

Each B-29 took 3,469 hours to modify to meet atomic bomb delivery specifications. These modifications consisted of:

New H-frame support to hold the A-bombs
C-6 bomb hoist
Sway braces
Carrier assembly
Antenna assembly
Junction box
British (RAF) type G shackle assembly
Winker-type bomb bay doors
SCR-718 radar altimeter[166]

By working seven days a week, Martin engineers completed these modifications in six weeks. Each design and modification step required approval by factory representatives from the AAF Technical Service Command, Wright Field, Ohio. Tibbets brought a boilerplate mockup of a large bomb with general dimensions to that of the uranium bomb *Little Boy* to the bomber plant for demonstration evaluations during modifications.[167]

Throughout the war, the Omaha-Martin plant hired large numbers of workers. Advertisements were aired on radio, printed in local newspapers, and posted on employment sheets in U.S. Employment Offices and Office of War Information, along with specialized Federal agencies. Many workers were hired right out of high school, along with others looking for higher paying jobs. The relatively high pay offered was a great incentive, but many workers just wanted to show their patriotism after the Japanese attack on Pearl Harbor. They wanted to join the war effort in some capacity.[168] There appeared to be some type of glamour and excitement in working in menial jobs at the plant. Seventy-five percent of the plant's workers were from the Omaha, Nebraska and Council Bluffs, Iowa area. Others came from surrounding states.[169]

New hires that had already passed a battery of pre-employment tests were impressed with the importance of their work by an introductory tour of the extensive bomber production facility. A representative from the Industrial Division of the Industrial Relations Department was placed in charge of new workers and their first activities at the plant: fingerprinting, photograph for an identification card, and issuance of a B-29 plant identification employee badge. The employee badge had a printed description of the badge holder. The badge included a series of numbers and a code of multi-colored disks and rims indicating the wearer's shift and access to work areas in the

Building D of the former Omaha-Martin B-26 and B-29 production facility, Offutt AFB. (Author)

Diorama of a B-29 rolling out of the Martin production facility at Fort Crook on display at the Strategic Air Command Museum. (Author)

Diorama of B-29 *Enola Gay*, built at the Omaha-Martin plant. On display at the Strategic Air Command Museum. (Author)

Diorama of the B-29 final assembly floor at the Omaha-Martin production facility on display at the Strategic Air Command Museum. (Author)

plant and equipment.[170] The plant itself has been compared to a small city. Several hundred telephones were installed at strategic locations throughout the plant. The telephone system had two master switchboards, over 150 miles of telephone wire, and twenty-two operators. Bomber plant departments were created for finance, fire, police, schools, sanitation and safety, utilities, streets and grounds, and first aid. The bomber plant maintained a post office, a hotel on site for VIPs visiting the plant, library, recreation, transportation, music department, and a war bonds sales office.[171]

The cafeteria served 10,000 to 11,000 meals each day, amounting to 12,000,000 meals per year.[172] Cafeteria workers served snacks and refreshments during rest breaks. Smoking was only allowed in the cafeteria and specified areas during thirty-minute lunches and two daily rest breaks.[173] Peak production was reached when plant workers filled all three production shifts, 22 1/2 hours per day, six days a week. The seventh day was for equipment maintenance.[174]

By January 1945, a total of 13,217 employees were working in the plant: 11,019 working in the main production area and 2,198 in the Modification Center. The overall labor force consisted of 5,306 women, 7,656 African-Americans, 682 inspectors, and 127 supervisors and technicians.[175] Job

Diorama of the B-29 final assembly hall with the forward fuselage and inboard wing sections with engines installed on display at Strategic Air Command Museum. (Author)

Diorama of the final assembly hall with B-29s waiting for attachment of outer wing sections. The tail has been added. On display at the Strategic Air Command Museum. (Author)

classifications reflected an incredible range of employees: not only administrative, clerical, and factory personnel, but tailors to alter guard uniforms, writers to compile training manuals and brochures, photographers, cooks, chauffeurs, upholsterers, and others. The average 1945 hourly wage was .994 cents, compared to .69 cents in January 1942, a 37 percent increase in three years. The cost of living during this same time period increased 12 1/4 percent.[176] A March 1945 survey of straight-time hourly wages at the Martin plant and at thirty representative companies in the Omaha area indicated that wages were consistently higher at the Martin bomber plant. The plant's wages were somewhat lower than at many other war industries near more populated areas, though, such as Wichita, Kansas, Des Moines, Iowa, and Chicago, Illinois.[177] Martin workers were eligible to join and participate in a cooperative Martin group insurance and pension plan administered by Connecticut General Life Insurance Company.[178]

The bomber plant contributed more than paychecks to the local economies; it also provided industrial training for thousands of workers, many whom had never been employed in a factory. Operations in the bomber assembly line were simplified to a great extent by Boeing engineers, who broke down the complicated process into individual tasks easily performed by unskilled workers. This step-by-step production process reduced errors, resulting in exceptional quality.[179]

The Martin Company established absolute control over parts to make certain they arrived when and where needed in the correct step of the assembly process. In its B-29 production, Martin was one of the first to adopt the statistical analysis of operations in a factory. Operations on the bomber assembly line were simplified by Process Engineers who broke down complicated production problems into simple tasks by using visual charts to indicate problem areas.[180] In March 1944, the bomber plant conducted its own overage training at no charge to the employees.[181] This training covered "shop or factory methods" taught at the plant by selected instructors.[182] The training program not only upgraded employees' skills, but also increased overall plant productivity to the point in war production where the War Department estimated: "each employed person must do twenty-five percent more work on average if both U.S./Allied defense war material and America's civilian needs are to be fulfilled."[183]

Area high schools and the University of Omaha offered classes in specialized skills vital to war plant operations, including drafting and blueprinting. In January 1941, Sidney Owens, Acting State Director of Vocational Education,

War production poster used in the three B-29 production plants to maintain output of as many Superfortresses as possible on schedule. It is on display at the Strategic Air Command Museum. (Author)

Former Omaha-Martin bomber plant B-26 and B-29 workers, many of them women, touring Building D's main level, where they worked during WWII. This part of the tour went through the Offutt AFB Motor Pool area. The group toured the building on September 27, 1991. (Author)

requested a representative be sent to the Martin Company at Baltimore, Maryland to confirm skills workers would need. This initial evaluation, as well as a regional meeting of vocational education officials with federal officials from 16 to 18 January 1941 in Chicago, was paid for with federal funds. The federal government also defrayed the costs of employee access to trade training classes.[184] In November 1944, over forty percent of the bomber plant's 12,000 employees were women, which made Martin the largest recruiter of women in the Nebraska's war industries.[185] Bellevue, Omaha, and Lincoln, Nebraska and Council Bluffs, Iowa were greatly impacted socially, politically, and economically. Until WWII, only twenty-five percent of American women working in the expanding industrial work force as military production rearmed America or for Lend Lease. Women proved they could work in other than low-paying jobs, trained in all technical skills to meet war production. The number of working women reach fifty percent by 1944.[186]

Bomber plant workers were highly motivated, not only out of patriotism and desire for good paying jobs, but also out of a sense of community they gained from participation in a huge war effort. Without their labors, the U.S. war economy would never have been able to turn out huge quantities of military equipment and munitions. Women's presence in the war industries sparked the beginnings of permanent social change, not only in the working roles of men versus women, but also in the living styles and home duties of men and women. In February 1943, Fowler B. Harper, Deputy Chairman of the War Manpower Commission, suggested school attendance time be extended through the afternoon and night shopping hours be longer to meet the schedules of working women.[187] At first, many women did not have basic skills necessary for the jobs applied in the plant. Less than ten percent of women applicants had any extensive experience with machinery of any type.[188]

Martin bomber officials wanted to hire women on the same basis as men, indicating that on the payroll "all Martineers are equal."[189] Classes in advanced technical skills were offered (aircraft electricity, instruments, and radio) and were available for all three shifts. The increase in women inspectors was one of the benefits for the number of women working in the plant. On 24 March 1942, Joan Catalano became the first woman inspector working in the bomber plant. Later, women became inspectors in other departments: receiving, detail manufacturing, general assembly, finishing and plating, hangars and flight test, and modifications.[190]

There were indications these gains for women might only be temporary. Eighty-three percent of the women hired were in the lowest classifications.[191] Women worked as drill operators, rivet handlers, bench electricians, floor timekeepers, dockhands, clerks, maintenance staff, cafeteria workers, and general work helpers. They were usually trainees in any department, assigned duties of a nature requiring no specific skill.[192] Women at the plant did have a higher rate of

Ethel S. Abbott Archival Library in the Strategic Air Command Museum. Its files contained valuable information on the Glen L. Martin B-26 and B-29 bomber production facility. (Author)

B-29 on display at the Lackland Air Park in San Antonio, Texas. (Author)

The former Strategic Air Command headquarters building became headquarters for the United States Strategic Command at Offutt AFB, Nebraska. The building sits on top of the former SAC underground command post. (Author)

turnover than men, perhaps due to family obligations.[193] In January 1944, the rate of turnover for women employees was 4.85 percent and for men 3.0 percent. By January 1945, the rate for men was 4.26 percent and women 7.57 percent.[194]

An article in the *Martin Star* (May 1944, reprint) noted this: "Women workers at the bomber plant had an inborn quality of patience and ability to make monotony an interesting thing, but stated that their intuition and originality could best be used at home. In 1941, national polls indicated about ninety-five percent of working women expected to leave the labor market after the war. However, as the war continued, this percentage dropped."[195] Women who worked in lower paying jobs in retail or home before the war were likely to want to keep on working. Clearly, for many women their work expectations conflicted with eventual postwar realities. When the

For many years, the only missile on display at the former SAC headquarters was the Minuteman III ICBM, seen in the background. When Offutt AFB became home to U.S. Strategic Command, it covered both Air Force and Navy missiles, such as the Trident SLBM in the front of the photograph. (Author)

war ended, so did the military service of millions of men and women. Women workers had given up their time and consumer goods for those in combat, so they were expected to give up their jobs for returning servicemen. Most returned to their former low-paying jobs or terminated from their war jobs. The prevailing attitude was that women should go home, raise children, and keep house. There are still opportunities for women from the war time work force to remain in America's skilled industrial work force, something that had not been available before to women.[196] Women learned how to build a complicated bomber and excelled.[197]

During its four years of operation, the Martin bomber plant regularly met its production goals and quotas, winning nine of thirty merit awards given out by the War Production Board to aircraft industries.[198] The War Department awarded the Martin-Nebraska bomber plant the Army-Navy "E" Production Award for operating twelve consecutive months of on schedule production.[199] On 18 September 1945, the last B-29 rolled off the production line.[200]

On 1 April 1946, the bomber plant's last one hundred employees completed their period of employment. During the plant's shut down, the Bellevue-Omaha-Council Bluffs economies faced the effects of postwar contract cancellation. A few workers were temporarily employed to remove B-29 production machinery, which was shipped back to Boeing in Renton, Washington. The bomber plant was used for machine tool storage from 1946 to 1948, and was later used for processing other war industry machine tools as temporary storage.[201]

Fort Crook's operations transferred to the United States Air Force, renamed Offutt AFB in 1948. SAC moved its first headquarters into Building D. After the new headquarters was completed in 1959, Building D was renovated into a guided missile maintenance and assembly facility. Today, Building D contains many support activities for Offutt AFB.[202]

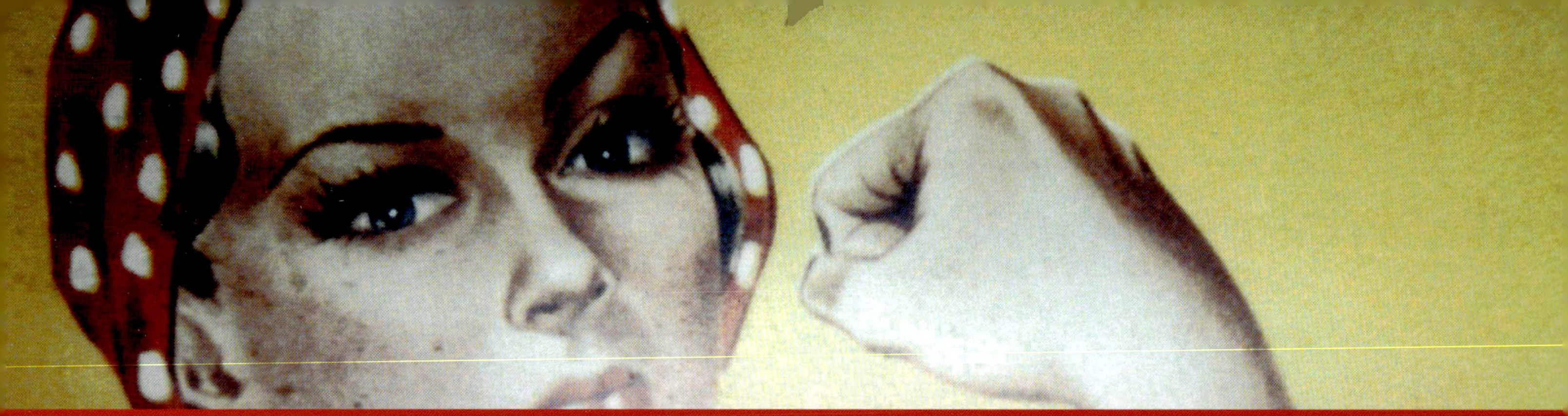

CHAPTER SIX
MUNITIONS PRODUCTION

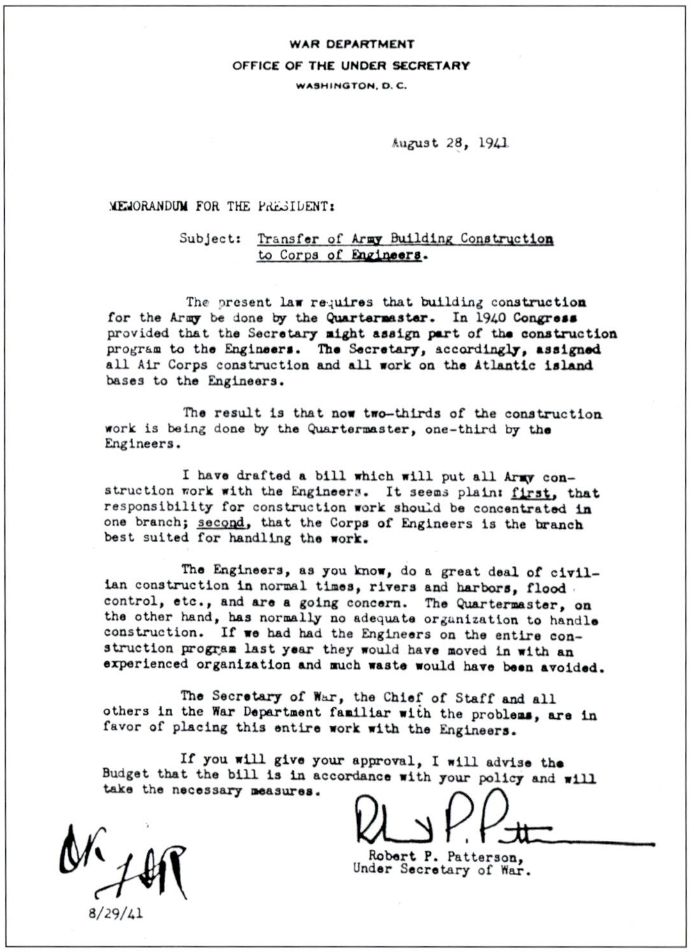

WAR DEPARTMENT
OFFICE OF THE UNDER SECRETARY
WASHINGTON, D. C.

August 28, 1941

MEMORANDUM FOR THE PRESIDENT:

Subject: Transfer of Army Building Construction to Corps of Engineers.

The present law requires that building construction for the Army be done by the Quartermaster. In 1940 Congress provided that the Secretary might assign part of the construction program to the Engineers. The Secretary, accordingly, assigned all Air Corps construction and all work on the Atlantic island bases to the Engineers.

The result is that now two-thirds of the construction work is being done by the Quartermaster, one-third by the Engineers.

I have drafted a bill which will put all Army construction work with the Engineers. It seems plain: first, that responsibility for construction work should be concentrated in one branch; second, that the Corps of Engineers is the branch best suited for handling the work.

The Engineers, as you know, do a great deal of civilian construction in normal times, rivers and harbors, flood control, etc., and are a going concern. The Quartermaster, on the other hand, has normally no adequate organization to handle construction. If we had had the Engineers on the entire construction program last year they would have moved in with an experienced organization and much waste would have been avoided.

The Secretary of War, the Chief of Staff and all others in the War Department familiar with the problems, are in favor of placing this entire work with the Engineers.

If you will give your approval, I will advise the Budget that the bill is in accordance with your policy and will take the necessary measures.

Robert P. Patterson,
Under Secretary of War.

8/29/41

Transfer of Army building construction to Corps of Engineers. (Author)

From 1939 to 1945, fighting in the European and Pacific Theaters of Operations consumed millions of tons of shells, bombs, ammunition, and other types of munitions. When England stood alone against Germany and Italy prior to 7 December 1941, U.S. ammunition and armament stocks were seriously depleted by Lend Lease shipments. As older stocks of munitions were shipped to England and China, there was an urgent need to replace munitions for the U.S. military and buildup for the expected involvement in the war. Munitions plants required large open areas in sparsely populated areas. Nebraska farm and ranch land was ideally suited for munitions plants, far enough from coastal areas to guarantee plant security. After Pearl Harbor, because of the large numbers of German and Italian immigrants in the United States, Army officers feared possible sabotage by hard core Nazi and Fascist individuals if large munitions plants were built near eastern industrial areas adjacent to large cities.[203] After the U.S. entered WWII, American Japanese were forcibly moved from west coast areas and shipped to relocation camps in the northern and Rocky Mountain portions of the United States (referred to as American POW camps). This was the dark part of American WWII history, although these Japanese Americans accepted their relocation and many joined the military to prove their patriotism and fight against a common enemy, while the majority of Germans and Italians were not similarly relocated. The Army wanted munitions plants located away from the U.S. coasts to prevent enemy attack, such as shelling by German submarines or commando raids. The War Department was also concerned that Imperial Japanese Navy submarines might sneak through U.S. air and sea reconnaissance patrols to shell West Coast defense plants. It is interesting these concerns were so open, considering the United States was not at war with these three countries until after Pearl Harbor. The War Department authorized the Nebraska Ordnance Plant's construction on 14 October 1941 at a cost of twenty-five million dollars.[204]

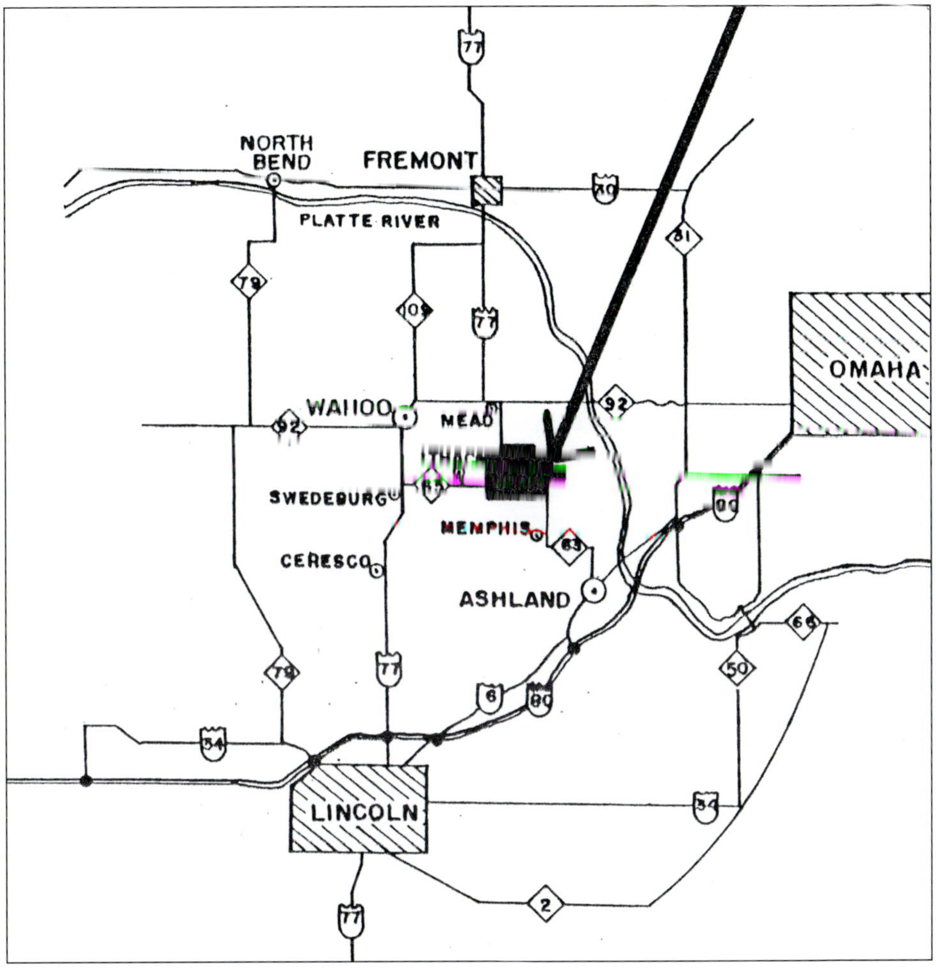

Map of Mead Ordnance Plant. Courtesy of Nebraska State Historical Society to author.

Signs were wired to the fence enclosing the ordnance, warning people not to enter. (Author)

On 14 October 1941, Mead residents heard on the radio that a large bomb loading plant would be built near the town. It did sound good, but it would require 17,000 acres of surrounding farm and ranch land. People would have to leave their farms and where they would go made landowners unhappy. By March 1942, five months after the War Department's announcement, the families in the construction area had vacated the land. Most of the buildings in the construction site were moved or destroyed. However, in the first phase of plant construction, the John Speckman home became a hospital and first aid station, the Bernard Johnson home became headquarters for Gifles-Vallet Inc., Architect-Engineers; and the David Gustaffson home was the guard headquarters.

Security was strict in the Ordnance Area, with vital areas well lighted and no one admitted except employees and those with a proper pass. All agricultural activities ceased. Guard towers were manned and patrolled. Mead, Nebraska, with a population of 260, found that a wartime boomtown was not all a golden tune in the cash register and a quick ride to prosperity; headaches resulted from bringing 1,500 people into a town keyed to accommodate 260. When the plant brought in 4,000 construction workers swarming over an area that a few months before was farmland, problems multiplied. For the city of Mead, the problem was one of housing, sanitation, and schools. Workers were faced with getting transportation, finding living accommodations, purchasing food, and obtaining recreational facilities.

As noted, housing became the most complex problem for the town. Anything that served as a shelter was used: chicken coops, hay storage areas in barns, a third floor attic, tents, trailers, and park stand shelters.

Fifty-two beds were set up in a commercial rooming house. About 90 percent of the town's residents opened their homes to accommodate the workers. One home had beds for eighteen men set up in the basement, with a family of six and two more roomers on the main floor. The town applied to the federal government for financial assistance for eighteen percent of the cost of an expanded sewer system. However, because of the temporary nature of the Ordnance Plant, it was denied. The city of Mead explored the possibilities of connecting the plant's facilities, but this was also denied because of security.

Construction workers were housed in dormitories in the area and often walked into town for ice cream at Jeppson Drug Store. The number of local restaurants increased from one to six. Sometimes it was impossible to walk on the sidewalk in downtown because of the number of construction workers and local residents shopping. Labor Union offices opened in a hotel and a small space in the southeast corner of Schneider's Grocery Store. From the standpoint of schools, the plant presented another problem. The area took out taxation of three of the twenty-three sections, or about 1/6th of its income. Workers' children made it necessary to hire more teachers.

Many workers commuted from Omaha, Lincoln, and surrounding towns. Many car pooled, paying 60-70 cents a day for their round trip. Workers' shifts on the construction site averaged ten hours on two shifts, seven days a week. Construction workers earned a good wage: $51.00 a week for a common laborer and $106.00 for carpenters and skilled journeymen. The large influx of workers and their families continued into town during construction for one year. After the Ordnance Plant began operations, the town's population leveled out, with critical housing problems easing dramatically. After the war, many of those employed at the Ordnance Plant moved to Omaha or Lincoln, with few remaining.

The Nebraska Ordnance Plant was constructed in 1942, under direction of the Army Corps of Engineers. Preliminary construction work began on 1 January 1942. A total of 177 tracts of land were purchased. Easements for roads and utilities were disposed of by completed negotiations, often after the land was condemned by federal government agencies for the Ordnance Plant's construction. The average price paid for the land was $127.00 per acre. The plant area consisted of twelve sections of Wahoo Project and fifteen sections of

View from the Ordnance Plant's main entrance looking west at the administrative office. In the rear is one of the main production lines in the Ordnance Plant. At this time, the area was still open (1991) and I was able to walk through the buildings. It was part of an EPA cleanup. (Author)

Entrance to a munitions storage bunker. (Author)

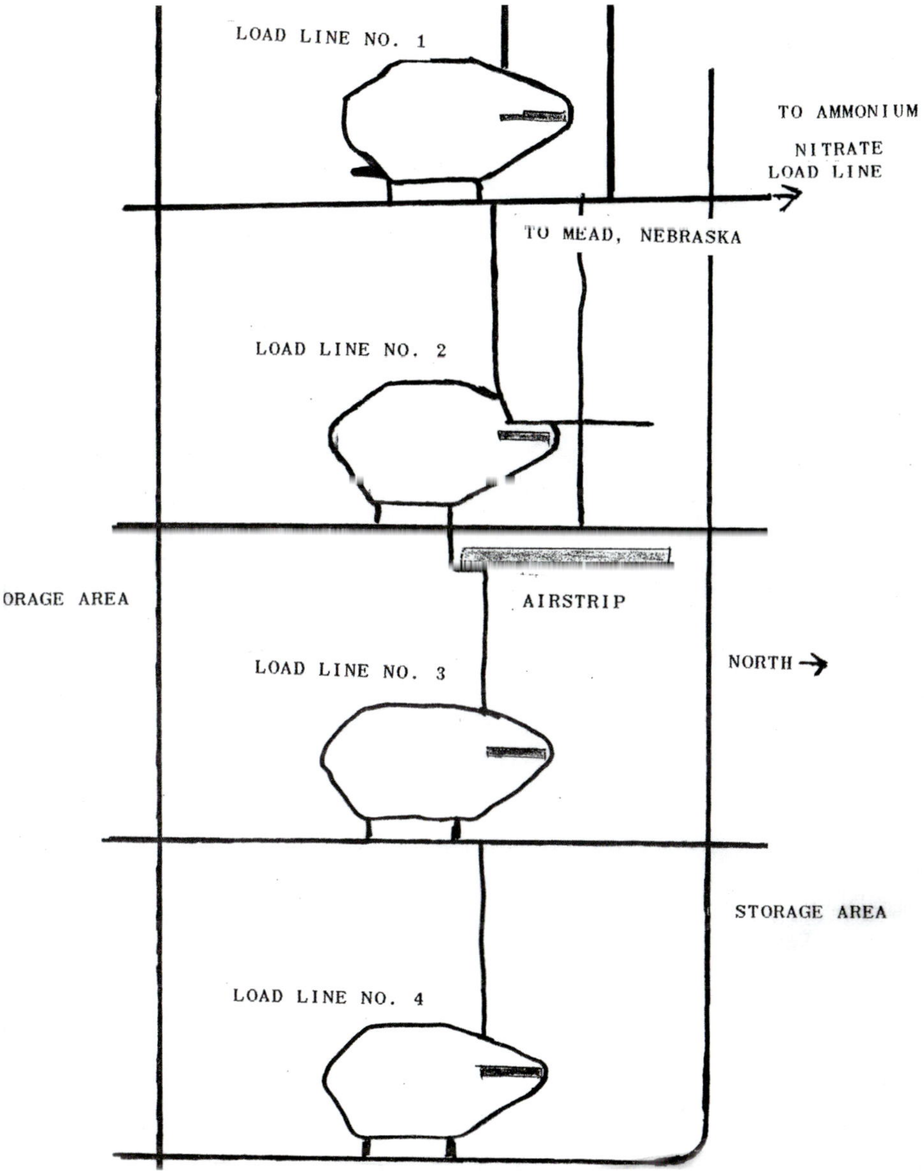

Drawing of the Mead Ordnance Plant. (Author)

The Mead Ordnance Plant complex was served by the Union Pacific Railroad track running west out of Omaha, Nebraska across the state. Much of the train traffic was a combination of freight and passenger service, except when large amounts of munitions were moved on separate trains, adequately spaced to prevent destruction of other trains and war cargo if a detonation occurred. Photograph on display at the Union Pacific Railroad Museum in Omaha, Nebraska. ((Museum Historian to Author.))

Most of the railroad traffic in the United States during WWII was moved by steam locomotives. This steam locomotive is being filled with coal at the Union Pacific terminal in Omaha, Nebraska. Photograph on display at the Union Pacific Railroad Museum in Omaha, Nebraska. (Museum Historian to Author.)

Marble Project. It was a new community, with its own railroad station, internal rail distribution tracks, streets, water distribution system, sewer processing plant, fire department (critical with the tons of explosives produced in wood buildings, even though they were protected from each other by earth berms), recreation hall, on-site dormitories, and twelve senior residences for military officers and plant supervisors.

The Ordnance Plant also contained four load lines, an ammonium nitrate plant, booster line, warehouses, administration building, and maintenance shops (automotive, diesel engine, carpenter, paint, machine, electric, laundry, etc.) pertinent to the plant's operations.

The Ordnance Plant was served by the Union Pacific Railroad from the north and Chicago, Burlington & Quincy Railroad from the south. Highway access was by US 30A (today Highway 92) and 77. WWII production started on 9 September 1942, continuing until V-J Day in August 1945. During the war, production was awesome: 2,839,778 bombs (90-pound fragmentation to 4,000-pound Block Busters used by the RAF) and 16,311,594 boosters. The plant was operated by the Nebraska Defense Corporation, a subsidiary of the Firestone Tire and Rubber Company. The plant employed an average of 3,000 workers. The contract was terminated and all property returned to the Ordnance Corporation on 28 November 1945. The plant was designated as a permanent standby ordnance depot to be used for storage of ammunition components. During 1946-1949, the Emergency Export Corporation produced 430,000 tons of ammonium nitrate for export shipment.

Even though WWII production contribution of the Ordnance Plant ceased with the end of the war, its story continued into the Korean War (Cold War) and the present. I selected this ordnance facility because of the opportunity to explore and photograph it before the area was closed due to the presence of hazardous chemicals remaining after years of munitions productions.

Women and men working on the 16-inch naval shell load line. Courtesy of NSHS

Women working on one of the pour booster lines. Courtesy of NSHS

After the United States became involved in the Korean War in 1950, the Ordnance Plant went back into production status in February 1950, producing practice rockets, 105mm howitzer shells, and bombs (350 to 12,000 pounds). By August 1953, the plant employed 3,162 workers. On June 1956, the Ordnance Plant was again deactivated.

From 1956-1960, the Ordnance Plant had a core of 255 workers maintaining the facility in a readiness status. In 1959, the USAF started construction in one corner of the facility for an Atlas ICBM site. USAF engineers were concerned that because of the site's radar emissions, radio transmissions, and other electronic disturbances, it would not be safe to concurrently operate an active ordnance

Covered wood walkways or connection passages allowed workers to transit from one production line to the next. This was critical to prevent moisture from rain and snow being introduced into the production lines, which could end in detonations and destruction. (Author)

plant nearby. At this time, the facility was becoming obsolete and the decision was made to declare the plant surplus (excess) federal property. A notice was published on 5 August 1960 of intention to dispose of the property. In December 1961, the General Services Administration auctioned 5,000 acres of land on the site, mostly the northern and eastern sections of the Ordnance Plant.

The federal auction land sale average $195 per acre. SAC retained control over 2,112 acres for the Atlas ICBM site; later this land was reassigned to the Nebraska Army National Guard and Army Reserve for training exercises when the ICBM site was deactivated.

In April 1962, the University of Nebraska was granted a deed to 9,400 acres of land. All this property was on a twenty-year grant and was used for education and research under the title Field Laboratory. The Field Laboratory contributed to the state's agricultural program research. Late in 1968, the Ordnance Plant's Administration Area was sold for use by small industry.[205]

Dirt-covered munitions storage bunker north of the main load lines. If an accidental explosion occurred, the force of the explosion went up through the wood roof, with adjacent bunkers protected by earth berms so as not to start secondary explosions. (Author)

The large area required by the Ordnance Plant was necessary for separation of production lines and handling and storage facilities. (Author)

In 1991, most of the former Ordnance Plant's buildings were in bad shape. I walked through the buildings taking photographs. Most had not been cleaned up and debris remained everywhere. No longer required, but at this time, the state had no funds to clean up the large facility. (Author)

By the late 1980s, the Lower Platte North Natural Resources District (NRD) became concerned about the possibility of ground water contamination at the previous Mead Ordnance Plant. Two other Nebraska ordnance plant locations will be discussed later (Hastings and Grand Island). These two facilities had previously been declared federal Superfund sites. NRD received assistance from Nebraska's congressional delegation to force the Army Corps of Engineers to investigate the former Mead Ordnance Plant site. The facility was investigated by the Army Corps of Engineers and Defense Environmental Restoration Program (DERP). The area is not currently owned by the federal government, leaving much to the state for some type of corrective action. Included in the Army Corps of Engineers' investigation was the Nebraska National Guard training area and the plant's administration area, bomb booster assembly area, burning ground (it was common practice to dig a pit into the ground to burn contaminated chemicals and old munitions, something only conducted in closed high-temperature facilities today), sewage treatment area, and ammonium nitrate plant.

In a study completed in April 1989, the Army Corps of Engineers identified areas of soil contaminated by dangerous PCBs and munitions waste, including Trinitrotoluene (TNT) and Cyclomethylence-Tritramine (RDX). The Army Corps of Engineers also detected TNT, RDX, and Trichloroethylene (TCE) in on site drilled monitoring wells and RDX and TCE in off-site drinking water wells. An estimated 400 people pulled their drinking water within three miles of the site. The Army Corps of Engineers started cleanup in 1994; from 1994-1996, they removed 1,250 tons of PCB tainted soil that was transported to a licensed waste landfill. For the RDX contaminated soil, a large incinerator was built on-site in 1997. From October to December 1997, more than 16,000 tons of soil were burned in the 1,700-degree incinerator, completely destroying the RDX. Remains of the cleaned soil were buried on-site. The load lines, ordnance storage igloos, and other buildings were demolished. This is

Liquid shell TNT filling building. (Author)

why my documentation of the facility is important to retaining WWII history.[206]

Naval Ordnance Depot

The City of Hastings, Nebraska was notified by U.S. Senator George Norris and Congressman Carl Curtis that the U.S. Navy would build a Naval Ammunition Depot (NAD) southeast of the town. The depot would be built on 48,753 acres, costing $45,000,000. Construction started on 4 July 1942 by the Maxon Construction Company, taking 18 months and using 5,000 construction workers. As with all wartime construction sites/projects, housing was short. The U.S. Navy built a twenty-acre trailer court at 14th and Burlington Street at the Adams County Fairgrounds and Spencer Park in southeast Hastings. This was a temporary fix to solve the housing shortage in this small town.

U.S. Marine Corps (USMC) guards arrived in December 1942, with U.S. Coast Guard K-9 dogs arriving in December 1943. Plant workers began to be hired in January 1943. NAD was commissioned by the U.S. Navy on 22 February 1943. The first

One of the munitions load buildings. (Author)

A Union Pacific Railroad passenger train travels west across Nebraska, moving troops to embarkation ports. Rail access was important to the location of an ammunition depot. Photograph on display at the Union Pacific Railroad Museum in Omaha, Nebraska. (Museum Historian to Author.)

production test load was made on 1 July 1943. On 4 July, the first production ammunition was completed, shipped by rail for U.S. Navy warship armaments. Employment and production reached maximum capacity in June-July 1945. The plant required large numbers of workers: 125 naval officers, 1,800 naval enlisted, and 6,692 civilians. Construction required over 2,000 contract workers. This was a large wartime hazardous industrial production operation.

In 1945, the first heavily guarded ammunition train left NAD for the West Coast with ammunition shipped out to the fleet for combat operations against Japan. NAD produced bombs, mines, rockets, 40mm shells, and large caliber 16-inch shells for battleships. NAD workers' starting pay was 74 cents per hour, 60 hours per week. In comparison, a Hastings retail sales clerk earned 25 cents per hour. There was always a need for workers to cover round-the-clock operation. This was a dangerous place to work, but considering the large amounts of ammunition, sooner or later something had to go wrong.

On 27 January 1944, a six-inch shell exploded in the Black Powder Room. Three Navy enlisted from the Negro Ordnance Battalion died: Adolph Johnson, Jesse Wilson, and J.C. Miles. On 6 April, 1,000 pounds of explosives blew up in the Bomb and Mine Loading Area. A railroad boxcar blew up and caused a second, near simultaneous explosion in the cooling shed containing sea mines and depth charges. Seven workers were killed: Chester Arthur Curtis, Norris Elmer Frey, Lida Sarah Mitchell, Lois Lillian, Nevins Adams, Vera E. Conant, Mary E. McQuaid, Keith Clark Mathiasen, and LaVerne L. Tompkins. The resulting series of explosions caused damage to the Glenvil, Harvard, Fairfield, and Clay Centers. On 10 June, a detonation in the 60mm building exploded, killing Walter Michaelson. The fourth explosion was on 15 September. The south railroad transfer depot blew up, resulting in a huge crater 550 feet long, 220 feet wide, and 50 feet deep. The explosion killed U.S. Coast Guardsman S1/C Bert E. Hugen, U.S. Navy Si/C Leslie Williams, S1/C Freeman Lorenzo Tull, S1/C Willie Williams, S2/C Daniel Casey, S2/C Frank William David, S2/C Samuel Burns, S2/C Clarence Randolph, and S2/C Ulysses Code, Jr., while injuring fifty-three others. Damage was extensive to

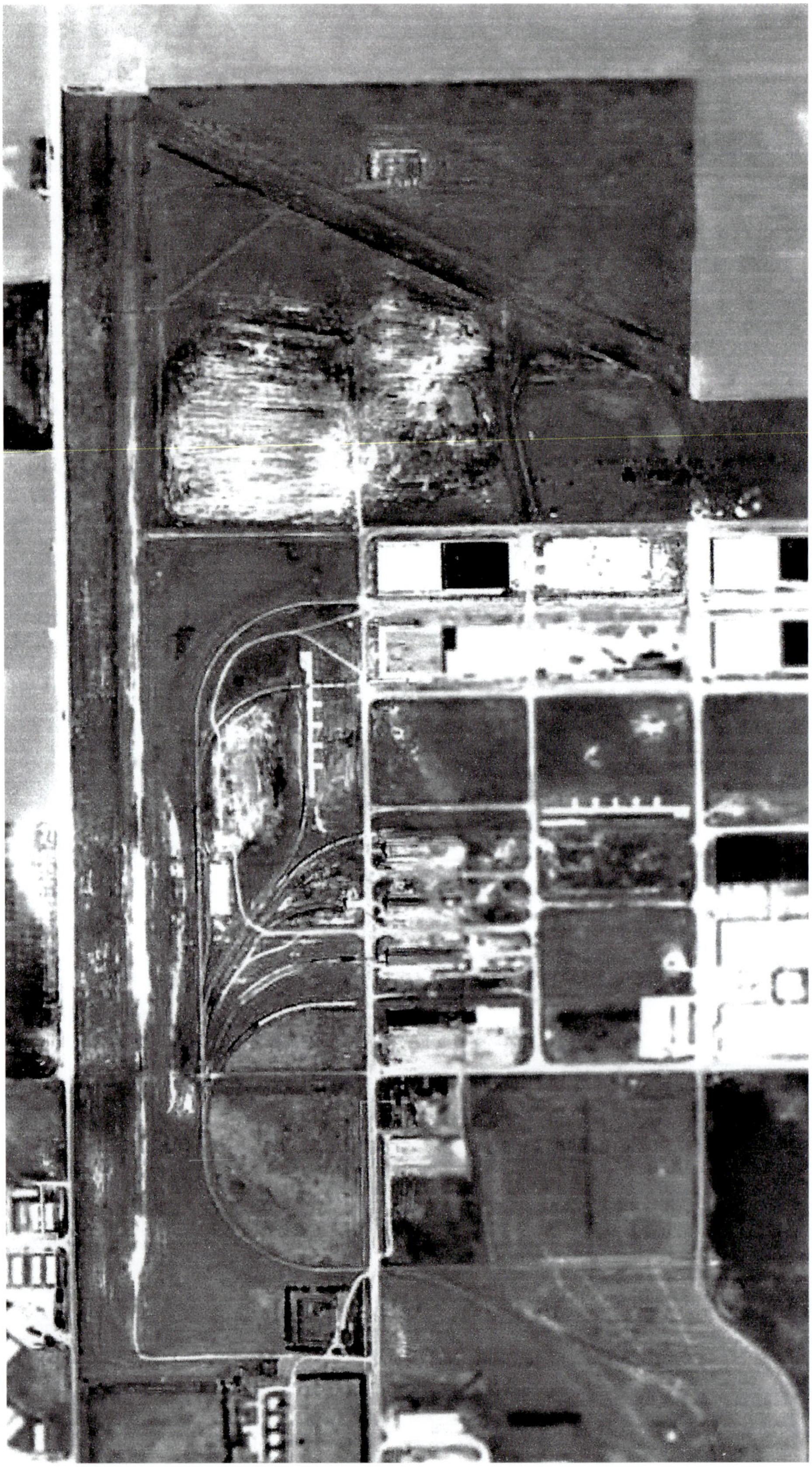

Overhead view of the Hastings Naval Ammunition Depot. Courtesy of United States Geological Survey.

surrounding towns. This was not as bad as it could have been due to earthen berms in front of the ammunition storage igloos that deflected the blast, shock waves, and debris upward and not out.

The depot consisted of 2,200 buildings, warehouses, and bunkers at a cost of $71,000,000 on 49,000 acres in Adams and Clay Counties. It employed 1,000 military and civilians. The facility was served by 207 miles of railroad tracks, 274 miles of haul and service roads, and ten miles of earth-covered igloo type ammunition storage bunkers. NAD was the largest Navy inland depot, producing forty percent of its WWII ordnance. The Navy also operated ammunition depots in Oklahoma, Indiana, and Nevada. Prior to the end of the war in the Pacific, as early as April work hours were reduced to 54 hours per week. In August, work hours were reduced to 40 hours, with the work force reduced to 3,000. By 1949, the work force dropped to 1,189.

As with the Mead Ordnance Plant, the outbreak of the Korean War resurrected the depot, with the work force increasing to 2,946 by January 1954. The Depot went into maintenance status in April 1957 and deactivated in December 1958. In September 1964, a total of 10,263 acres near Clay Center was transferred to the U.S. Department of Agriculture for a meat animal research center. The administrative headquarters area was transferred to Central Community College in 1966. Between 1966 and 1967 the remaining surplus land was sold.[207]

Sioux Army Depot

There was an ordnance plant in Sidney, Nebraska, in the western part of the state called the Sioux Army Depot (airfield and ordnance). The depot was established on 23 March 1942, under the U.S. Army Ordnance Department. With its extensive railroad network the depot received, stored, and shipped out ammunition and military supplies. This was also a large complex of 19,771 acres, 801 ammunition storage igloo bunkers, 392 support and administrative buildings, 22 warehouses, 225 on-site family housing units, 51 miles of railroad track, and 203 miles of haul and service roads. The depot was also serviced by a short airfield

At the peak of operation, 2,161 workers were employed at the Sioux Army Depot, but there were never enough workers in the depot. After Italy surrendered and became allied with the United States, Italian POWs from the nearby POW camp at Scotts Bluff were allowed to work in the depot. In addition, Japanese American internees were also allowed to work in the depot. Courtesy of NSHS

(4,400 feet long) along a north/south line. The depot employed 2,161 civilians and 57 military personnel.[208]

The depot did not have enough civilian labor to meet production schedules, forcing the U.S. Army to bring in German and Italian POWs to assist ordnance plant non-production or load line functions. Nebraska's POW camps will be discussed later. Under Title II of the Geneva Convention's General Provisions: "Prisoners of War may be interned in closed camps but may not be confined or imprisoned except as an indispensable measure or sanitation. POW camp installations shall provide housing which will afford all possible guarantees of hygiene and healthfulness, adequate heating, lighting, and fire protection. In addition, space allowances and other housing conditions must conform to the facilities, which are provided troops, and base camps of the detaining power... prisoners could volunteer to work on military installations (non-war related jobs), private industry or in agriculture."[209]

The Sidney Branch POW camp was a satellite POW camp of the main POW camp at Scotts Bluff, referred to as Side Camp Number Nine, consisting of temporary barracks constructed south of the Sioux Ordnance Plant. It was secured with a barbed wire stockade and guarded. Many of the branch camp's prisoners were processed through and out of Scotts Bluff to Sidney. The Sioux Ordnance Plant's POW camp initially held 300 Italian and 306 German POWs. These POWs worked as common laborers, engineers, carpenters, post exchange cooks, landscape gardeners, and unloading trucks and railroad cars. By January 1945, POWs were transferred back to the main Scotts Bluff POW camp.[210] The ordnance plant at Sidney was deactivated on 30 June 1967.

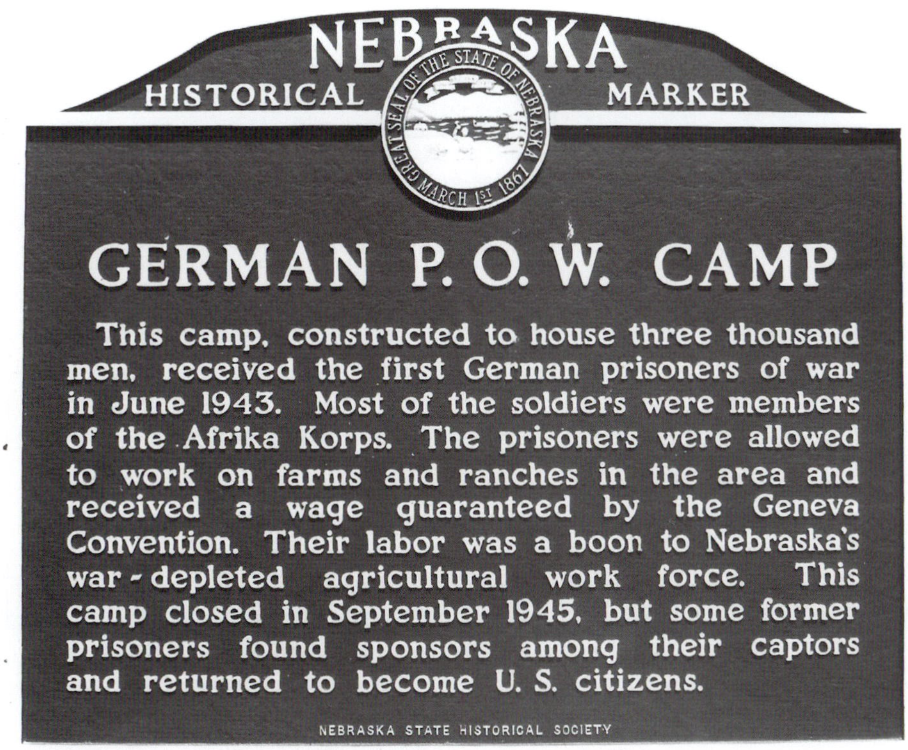

Historical marker at the Scotts Bluff WWII POW camp. (Author)

Cornhusker Ordnance Plant

On 24 March 1942, the Army Corps of Engineers started construction on the Cornhusker Ordnance Plant in Grand Island, Nebraska. The plant was completed in November 1942, with the first bomb poured on 11 November. The rapidly created plant on twenty square miles was a good example of wartime construction. The Army Ordnance Corps provided standardized plans for construction at other ordnance plants. These uniform plans were used whenever and wherever possible to eliminate construction delays, beginning ordnance production in the shortest time. The plant had four loading lines, a booster line, and an ammonium nitrate line for production of 105mm ammunition and bombs. The main complex covered 12,788 acres with 15 on-site staff quarters, five dormitories with 440 rooms, six barracks for 240 construction workers, an eight-bed hospital, two recreation rooms, and ten cafeterias.

The Army Corps of Engineers built many other facilities to support munitions production: machine, carpenter, and maintenance shops; four motor vehicle sheds; a laundry facility; 41 warehouses totaling 500,000 square feet; and 219 ammunition magazines with a storage capacity of 2,780,800 square feet.[211] Production continued until 16 August 1945. During WWII, the plant employed a maximum work force of 4,229. They loaded 90 and 260-pound fragmentation bombs, 1,000 and 2,000-pound general purpose bombs, and 105mm artillery shells. The plant's operations were managed by the Q.O. Ordnance Company, a subsidiary of the Quarter Oaks Company. After WWII, the ordnance plant was decontaminated and went into standby status. In the 1950s, the Silas Mason Company operated the plant to manufacture rockets. During the Korean and Vietnam Wars, the plant produced 500 and 750-pound bombs.[212]

The ordnance plant was added to the EPA's National Priorities List (NPL) for hazardous waste sites in 1987. The Agency for Toxic Substances and Disease Registry (ATSDR) prepared a preliminary public health assessment in 1988. The isolation and access to former

Two African American men assigned to the Negro Ordnance Battalion load 105mm shells onto a pallet for transport. Courtesy of NSHS

Women working at the Cornhusker Ordnance Plant at Grand Island, Nebraska. Work started in 1942, under supervision of the Quarter Oaks Company. The bomb loading plant processed 800,000 pounds of TNT every twenty-four hours. Courtesy of NSHS

on-site plant areas limits the chances local populations have for coming into contact with volatile organic compounds (VOCs), such as RDX, TNT, or HMX. There is a concern about the number of local residents possibly exposed to contaminated drinking water after the plant closed. Alternate sources of drinking water have been provided for local residents around the plant. Removal of contaminated soil and its incineration began in August 1987, near north load lines 2 and 3, as well as south of the north magazine area. This amounted to 44,722 tons of soil removed and incinerated.[213]

Union Pacific rail passenger cars were a common sight on the tracks in Nebraska during WWII. Passenger car on display at the Union Pacific Railroad Museum in Omaha, Nebraska. (Author)

When workers relaxed, they often used the recreational hall's juke box to play records. Even this building carried war posters to increase production. On display at the Nebraska State Historical Society in Lincoln, Nebraska. (Author)

CHAPTER SEVEN
GRAND ISLAND AIR BASE

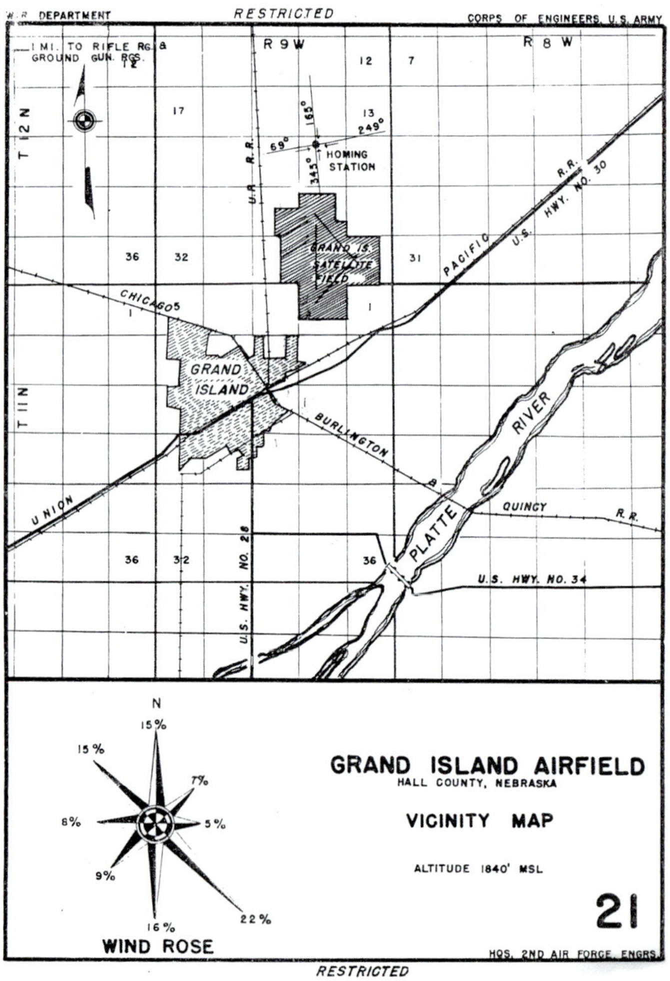

Grand Island World War II vicinity map. (Author)

Grand Island Air Base was built on the pre-war site of the City of Grand Island's Municipal Airport, located four miles northeast of the town.[214] The new air base was serviced along its western boundary by an oil-surface road connecting to Grand Island's paved city streets, providing all-weather vehicular access from the local airport to the city. No railroad facilities led directly to the proposed airfield construction site. A railroad siding was available at Cary, adjacent to the gasoline storage and service station 1 1/4 miles from the airport's hangar and administration buildings. The construction site comprised one full section of land.

The original construction site was graded and leveled for overall landing operations. Runways at the time had been under construction in Grand Island by an accepted Works Project Administration (WPA) project at the initiation of the satellite construction operations for a military airfield. Although the original runway under construction by the WPA was not at the desired location for a large military training base, it did provide some benefit on work completed. This required acquisition of additional land for the extension of runways and clear zones required for safe aircraft operations. The architecture and engineering work began on site on 3 September 1942. Construction bids were opened on 10 September, with work starting on 14 September. There were many technical requirements completed in a short time because of critical war mobilization requirements. Architecture and engineering work was conducted by R.J. Tipton (consulting engineering company), with site work conducted by Ed. H. Honner Construction Company. As with other Nebraska wartime construction projects, a critical shortage of common laborers remained throughout the project. This was partially compensated for by hiring part time workers for morning, evening, and weekend shifts. This allowed these laborers to work at their regular jobs on farms, ranches, businesses, schools, and city government agencies. There was no difficulty in locating and recruiting skilled construction workers.

WPA constructed hangar at the south end of the aircraft parking ramp. It was operational prior to construction of the military airfield. (Author)

Military facilities consisted of three concrete runways 7,000 feet long and 180 feet wide; concrete taxiways to serve each end of the separate runways; sixteen aircraft hardstands 75 feet in diameter adjacent to the north-south taxiway; and one 370 foot long and 245 foot wide aircraft parking apron east of the existing municipal hangar.

Original architecture/engineering plans specified fifty-foot wide concrete taxiways modified to 75 feet, with a 12 1/2 foot section of 5-inch thick stabilized base on either side to support heavy bomber aircraft. Construction workers built eighty-six buildings for housing, technical, and operational facilities for 217 officers and 692 enlisted. With the exception of the bombsight storage building, all others were considered temporary. Workers used Theater of Operations building designs with standardized plans provided by the Army Corps of Engineers Office of the Chief of Engineers. These buildings had an expected life span of five to seven years and were built as quickly and cheaply as possible to meet AAF training requirements.

Runway R-13 at Grand Island. (Author)

Workers modified the standard plans to meet local building materials acquisition: one-half inch thick Gypsum board and 7/8-inch thick surfaced Celotex to replace or substitute for dimensional lumber sheeting, Gypsum board, and felt with wood battens. The existing hangar and administration buildings were constructed of architectural concrete large enough to support military operations. Construction provided an AAF warehouse, one Army Quartermaster Corps warehouse, post exchange, open storage area capacity of 1,800 tons located northeast of the municipal hangar, and an open coal storage area with a capacity of 238 tons located in the administrative area to provide heating material.

Water was available from two on-site wells. No natural gas was available for cooking or heating. Electric power came from an existing 2,300-volt circuit purchased from the city of Grand Island. All runway, boundary, and range lights were powered by semi-portable electric generators provided by the AAF. An external storm sewer system drained or channeled runoff from the runways, taxiways, hardstands, parking apron, and along the eastern edge of the construction site. The air base had its own sewage treatment facility, consisting of an Inhofe tank, sludge drying bed, and irrigation field. The installation of the base telephone system was completed by Army Signal Corps personnel at a cost of $24,000. Telephone lines were carried on existing electric distribution poles on the base. Primary construction was completed on the base by 8 November 1942, with support buildings available by 15 November, followed by remaining construction by 8 January 1943.[215] There still was a lot of cleanup of construction debris to make the base's appearance more acceptable and improve training capabilities. It is remarkable that most of the primary or operational runways, taxiways, and hardstands (improved) survived long past the end of WWII, especially as a functioning modern airport. The volume of aircraft operations does not come close to that of AAF training during the war.

Runway 17 with a wide aircraft parking apron with markings for commercial passenger aircraft operations. (Author)

Bombardment Groups Assigned to Grand Island Air Base

Bomb Group	Bomb Squadron	Date Assigned
6th (B-29)	24th	26 May to 18 November 1944
	39th	
	40th	
376th (B-29)	512th	25 June to 10 November 1944
	513th	
	514th	
502nd (B-29)	402nd	26 September 1944 to 7 April 1945
	411th	
	430th	
28th (B-29)	77th	4 August to 6 October 1945[216]

Runway 35 view out of the passenger terminal at Grand Island. (Author)

Training at Grand Island AB for B-29 aircrews provides a great view of the AAF concept for Superfortress crew combat preparation. Records from USAFHRC recreate the B-29 training program for the 6th BG:

Ordnance Training

Class Designation	Hours
Motor vehicle operation	6
Safety regulations	4
Principles of ordnance supply	2
Ordnance publications for supply	2
Property accounting	1
Authorized and initial allowance	2
Ammunition (general)	12

Runway 35. (Author)

One of the few surviving examples of a maintenance operations building at a WWII base in Nebraska. This type of building was located near the flight line with adjacent parts storage warehouses for maintenance scheduling. Except for the filling in of one window with plywood for a room air conditioner, the building retains its WWII appearance. (Author)

Munitions Training

Class Designation	Hours
Typical layout	4
Packing and marking	2
Bombs	14
Military explosives	8
Fuses (nose)	10
Fuses (tail)	10
Bomb handling drill	32
Disposal and demolition of bombs	4

Armament Training

Class designation	Hours
Rifle (.30 caliber)	2
Carbine (.30 caliber)	1
Pistol, automatic (.45 caliber)	4
Guns, submachine (.45 caliber)	8
& Thompson machine gun (1929-A1)	
Gun, machine (.50 caliber)	22
Browning M2 AC	
Gun, automatic (20mm ANM-2) 22	
Accessories and mounts	3 1/2

In 1991, one of the B-29-sized hangars at Grand Island. (Author)

Intelligence Training

Class designation	Hours
Aircraft recognition	2
Safeguarding military information	1
Censorship	1
Camouflage	2
Briefing and interrogation	2
Situation maps	1
Office procedure	1

View of Grand Island Airport's flight line showing the B-29 hangars in the background, with modern light/commercial aircraft storage buildings, parking apron, and the northern taxiway. (Author)

Beginning with the first military arrivals at Grand Island, training officers had to overcome many obstacles. By 31 July 1944, all but one of the required ground echelon training blocks had been completed, with 20 percent of the standard Army Orientation Course (gunnery) completed. As with any new military organization in a training environment, it was difficult to pull personnel from their duties for required training allotments, frequently and usually complicated by shortages of on base training aids. This was only corrected by expenditure of scarce manpower on self-help construction projects.

Communications training was complicated: radio operators and mechanics received 78 hours of classroom instruction and 156 hours of practical line maintenance; telephone operators received 208 hours of practical operation; ground-based radio operators received 78 hours of classroom instruction; and teletype operators and mechanics received practical line maintenance and daily operational experience. For those working in the Orderly Room support area, enlisted personnel took training courses on Malaria control, field sanitation, first aid, censorship, camouflage, identification of friendly and enemy aircraft, and the importance of combat intelligence.

Flight crews were heavily engaged in training, although no navigators were assigned. The first ten bombardiers arrived on 27 July 1944, assigned right out of initial school training. Because B-29s were in short supply, B-17s were used by staff bombardiers to train these new arrivals. Each bombardier received seven hours of release procedures at 20,000 feet. As training progressed, 300-pound dummy practice bombs were dropped. By 31 July 1944, forty-one pilots were on base, recently graduated from B-17 pilot training. However, only three had been checked out in B-29s.

Armament Training

Class designation	Hours
Use of technical orders	2
AAF procedure & technique	3
Familiarization of tools & equipment	2
Supply procedure	2
General maintenance procedure	1
B-29 operation & maintenance	3
Aircraft combat material (general)	1
Bomb racks	8
.50 caliber machine gun, M2 (basic)	5 3/4
20mm cannon (aircraft)	6 1/2
Turrets	3 1/2
Small arms	6 1/4
Bombs and fuses	2

High-ranking AAF officers at Grand Island Air Base during its dedication ceremony (L to R): Brigadier General Frank A. Armstrong, 17th BG, Operational Training Wing; Colonel Downs E. Ingram, Commander Grand Island Air Base; and Colonel Kenneth H. Gibson, Commander 6th BG Courtesy of Nebraska State Historical Society.

Looking inside one of the large B-29 hangars. (Author)

As noted above, B-29 armament training was an extensive part of a bomb group's required instruction. This training was followed by the Group's Bombsight Officer's close supervision of the bombsight maintenance mechanics and the required procedures to accurately maintain the B-29's bombsight to factory specifications, working on the delicate equipment under an officer's supervision.

Bombsight Maintenance Training

Class designation	Hours
Bombsight and maintenance	10
M Series Sights trouble shooting	3
Auto pilot trouble shooting	10

The bomb group's Central Fire Control Officer set up a maintenance program with courses to bring maintenance personnel up to proficiency levels in order for them to be CFC certified.

B-29 hangar at the north end of the aircraft parking apron. (Author)

Bivouac training. Courtesy of NSHS

CFC Maintenance Training

Class designation	Hours
Basic electricity	8
CFC theory	4
Sighting station	4
Servo theory	4
Servo	4
Amplidyne	8
Power motor	4
Wiring diagrams	20
Turret assembly & disassembly	4
Sight assembly	4
Harmonization	8
Review on CFC	12[217]

Beginning in August 1944, training intensified, including ground training. Ground training consisted of three days of bivouac encampment, one day for each squadron. Squadron officers and enlisted personnel marched nine miles from the base to the designated bivouac area near the North Platte River. Each carried a shelter half, one blanket, and one canteen of water. The noon meal consisted of Army K rations. Once at the bivouac area, dummy land mines had been scattered throughout the area to simulate the dangers of a combat zone and make personnel aware of dangers on the ground, requiring caution and diligence when moving through and setting up a temporary camp. Periodically, B-17s or UC-78s dropped one-pound dummy flour sack bombs to simulate enemy air raids. Every man had to dig a foxhole to provide protection against the simulated bombings when an air raid warning sounded. This was usually someone banging together metal pots or mess kits. The evening meal was provided from a mobile Army field kitchen unit. Communications personnel set up a field switchboard; supply personnel checked out tools and equipment used during the bivouac; and dispensary personnel took care of field related injuries or medical problems. When it turned dark, an infantry detachment assigned to the Second Air Force initiated a commando raid on the encampment, firing blanks. They lobbed teargas grenades into the camp area, forcing those inside to don their gas masks. Even though gas attacks had not been used by the enemy in combat as during WWI, there was still a fear of such attacks when the war started going against the Axis. In the morning, after breakfast, they filled in the foxholes, cleaned the camp area, and marched the nine miles back to base.

Airplane Commander Training

Class designation	Hours
Physical training (PT)	12
Intelligence	2
Critique of airplane identification	10
Medicine	2
Bombing	2
Engineering	14
Weight & balance	4
Crucial control	4
Communications	2
Navigation	4
Link trainer	4
Meteorology	2

Pilot Training

Class designation	Hours
Physical training	12
Intelligence	2
Critique	10
Navigation	28
Radar	5
Bombing	8
Gunnery	10

Navigator Training

Class designation	Hours
Physical training	10
Intelligence	2
Critique	10
Medical	2
Radar	28
Bombing	8
Gunnery	2

Bombardier Training

Class designation	Hours
Physical training	10
Intelligence	2
Critique	10
Medical subjects	2
Gunnery	12
Bombing	26
Navigation	10
Radar	3

Flight Engineer Training

Class designation	Hours
Physical training	10
Intelligence	2
Critique	10
Medical subjects	2
Powerplant	15
Electrical	14
Structural	14
Crucial control	4
Weight & balance	4

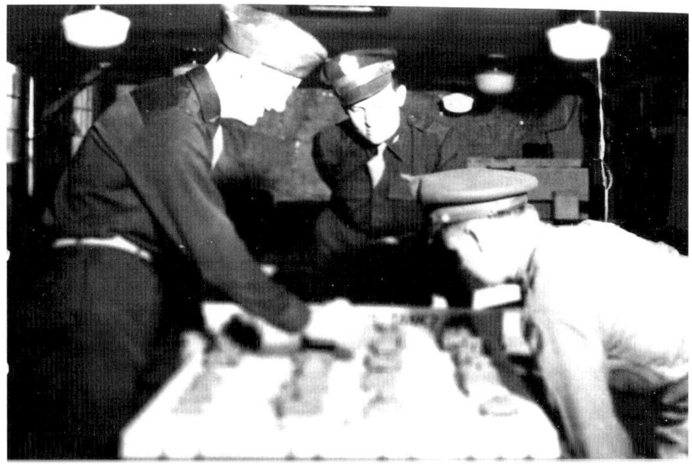

Officers taking ground equipment training. Courtesy of NSHS

Enlisted personnel taking code training. Courtesy of NSHS

View from Grand Island's control tower. The pre-WWII municipal hangar is in the center with light commercial aircraft parked in front. A light aircraft hangar is to the left center of the photograph. (Author)

Radar Operator Training

Class designation	Hours
Physical training	10
Intelligence	2
Critique	10
Medical subjects	2
Radar	4
Radio	37
Turret maintenance	8

Central Fire Control Operator Training

Class designation	Hours
Physical training	10
Intelligence	2
Critique	10
Medical subjects	2
CFC	27
Gunnery	22

Electrical Specialist/Gunner Training

Class designation	Hours
Physical training	10
Intelligence	2
Critique	10
Medical subjects	2
Electrical	15
Gunnery	34

Power Plant/Gunner Training

Class designation	Hours
Physical training	10
Intelligence	2
Critique	10
Medical subjects	2
Powerplant	15
Gunnery	34

Structural Specialist/Tail Gunner Training

Class designation	Hours
Physical training	10
Intelligence	2
Critique	10
Medical subjects	2
Structure	15
Gunnery	34[218]

The 376th BG was the next to arrive at Grand Island AB, remaining in training status from 25 June to 10 November 1944. It had to share base facilities and training time with the still on station 6th BG. The 502nd BG arrived on 26 September 1944, training on the base until 7 April 1945. Its September training schedule and activities demonstrated the strain to get ready for Pacific combat operations. Schooling for the bomb group's cadre was the Very Heavy Orientation Course held at Orlando, Florida on 2 September; a select number of officers and enlisted were removed from the bomb group's three squadrons. They were at Dalhart, Texas, and not transferred to Grand Island at this time. They attended a thirty-day B-29 Orientation and Applied Tactics course. This course was to train key bomb group personnel.

Commanding officer	Operations officer
Deputy commanding officer	Section heads
Squadron commanding officer	

The course was divided into two phases: two weeks of academics and twelve days of flying in simulated combat. Phase one gave instruction on theory and operation of a VH bomb group. To accomplish this, a schedule was set up to divide personnel according to assigned duties. This allowed each section to receive specialized instruction pertinent to its function in the bomb group. The last three days of the phase concentrated on planning and briefing of simulated combat missions. These training missions were theoretical, requiring all to participate to demonstrate combat operations and capabilities.

Phase II was the application of Phase I's academic training, testing knowledge in aerial missions. The 502nd BG flew to Pine Castle, Florida to set up its operational organization in tents and hutments. From this base set up, simulated combat missions were flown against targets located over a wide area: Lake Charles, Louisiana to Wilmington, North Carolina. These combat missions were primarily against industrial targets selected to simulate similar targets expected to be attacked in the Japanese home islands from runways on Tinian, Saipan, and Guam. Camera bombing assisted in determining estimated target destruction, similar to post-WWII SAC radar bombing of U.S. cities in training to deliver thermonuclear weapons against targets in the Soviet Union. The only variable not able to be experienced was the high-speed jet stream winds over Japan, which decreased target accuracy when using the Norden bombsight at high altitude. When flying with the wind B-29s sped so fast over the target that bombs released usually missed the target. If B-29s turned into the wind, they slowed down to the point of making them easy targets for Japanese fighters.

To assist in B-29 aircrew training for combat, specialized schools were set up:

- B-29 Factory Airframe Course at Boeing Aircraft in Renton, Washington
- R-3350 Engine Course at Amarillo, Texas
- Fluxgate Compass and Air Position Indicator Courses at Chanute Field, Illinois
- Turbo-supercharger Course at Lincoln School in West Lynn, Massachusetts
- C-1 Automatic Pilot Course at Minneapolis Honeywell Regulators Company in Minneapolis, Minnesota
- Second Air Force Unit Gas Officers and Non-commissioned Officers Course at Davis Monthan Field, Tucson, Arizona

At the same time, the 502nd's ground echelon training started; they were temporarily assigned to the 6th BG. Further breakdown of assignments placed each man within the framework of a

During the Cold War with the Soviet Union, SAC built a nuclear weapons storage facility at the northeast end of the airport. The airport served as a satellite bomber dispersal base to complicate the Soviet Union's nuclear targeting of America's nuclear deterrent striking force using manned bombers. Periodically, SAC B-47 medium, six turbojet bombers deployed to Grand Island. These B-47s were part of SAC's contribution to the Single Integrated Operations Plan (SIOP) to disperse its bombers away from main bases. The airport has the historical atmosphere of a WWII base with the presence of a modern civilian airport. (Author)

squadron, with group personnel detailed to the proper section of the Military Occupation Specialty (MOS) number. This procedure, which dovetailed the two groups together, placed men of the 502nd BG under direction of 6th BG Section Heads. For the various departments of the Engineering Section, this was the preferred training method, with heavy emphasis placed on on-the-job training. Maintenance crews were designated for the 6th BG's aircraft, irrespective of the group to which personnel belonged. This training in maintenance, communications, ordnance, armament, etc., was in reality achieved directly under the supervision of the parent bomb group. Academic training at Grand Island presented some problems. Originally, the Grand Island Base Unit was to provide classroom instruction in the various phases of V.H. bomber maintenance, communications, radar, etc. However, facilities proved inadequate, which required correction. For communications work, results were excellent and aided by the arrival at the end of September 1944 of a Mobile Training Unit from Second Air Force Headquarters. This unit provided specialized training for ground radio mechanics. All assigned 502nd BG personnel in this category were required to attend. The Grand Island AAF Radar School assisted in radio mechanic training.[219]

After the end of the war, many former military base buildings were removed, reassembled, and upgraded in Grand Island for civilian use to ease the postwar housing shortage. The WPA hangar survived, along with three B-29 hangars. There are WWII-era buildings scattered around the former air base. The runways have been modernized and support an active civilian commercial airport operations under the name Central Nebraska Regional Airport with three active runways.

CHAPTER EIGHT
HARVARD AIR BASE

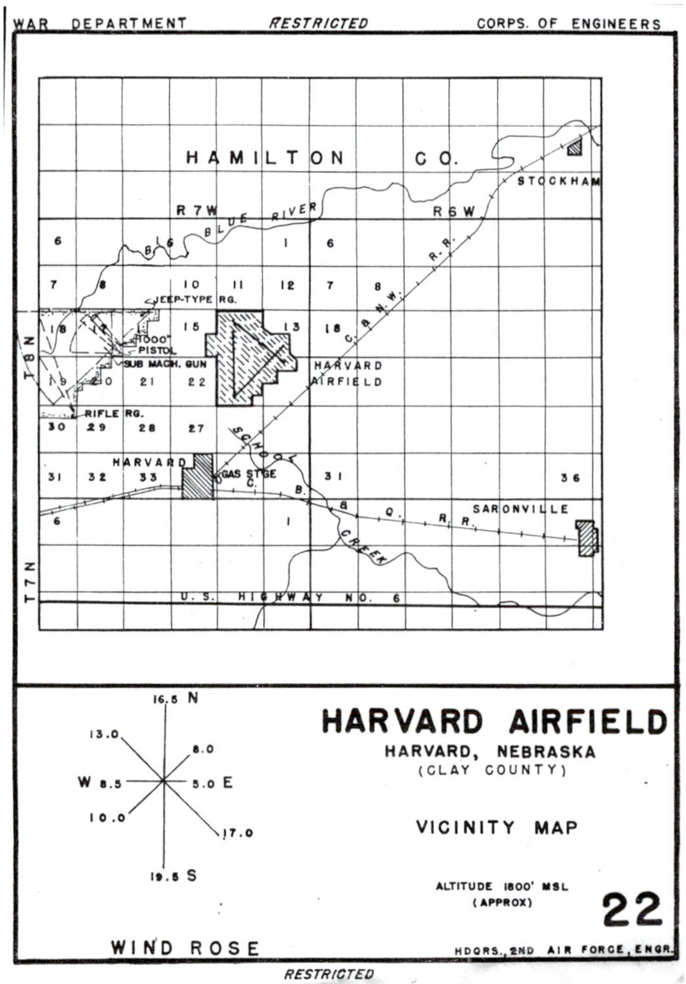

Harvard Airfield vicinity map. (Author)

On 2 September 1942, the AAF announced a satellite Army airfield would be built northeast of Harvard on 1,600-1,700 acres. The AAF also released build sites for air bases at McCook, Fairmont, and Bruning, with three others to be built at future disclosed locations in Nebraska. The day the city of Harvard received confirmation an AAF base would be built near their town, the federal government started contacting local farmers owning land on the proposed air base site that would have to vacate. By 17 September, construction workers set off a cascading effect on local housing in Harvard that was strained beyond capacity, with more workers than rooms. Harvard's post office became a very popular destination in town, as did most of the shops and stores.[220] Contractors working on the air base were Peter Kiewit & Sons, Condon & Cunningham as prime, assisted by smaller companies. Because of a lack of housing in town, temporary labor barracks were set up in an open area of the northwest part of Harvard. A temporary trailer park camp was set up on the town's athletic field to ease immediate housing needs. Two large buildings in the downtown area were turned into dining halls to feed construction workers.[221]

By 1 October 1942, Harvard's population doubled. By 19 November, construction work had been completed, with workers leaving the airfield area, as well as temporary living facilities in Harvard. The Army invited local Harvard businessmen to the base for a tour of the new facility with briefings and demonstrations on the air base's training mission, including its importance to the war effort.[222]

Runway 35 north. (Author)

Bomb Groups Trained at Harvard AB

Bomb Group	Squadron	Date Assigned
447th (B-17)	708th	14 August to 11 November 1943
	709th	
	710th	
	711th	
484th (B-24)	824th	20 September 1943 to 2 March 1944
	825th	
	826th	
	827th	
505th (B-29)	482nd	12 March to 6 November 1944
	483rd	
	484th	
501st (B-29)	21st	23 August 1944 to 7 March 1945
	41st	
376th (B-29)	512th	8 May to June 1945
	513th	
	514th	
	515th	
450th (B-29)	720th	26 July to 15 October 1945
	721st	
	722nd, [223]	

By early 1943, the new air base was operating 24 hours a day, seven days a week training B-17 aircrews. The base's classification changed from satellite to full OTU on 29 January, with the establishment of a headquarters and air base squadron. At least once a week on the base, a day was declared or designated as a "gas day" when an alarm sounded. This could be sounded once or multiple times, depending on the scenario selected. At the sound of the alarm, everyone on the base put on their gas mask, simulating a poison gas attack that might be expected in combat.[224]

B-17s flown at Harvard were part of an OTU with the 2AF. The B-17s were assigned to the 447th BG to prepare aircrews for combat with the Eighth Air Force in England. The 447th was activated on 6 April 1943, effective 1 May 1943, at Ephrata AAB, Washington. From 30-31 May, the bomb group's ground and air echelon of 59 officers and 80 enlisted traveled to the AAF School of Applied Tactics in Orlando, Florida. Classroom lectures started on 9 June. The first two days of instruction consisted of lectures on current Army, Navy, and Air Force organization, stressing inter-relationship between air, ground, and naval forces as they had been developed to date and determined expedient in actual Theaters of Operations during

Large aircraft parking apron. (Author)

WWII. After these first two days of orientation, class schedules were set up to provide lectures, classroom exercises, and classroom demonstrations relating to their duties. An average of one class or field trip each day of instruction brought the entire bomb group's cadre together for demonstrations on camouflage, ordnance weapons, synthetic devices, and displays of heavy bombardment equipment.

On 19 July, four 447th BG crews, along with aircraft assigned to the 9th BG (assigned to Signal Hill in Orlando, Florida), ferried the personnel of the bomb group to Brooksville, Florida, for field training. Officers and enlisted were quartered in a simulated combat area, with tents, an operations building, and a control tower. Life and work on the base was considered excellent training. A total of nine simulated bombing missions were flown between 19 and 30 June 1943. Procedures were followed as those expected to be encountered after moving to England, assigned to the Eighth Air Force. Field orders were received at Brooksville by coded messages at any time during the day or night for missions to be carried out in accordance with said order. Usually, this had to be executed within a few hours after the message was received. Simulated wartime combat mission objectives were New Orleans, Louisiana; Charleston, South Carolina; Mobile, Alabama; and other southern cities. Simulated combat missions were flown by the 448th and 449th BS. A change came with orders for sea search patrols off the coasts of Florida. S2 (intelligence) and S3 (training and operations) worked together in planning, briefing, conducting, and debriefing after each mission. Formation flying was practiced and performance evaluated. At night, aircrews flew against radar-controlled searchlights around the base to be exposed to expected German defenses, although at a reduced number.

To gain training not available, the 447th BG's ground echelon departed Brooksville by train to Camp Rapid, Rapid City, South Dakota, to train with the 17th BG Cadre Training Command, arriving on 13 June 1943. Once training was completed for the air echelon at Brooksville, they departed on 1 July, arriving at Camp Rapid on 4 July. The remaining section of the ground echelon arrived by train on 5 July, taking trucks from Rapid City to the air base. Camp Rapid and the Cadre Training Command were set to give heavy bomb group personnel training in the use of weapons, stressing military discipline and bearing and developing a war mind set for combat aircrews. All personnel participated in close order drills, calisthenics, and body building exercises, along with training practice with rifles and pistols. Revile sounded at 4:30 a.m. each morning, and by 7 a.m., every officer and enlisted man was engaged in strenuous activity. Formal retreats were held three days a week. Administrative routines were established and followed to improve training scheduling, implementation, and evaluation.

South taxiway. (Author)

On 31 July, the 447th BG departed Camp Rapid, reaching Harvard on 2 August 1943 to begin its first phase of training. During the first week, it was necessary for the bomb group's personnel to clean up supposed finished or newly constructed buildings that contractors left as is for occupancy and training. There were no post construction punch lists requiring contractors to clean up buildings and their construction areas prior to AAF occupancy. Group S-2 set up intelligence operations in a designated war room building.

While at Harvard, the bomb group suffered two aerial accidents. On 28 August, two B-17Fs (42-30239 and 42-3309) collided in mid-air, killing six officers and eight enlisted. On 22 October, five officers and nine enlisted were killed when a B-17G (42-31190) crashed when the aircraft was forced to the ground during severe weather, with a probable violent wind shear and down draft the cause of the accident.

Because of Harvard's relative isolation, on base recreational facilities were established. Army Special Services set up a Service Club with a snack bar and library and arranged weekly dances and athletic competitions. As the third phase of the bomb group's training neared completion, AAF inspectors made several visits to investigate training operations and overall status was determined to be superior and exceptional.

On 24 October 1943, one of the bomb group's officers, Major J. McNaboe, returned to Harvard from an overseas trip to England, Eighth Air Force Headquarters, visiting the 91st BG. The Major had meetings and briefings with the bomb group at Harvard on Eighth Air Force procedures: briefings and post mission combat interrogation and intelligence on attacking German fighters. On 7 November, the first echelon of the bomb group's officers comprising the advance staff departed for England, arriving on 12 November via Air Transport Command aircraft.

The remaining officers and enlisted men departed Harvard Air Base in squadron order.

Bomb Squadron	Departure date (1943)
711th	8 November
708th	9 November
709th	10 November
710th	11 November

After leaving Harvard Air Base, the squadron's aircraft made the flight to England in stages:

- Harvard to east coast staging bases
- East coast staging bases to Newfoundland (Harmon or Gander)
- Newfoundland to Labrador (Goose Bay)
- Labrador to England (Eighth Air Force bases)

WWII warehouse located west of the main flight line. The building retains most of its WWII appearance. This is remarkable, as when this photograph was taken in 1991, the building had survived from 1943, when Army Corps of Engineers designed the buildings for a life span of five to seven years. Everything was built in haste to begin training as soon as possible. (Author)

The first 447th BG B-17F arrived in England on 16 November. One B-17F with four officers and six enlisted men assigned to the 710th BS crashed in the North Atlantic. The bomb group's ground echelon departed Harvard on 11 November. Its route to England was similar to that taken by many bomb groups assigned to England and the Eighth Air Force, although the name of the sea transports differed. The bomb group's ground echelon arrived by railroad transport to Camp Shank, Orangeburg, New York, on 13 November, remaining there for one week. The ground echelon boarded what was probably the most famous North Atlantic transport of WWII, HMS *Queen Elizabeth*. The 447th BG's ground echelon departed New York on 23 November on the *Queen Elizabeth*, arriving at Greenock, Firth of Clyde, Scotland, on 29 November. The ground echelon boarded a train to Stowmark, Suffolk, England on 30 November, transferring to trucks for the drive to Station 126 at Rattlesden and joining the air echelon.[225]

The 484th BG next occupied Harvard Air Base on 7 November 1943, with 120 officers and 939 enlisted men. Its advanced cadre arrived on base in late September. The bomb group trained with B-24s. During November, the group's initial efforts were on ground training, with no flying. The group concentrated on small arms training—normally administered by base personnel, but was taken over by the bomb group by building their own small arms training ranges. By the end of September, the group completed training on the Thompson sub-machine gun. Gunners practiced at the base skeet range. Chemical warfare training was given to all group personnel.[226]

The 505th BG was the next group to occupy Harvard AB. Their first objective was to clean up the base after the 484th's departure, a usual occurrence after the departure of one bomb group and the arrival of the next. Departing bomb group personnel were not interested in cleaning for the next arriving bomb group. Some bomb group commanders maintained the base they trained at in better condition than others did. It seemed a random draw as to what base retained an acceptable military appearance and neatness versus other training bases. The 505th moved into its administrative offices, barracks, and

The wood framing and covering of the WWII hangar has been removed with the concrete floor retained and a metal grain storage building erected. The concrete side bays of the former hangar remain and are used for equipment storage. A surviving intact WWII hangar is visible in the background of the photograph. (Author)

maintenance shops in the hangars, getting everything ready for maximum training operations. Many of the repairs to buildings were necessary to rehabilitate for round-the-clock training to get ready for combat. The group had to fly B-17s until factory B-24s were flown in for transition standardization and instrument training.[227]

Transition training with B-17s for the bomb group consumed a daily average of 25,000 gallons of aviation fuel each day. It took a huge home front effort to produce enough aviation fuel for civilian air transport (limited), military training, Air Transport Command, U.S. combat operations, and Allied air support. The shipment of aviation gasoline from refineries to Harvard AB, as well as other training bases, required precision shipment timing over an already over-burdened U.S. rail network to keep the base's aviation fuel tanks full for training operations.

The 501st BG arrived at Harvard AB in August 1944. In getting ready for combat, the bomb group began a staggered training program. The following depicts what it took to train a B-29 group. From 1-3 December, nineteen aircrews began

Surviving B-29 hangar at Harvard Air Base. It is used for grain storage. The hangar is in relatively good shape. (Author)

A surviving WWII squadron operations building next to the demolished hangar was rebuilt as a grain storage building. Squadron operations buildings were built between each hangar, one per squadron assigned to the training base. This building is in good shape, including the brick chimney from the heating plant. (Author)

flight training. Briefings started at 6:30 a.m. and again at 4:30 p.m., with each squadron's schedule staggered so it could fly and attend ground school. The 21st BS training schedule is an example of a tightly organized program under tight time constraints. The squadron flew morning training flights, with mission briefings at 6:30 a.m. on 5 December, flying again at 4:30 p.m. on 6 December. Ground school was at 10 a.m. on 7 December, continuing until 10 p.m. If ground school for any training fell on a Sunday, it was considered a day off. Each squadron divided its aircrews into three flights.

This type of scheduling allowed a bomb group to fly a total of 1,026 training hours, averaging 20 1/2 per aircrew each month. Unfortunately, this was only approximately 50 percent of the training schedule, primarily because of a 74 percent availability of aircraft. The Second AF training program was based on a daily squadron average of 70 flying hours, using eighteen aircraft at each OTU base. As the new B-29s were delivered to train bomb groups, training hours improved. This was set up to permit a bomb group to complete training in an average of 90 days. At Harvard AB, by December 1944, only thirteen B-29s were available for group training. The only option was for the 501st to fly eight B-29s on seven-hour training missions or four B-29s on two seven-hour training missions each. In this manner, the bomb group could accumulate 56 flying hours per day. However, this resulted in no slack to replace or make up flying hours lost to severe weather, which occurred when 668 hours were lost to inclement weather. For navigation training twenty hours were flown, a fraction of the required 1,034 hours.

During December, the bomb group's three squadrons dropped 145 dummy practice bombs, of which 45 were scored by photographs, with the remainder estimated by the squadron bombardier. Interestingly, circular error probable (CEP) average for the bombs scored by estimate was 428 feet and 406 feet scored by photograph. From the practice bombs dropped, 123 were released at an altitude of 20,000 feet, while 22 were released from 10,000 feet. Thirty camera bombing attacks were conducted at an altitude of 20,000 feet, but this did not go as planned. The K-24 camera used at the start of bombing training developed malfunctions. Bomb group camera technicians switched to the K-22 camera. The K-24, used during winter training operations, resulted in brittle film because of the cold temperatures at high altitude and frequently broke. The shutter also stuck, creating

A B-29 hangar in the final stage of demolition in 1991. The wood frame roof and siding have been removed and salvaged for resale. The brick chimney from the heating plant remains intact at the back of the hangar. Most of the concrete wall sections have been knocked down and broken into pieces for resale as construction fill material. (Author)

double exposures and making the developed film useless for bomb scoring and bombardier/aircrew coordination evaluation. The camera had operational limits, in that it exposed one frame of film at the moment of bomb impact. Limitations resulted in an inability to score bomb missions because the practice bomb did not impact and detonate at the second of film exposure. In addition, frequently the spotting charge in the nose of the training bomb did not detonate, so it was not visible in the photograph. The problem was corrected by adding two more seconds to the intervalometer, permitting the bombs to hit the ground, detonate, and be photographed for scoring. The base photo lab reported the K-24 did not maintain nor hold a sufficient vacuum to keep the film flat against the camera's focal plane shutter mechanism.

Technical ground training for December 1944 amounted to 27 percent of the 90-day training period. The Radar Section set up a synthetic radar bombing training for the bomb group's bombardiers in order to sharpen their synchronizing principles required on a bomb run to target. There was a problem encountered in setting up a definite optic angle presentation. Bomb group personnel corrected the problem by painting a course line on the radar bombing trainer's building floor with the optic angles crossing it. These angle lines were determined from the height of an ordinary bomb trainer with the assistance of the Norden bombsight. Also, modified inter-phone hookups were installed consisting of a field telephone to be used by the radar operator to call the angles and a headset for the bombardier's use. The movement of the trainer did not change. The difference was that the navigator called out the optic angles as the trainer crossed the optic angle lines while following the course line. The angles were noted by the bombardier and served to see if the indices pointed at the correct angle. If not the correct angle, correction was made. A course for radar and RCM officers in LORAN and operation of APQ-13 was taught at the Base Radar School.

The bomb group's ordnance training program progressed into its third phase in December 1944, with 92 hours of instruction completed. This was for those with 511 MOS, classified as an Ordnance Specialist. The Ordnance Training Program was based on a bomb group, not a bomb squadron. The size of classes caused difficulty in getting classrooms large enough to hold the students. Most of the trainees lacked a general knowledge of their duties in aviation ordnance, requiring considerable training

In 1991, the southern hangar at Harvard Air Base was totally demolished with part of the concrete hauled away. (Author)

time to bring their basic ordnance knowledge up to acceptable standards. There was difficulty in scheduling classes so as not to conflict with ground school. This led to holding overflow classes at night, extending the training day, which was already considered long and exhausting.[228]

Beginning in January 1945, the bomb group's training moved to phase two. During the month, the bomb group flew 1,115 hours in their B-29s—only 51 percent of the scheduled hours—limited by having only thirteen hours, instead of the eighteen authorized. The bomb group was directed by Second AF to remove designated equipment from their B-29s to reduce weight, increase bomb load carrying capabilities, and decrease strain on the engines in preparation for combat missions against the Japanese home islands.[229]

Ed Henry, 485th BS, commented on the B-29 conversion process: "I found out after WWII that Colonel Paul Tibbets had flown a stripped-down B-29 during a test project, getting the 509th CG combat ready to drop atomic bombs on Japan. Also, it was General Curtis LeMay's decision to remove excess weight in order to lessen strain on the engines and increasing bomb load capacity on low-level, night incendiary missions. As an armament chief, I directed the removal of CFC equipment: gun turrets, sighting stations, the 20mm tail cannon, and all .50 caliber machine guns except the two in the tail turret."[230]

For B-29 bomb groups in training, starting in February 1945, a new Second AF flight training directive was published, changing the character of training missions. The directive specified that five 3,000-mile training missions would be flown, replicating round trip distances from the Marianas Islands to the Japanese home islands.[231]

Glen Clark, 485th BS, noted:

> As a B-29 pilot, our crew completed (ten) three thousand mile round trip navigational practice bombing missions at 33,000 feet. For the most part, the missions went well. Sometimes it was difficult to get

Central wood framework of the hangar removed, awaiting demolition of the concrete walls to be sold for construction fill. (Author)

the proper altitude because of a balking turbo-charger. Once we were able to get to 38,000 feet. The B-29's ceiling was supposed to be 42,000 feet. Our combat aircraft could probably have easily reached this ceiling, but we never had the opportunity to try. One time, we were returning to Harvard from Salt Lake City and the weather was really socked in. In that area weather and wind conditions can be very unpredictable. We missed a radio beacon and I asked the navigator for a corrected heading to Harvard and he could not immediately give it to me. We were not near the mountains, so we let down to see if we could break through the thick overcast. When we broke out at an altitude of 1,800 feet a small town showed up, with its name on the water tower.

On one other mission, we were camera bombing a bridge in New Orleans, Louisiana at 33,000 feet when an oil leak in number two engine caused us to feather the propeller. At that same instant we lost pressurization and intercom. We started a fast let down and I turned over controls to the copilot. I grabbed a walk-around oxygen bottle and crawled through the tunnel to make sure the scanners had their oxygen masks on. They felt the pressure leave the aircraft and had donned their oxygen masks and were sitting on the floor. One does not live but about four minutes at 33,000 feet without oxygen. We headed back to Harvard at a lower altitude, fully intending to take our crippled plane home. When we reached Tulsa, Oklahoma we were told to land. We landed at about 9 p.m. There were eight inches of snow on the runway. We called back to Harvard about the engine and a couple days later, after the weather cleared, engine parts and mechanics were flown into Tulsa. The engine was repaired and we returned to Harvard.

We flew to Jamaica for over-water navigational training missions. Our flight plan routed us via Fort

At the former barracks area: the lavatory, shower room, and toilet facilities building with only the concrete flooring remaining from 1943. At the time of this photo in 1991, the wood walls and roof had long been removed. This was one of the few remaining concrete floors at the former air base, except for the aircraft hangars. Grass and weeds are slowly destroying the remaining concrete. (Author)

Worth, Texas; Galveston, Texas; and Miami, Florida, then on to Jamaica. When approaching Fort Worth, we could see a tremendous thunderstorm in our flight path. I requested Air Traffic Control for a change of flight plan to fly around the squall line. They would not approve the change and ordered me to climb to 27,000 feet, at which altitude we could fly over the storm. We climbed to the designated altitude, but the storm towered above us at least eight to ten thousand feet. We tried to get higher, but a stubborn turbo-charger would not let us go higher. We proceeded on course to Galveston. I have flown through a lot of severe storms, but never anything like that one. We were forced up 6,000 feet per minute, then down 6,000 feet per minute. I told the radar operator to pick out the light and dark spots on the radarscope and steer us through the dark spots. We finally maneuvered through the storm and came out at Galveston. I believe that if we had not followed the radar operator's directions, our flying careers would have ended in the thunderstorm.

Our training schedule in Jamaica was very rigid. We had to fly every day to meet the training schedule. However, one day, the recreation officer arranged for us to go out on a boat to fish. It was different and fun when off duty, and we caught a lot of Mackerel Jacks and Barracuda. Later, we made a short trip by train to Kingston. It was very interesting, but there was not enough time to see everything. During training, we were the first aircraft to take off. We discovered we had no airspeed indicator. The runways were extremely short, so we went ahead with the take-off and I called to the tower to alert them to our problem. I had the pitot tube cover in my lap, so that was not the problem. They worried about sabotage in that area. They told me to just fly around a while. They came back on the radio and told us that when checking other aircraft, they found a swarm of bees had filled the static tubes with beeswax. Mechanics cleaned the tubes, installed wire screen to keep out the bees, and recalibrated airspeed indicators. We finished training, flying back to Harvard.[232]

[illegible] assigned to Clark's B-29, added:

We took our gunnery training in Jamaica. We flew the B-29 there and back along with a B-17 with a transport crew. We landed in Cuba, Puerto Rico, and Orlando, Florida. We took off from Orlando to Harvard, but did not make it all the way due to weather. The Air Transport Command crew was not very efficient and we became lost near the Nebraska and Kansas border. Because of the bad weather, we had to fly above the heavy clouds at 16,000 feet. The navigator became useless, as we had no oxygen and kept passing out. The radio operator could not locate any stations for help. Finally, our B-29 pilot convinced the B-17 pilot to let his B-29 radio operator see what he could do. Our radio operator, Corporal Jarrett, was finally able to contact an Emergency Air Line Station at North Platte, Nebraska. We finally let down through the clouds and found North Platte. The B-17's crew chief said we were getting very low on fuel. The pilot attempted a landing over the flood-swollen North Platte River. Landing was finally made on the shortest runway, which led to the big hangar. With the engines' controls and brakes, we turned just short of the hangar, and at that instant all four engines quit, out of fuel. The rest of the trip back to Harvard was made by train.[233]

Clark continued: "We finished our training at Harvard and we went to the staging area at Kearney, Nebraska, where we received our B-29 combat aircraft, made some shake down flights, and then were off to Mather Field, California, for subsequent flight on to Guam."[234]

The 376th BG was next at Harvard AB from 8 May to 25 June 1945. It never deployed to the Pacific. The last B-29 BG to train at Harvard was the 450th, which was on the base from 26 July to 15 October 1945, when it was inactivated.[235]

By the end of the war, Harvard AB had trained three Air Service Groups, three heavy bomb groups (B-17 and B-24), and four very heavy bomb groups (B-29). Harvard was used to separate personnel out of the military, which by 11 February 1945 had reached a total of 3,567. Harvard AB was declared surplus federal property on 21 May 1946, retaining only a small servicing military support staff. All Army material and equipment that could be removed was packed and shipped out to a federal warehouse facility. Surplus property sales were held on the base, administered by the state of Nebraska. Most of the buildings (barracks, gymnasium, movie theater, service club, chapel, and others) were moved, dismantled, or sold for lumber. The City of Harvard kept the USO building functioning with funds from the national USO organization. The federal government, which created the large housing area northeast of Harvard, also turned this over to the city, renaming it Harvard Courts, and it was remodeled and updated. The former air base came under control of Nebraska's Department of Aeronautics.[236]

CHAPTER NINE
KEARNEY AIR BASE

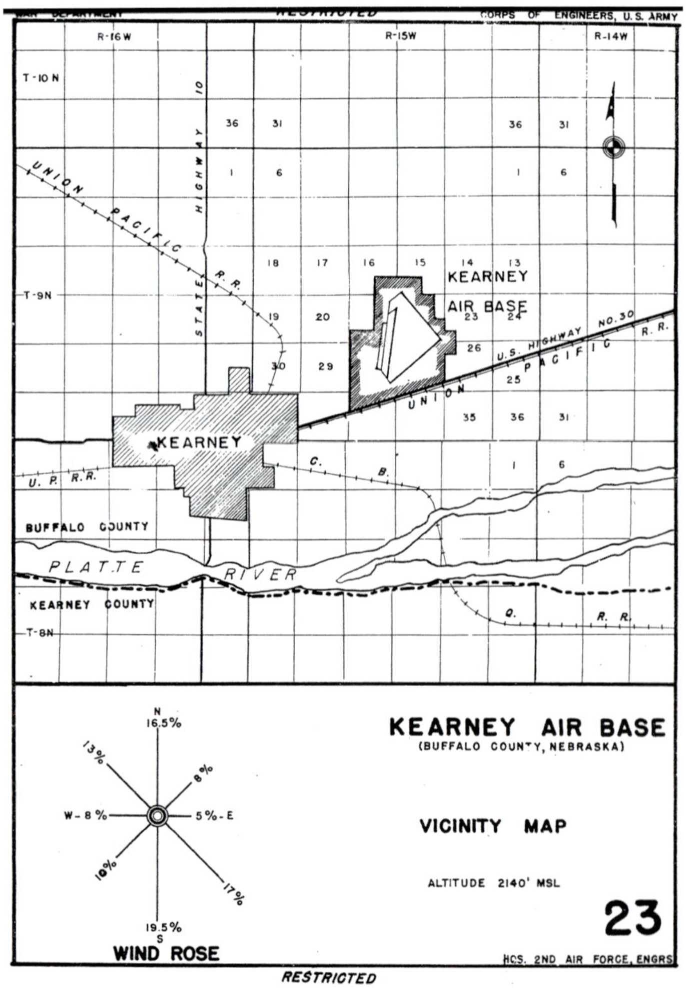

Kearney Air Base vicinity map. (Author)

In 1940, Kearney's population was 10,000, respectable for a town in the middle of Nebraska. Many business leaders in the town recognized the potential economic impact and growth opportunities that could result if the War Department decided to build a war plant or air base near their town. Three Nebraska city committees pooled funds (Kearney, Grand Island, and Hastings) to create the Central Nebraska Defense Council to lobby the War Department to acquire defense plants and air bases. Kearney's Chamber of Commerce created a special committee, which in turn formed six subcommittees tasked to assemble information and prepare a report on the advantages of building a defense installation in or near their town. Kearney committee members traveled by train to Washington, D.C., to meet with federal agencies and War Department officials, along with the state's Congressional members (House of Representatives and Senate), delivering copies of the Central Nebraska Defense Council's report on the suitability for war plants and air bases near their towns. Although Kearney, Grand Island, and Hastings cooperated in lobbying to secure defense installations for central Nebraska, they still competed directly against each other for a military installation.[237]

By late 1940, rumors circulated throughout town that an aviation training school would be located somewhere in the middle of Nebraska. Lincoln's newspapers reported local businessmen would be asked to purchase land for or develop facilities for a military training school. For Kearney to be considered, a suitable airfield had to be ready as soon as possible to edge out Grand Island and/or North Platte from being selected by the War Department to build an air base. In April 1941, the City of Kearney held a bond election, guaranteeing up to $60,000 to finance the building of a municipal airport. The airport's cost would far exceed this amount, estimated at $360,000, with the remaining balance of $300,000 to be funded by the federal government's WPA. On 1 September 1941, the *McCook*

Aerial photo of downtown Kearney, Nebraska in 1942, looking south towards 25th street to 1st avenue. Courtesy of Kearney Army Air Base Reunion Committee.

Gazette reported Kearney and several Nebraska cites had been selected for construction sites for AAF bases. On 10 September 1941, Captain Lyman G. Young, Omaha District, U.S. Army Corps of Engineers traveled to Kearney to examine Kearney Municipal Airport's facilities. Although the Corps of Engineers issued no official announcement, their on-site inspection raised expectations an air base would be built near the town.

On 6 October 1942, United States Senator (Nebraska) George W. Norris made it official; a War Department construction contract had been awarded to build an air base at Kearney costing three million dollars. The primary construction contract was awarded to Peter Kiewit & Sons and Condon Cunningham Company of Omaha, Nebraska; both were heavily involved in wartime construction throughout the state. There was a cost plus fixed fee contract awarded to A. Guthrie and Son Incorporated of St. Paul, Minnesota. Corps of Engineers, Omaha District supervised the overall construction project.[238]

The City of Kearney offered 352 acres at the Keens Municipal Airport under long-term lease to the U.S. Army for one dollar per year for as long as the air base was in operation as an active training base. More land was required for safe military aircraft operations than available at the municipal airport. The Army condemned 2,275 and a half acres of additional land to increase the proposed air base's size. On 10 September, the Corps of Engineers set up a temporary operations office in Kearney. Preliminary work on the airfield site consisted of digging four miles of drainage ditches to dry up surrounding sugar beet and corn fields prior to grading the runways and other facilities. The contract for construction of buildings and utilities for the air base was awarded to A. Guthrie and Son, Incorporated on 14 September 1942. On 22 September, a contract was signed with Peter & Condon Company to complete grading and paving of the runways, taxiways, and aircraft parking aprons. Construction required the existing asphalt runway at the municipal airport be

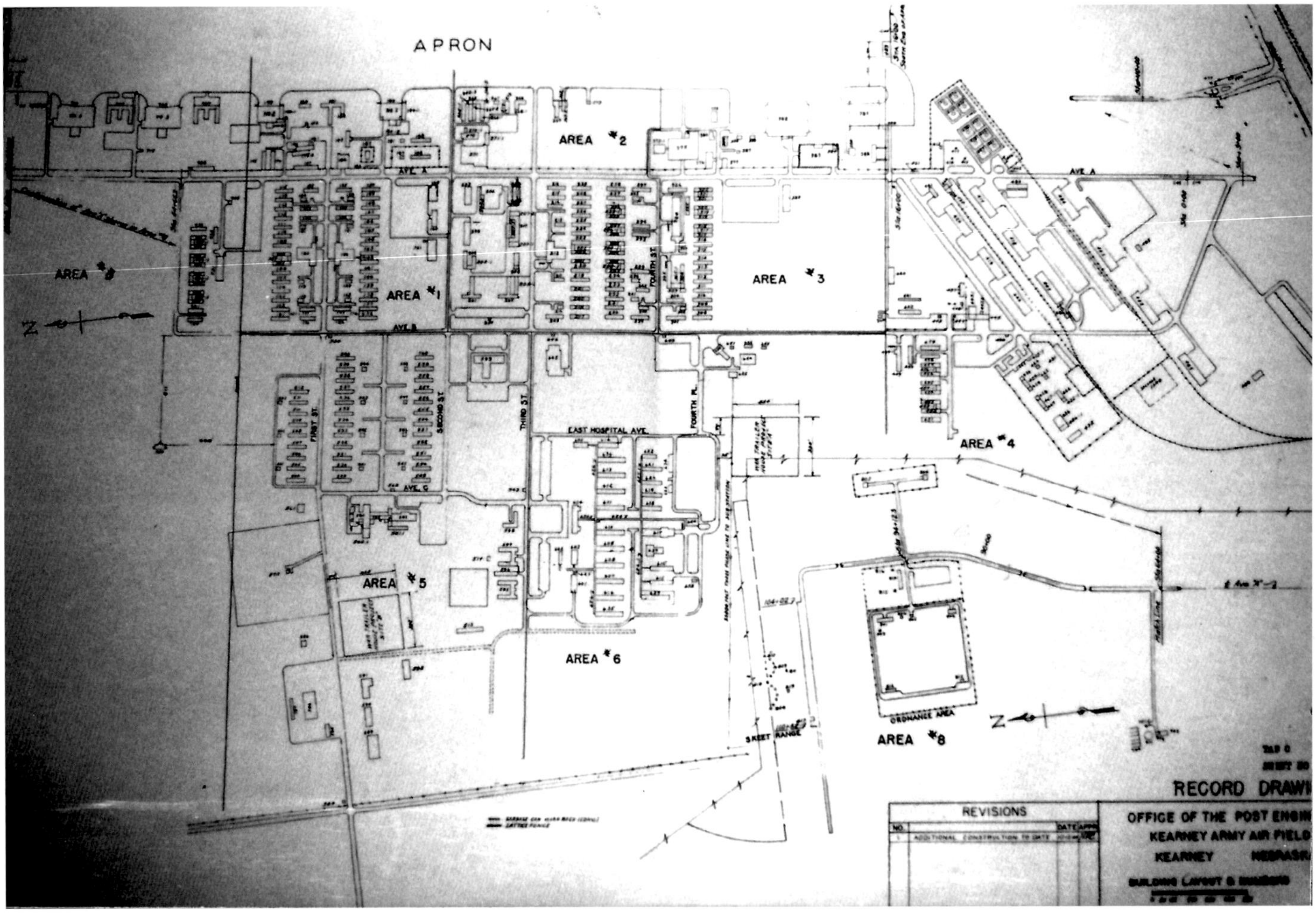

U.S. Army Corps of Engineers plan for the construction of Kearny Air Base, maintained on site by the Office of Post Engineer, Kearny Army Air Field. The blueprint shows the complexity of building an air base on a site where no previous military installation existed. Courtesy of NSHS

torn up and trucked away, with new grading and sub-surface fill to prepare for pavement thick enough to support heavy bomber training operations.

As throughout the state, the immediate problem at Kearney was the sudden influx of construction workers and a shortage of workers' housing. Civilian housing vacancies were rapidly filled, including the Kearney Military Academy, but even this was not enough. The city set up a 150-unit trailer park at the county fairgrounds. The vacant Safeway food store was turned into a recreational facility for the workers on 15 January 1943. After the city set up operations during construction of the base, the USO took over its operations after the base began training operations. The 1940s was still a period of segregation. After the arrival of African American Army personnel at the air base, a separate USO facility was set up for them and a hotel for sleeping accommodations. The U.S. military did not mix African Americans in the same units as Caucasians at this time, although African American Service Battalions worked on Nebraska's military installations.[239]

The Municipal Airport's hangar was turned into a machine shop for the air base's Ordnance Repair Depot. Concrete paving commenced on 6 October 1942, continuing to 24 November. Paving work required the delivery of 1,000 railroad Hopper cars of cement, the equivalent of pouring a standard two-lane concrete highway from Kearney to McCook—a distance of 100 miles.

While paving work was in progress, workers built many of the air base's wood buildings. They also worked on the utility distribution system on the air base. By 1 October, over 1,000 workers were on the air base. By the end of November, the number of workers increased to 3,000. The large base had eight support areas. The first group of completed buildings was used to house construction workers unable to find lodging in the surrounding area. As other barracks and support buildings were completed, construction began on the post office, recreation and service club, hospital, theater, chapel, and post exchange. The majority of the air base's primary buildings were finished by the end of November.[240]

The Union Pacific Railroad Depot became the unloading point for military personnel when they arrived in Kearney. Construction of Kearney Air Base started on 14 September 1942, with the first train with military personnel assigned to the base arriving on 30 January 1943. Until the early 1950s, the railroad depot handled thousands of military personnel. Courtesy of NSHS

A bus from the base's transportation department leaving the air base for the trip to Kearney with AAF personnel on a pass, then picking up others at the Union Pacific Railroad Depot for the trip back to base. Courtesy of NSHS

Aerial view of Kearney Air Base. At the center of the photograph is a warehouse and support area. The flight line is to the right, with a partial view of the aircraft parking apron, taxiways, and runways. Courtesy of Kearney Army Air Base Reunion Committee.

After the air base became operational, the AAF opened it for employment, hiring 800 civilians. This was a great boost to Kearney's economy. The air base had many local organizations supporting wartime training operations. The Aero Shop repaired wheel assemblies, deicer equipment, performed fuel tank installation, and aircraft cleaning. The Machine Shop repaired or manufactured unavailable parts, made adjustments and modifications as directed by Second AF, and cleaned and checked oil cleaners on each aircraft passing through the air base's depot (B-17s, B-24s, and B-29s). The Paint Shop added AAF stars, insignia, call letters, camouflage, and anything else required on AAF aircraft. The Propeller Shop overhauled, repaired, and balanced aircraft propellers. The Instrument Shop maintained the aircraft's instruments and salvaged equipment from wrecked aircraft. The Reclamation Shop kept many aircraft flying by pulling parts from wrecked or badly damaged aircraft. The Parachute Shop folded and repaired parachutes, cut and spliced leather earphone covers, tested life and safety belts, and sewed gun covers and ammunition bags while repairing and maintaining aircrew clothing.[241]

On June 1, 1988, the *Kearney Daily Hub* printed a special insert about the former WWII Kearney Army Air Base and a reunion of former members to be held 3-5 June 1988.

Women in the Parachute Shop took the lives of military men in their hands every day when packing parachutes. In order to work on parachutes, each person assigned had to be trained for three months before certification to be allowed to independently pack parachutes. Each parachute took approximately one hour or slightly less to pack, with each section packing from 12-13 parachutes per 12-hour shift. Packing a parachute was an exact, systematic process, both technical and complicated. Individual shroud lines were inspected for defects or wear and replaced as required. The silk fabric (prior to

An Aviation Squadron building at the air base. Simple wood building with inexpensive single-pane glass windows, hinged on the bottom to swing open and positioned at an angle when opened by rope or chain, or whatever was available. There were no gutters, just angled wood strips over each window to channel rainwater away from the windows. Each squadron organization made some effort to spruce up the outside of each building. Courtesy of NSHS

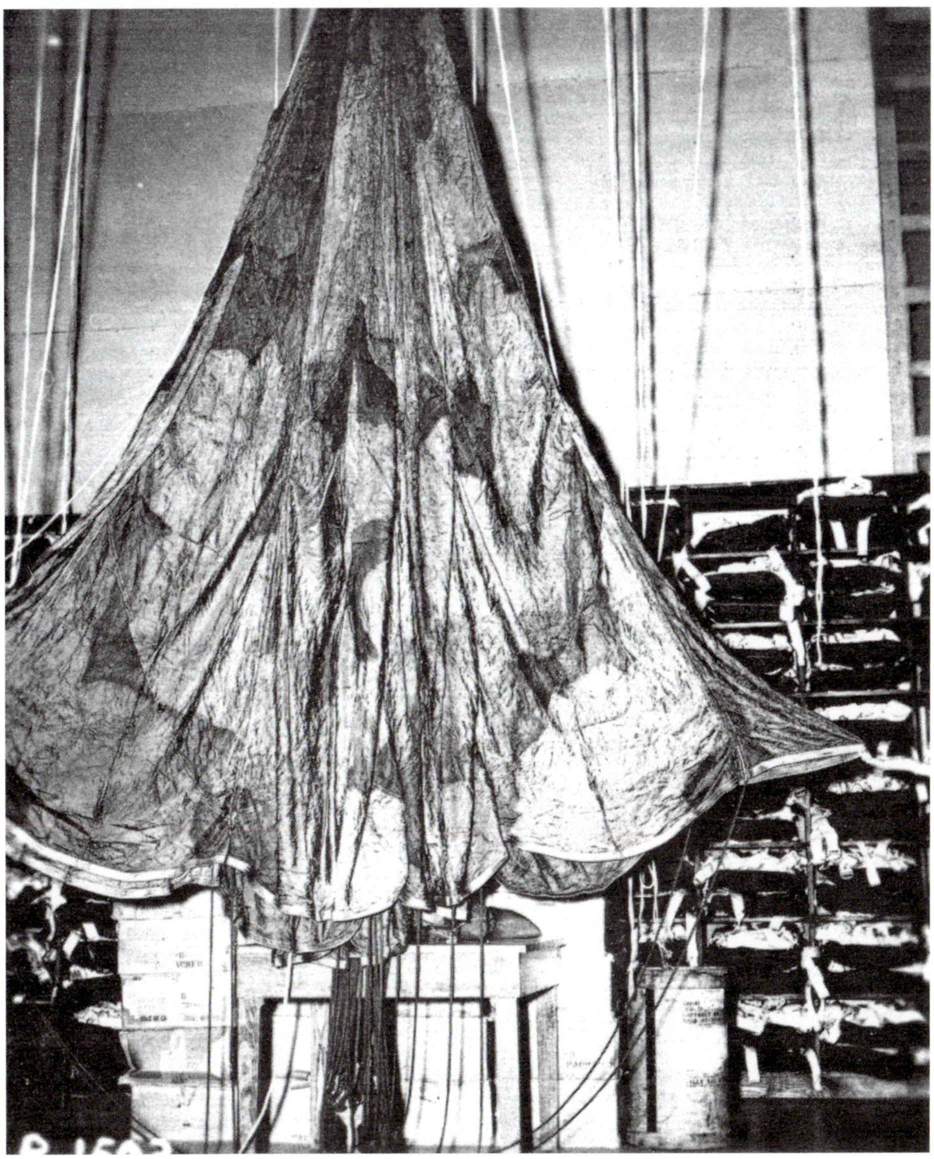

A parachute hanging from the loft ceiling of the Parachute Shop. Courtesy of NSHS

the introduction of nylon fabric) was fanned out on a long table to prevent wrinkle tears or rips; its surface was inspected for damp spots, holes, or fabric flaws. The long tables allowed the parachute to be secured at its top, with the lines pulled tight. There were twelve silk panels per parachute, each carefully folded and packed with a ripcord and signed safety seal. Each packer placed her name inside the packed parachute. If a crewman used the parachute in an emergency to save his life, the packer was eligible for the Cocoon Club for saving his life.[242]

The base's eight supply warehouses provided stock to support training operations and individual crew equipment issue. Every crewman processed through base supply to receive his combat equipment: uniforms, heated flying boots, gloves, side arm, ammunition, and many other items needed for assignment to a specific combat Theater of Operations.

On 17 January 1943, the Chemical Section started training aircrews and ground support personnel on how to use and care for gas masks, how to identify the odor of airborne gases and effects, and decontamination procedures. The first Army training units arrived on 30 January to begin training operations.

One of eight base supply warehouses. (Author)

The base also had to support various operations at the Kearney Union Pacific Railroad Depot. Troop trains were often routed from the Union Pacific's main line through the base to pick up supplies, such as clothing and K-rations. Periodically, a military service person was removed from a Union Pacific train for emergency medical treatment. Sometimes a train made short stops to pick up supplies for transshipment.[243]

Bomb Groups Assigned to Kearney Air Base

Bomb Group	Bomb Squadron	Date Assigned
100th	349th	30 January to
(B-17)	350th	1 May 1943
	351st	
	418th	
393rd	580th	1 August to
(B-17)	581st	1 November 1943
	582nd	
	583rd	
488th	818th	1 October 1943
(B-17)	(formerly 840th)	1 May 1944[244]

In early February 1943, the 110th BG started arriving at Kearney AB. The ground echelon went directly to work: not training, but cleaning. The one story wood barracks were as the construction workers left them, littered with debris. The task of cleaning or policing these buildings and surrounding grounds required many days of hard work. Double-deck bunks were installed, along with coal heating stoves (two per barracks). The barracks became reasonably comfortable with Army supplied sheets, pillows, blankets, footlockers, and allowed personal items. The bomb group was fed in two large mess halls, with two squadrons sharing one mess hall. The bomb group rated their food as excellent until the garrison allowance was replaced by a field ration allowance, with food then downgraded to good or fair.

After the base areas were cleaned up and men settled into their barracks and shops they began their processing duties, which consisted of inventory, inspecting aircraft, equipment, personnel, and operational aircraft of air echelons headed for combat. Shortages of equipment had to be made up with shipments from other bases or new production. Every aircraft

There were frequent parades on the base. Members of the 100th BG are forming in squadron order on the base parade ground. Courtesy of NSHS

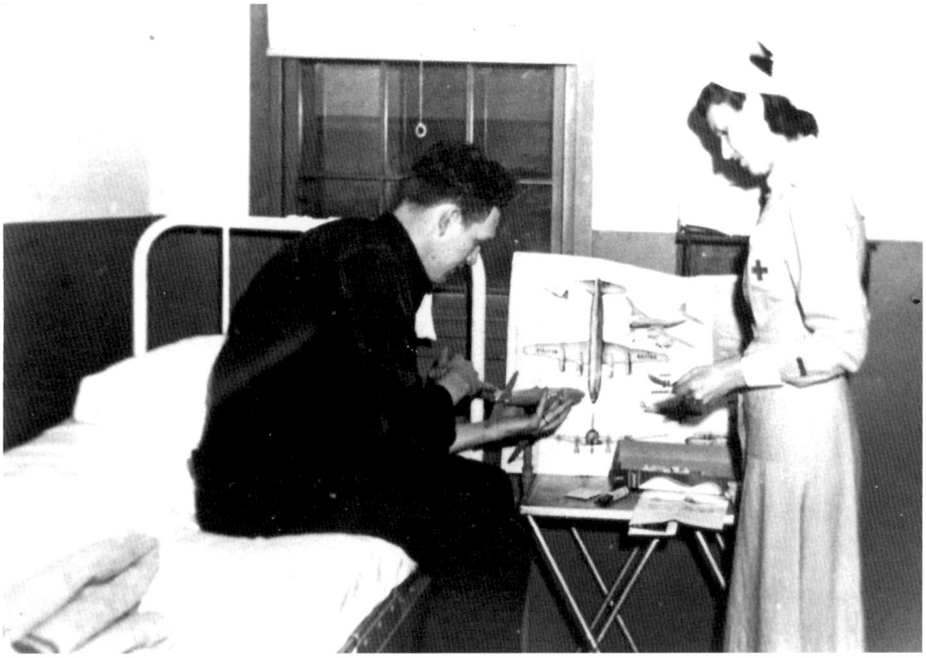

In the base's hospital, an enlisted man puts together a model aircraft as a Red Cross volunteer looks on. Courtesy of NSHS

Aircrew and ground personnel on the base firing range. Courtesy of NSHS

Kearney Air Base processed many B-17 aircrews during WWII, including Lieutenant Clark Gable. Courtesy of NSHS

had to be checked and prepared for over-ocean flights to combat zones. Aircrews were given classroom instruction by the Intelligence Section. They practiced the care of their equipment, including machine guns, which they had to strip and clean. Many gunners were not familiar with the technical operations and required maintenance of their weapons. While the 100th BG had no aircraft of its own for training, the bomb group's officers did get in some flying time in the few aircraft available, while the group's personnel processed on base flew a limited number of practice missions during their stay of two to three weeks. Each transient bomb group made one long mission from Kearney to the Gulf of Mexico for navigational and gunnery practice before movement to overseas combat. The 100th BG processed the 2nd, 95th, and 351st BGs. One famous member of the 351st BG was Hollywood actor Clark Gable.[245]

As previously noted, Kearney AB processed many B-17 aircrews during WWII, including Lieutenant Clark Gable. One of the women working at the air base from Kearney (Marian Wardrop, assigned to the Supply Department) processed the Lieutenant through the base. As a nineteen-year-old, she became excited just asking Gable for his name, rank, and serial number and processing the Lieutenant through the base supply system before he climbed into a B-17 for the long flight to England, assigned with the eighth Air Force.[246]

Metal hangar roof attached to concrete walls, with external concrete bracing to hold up the walls, along with the weight and pressure of the roof structure. (Author)

Weather at Kearney affected the 100th BG's training. Even during February and March 1943, there were many days of good weather, sunshine, and warm temperatures. There were also periods of good flying weather in winter and spring. At the opposite end of the spectrum were spring dust storms, which filled buildings with microscopic dust particles, making life and training miserable. By the end of March, the bomb group's pre-overseas movement unit inspections started. On 20 April, thirty-seven aircrews led by Colonel Darr H. Alkire took off on a training mission to Hamilton Field, California to check out the bomb group on high altitude formation flying. All but three of the aircrews completed the training mission, which allowed combat flights at high altitude. Three aircraft did not complete the training mission: one B-17 broke off a section of its tail when landing at Hamilton Field, with the tail gunner surviving, suffering scratches and bruises; the second B-17 was hit by stray .50 caliber machine gun shells when its gunners test fired their guns; and the third B-17 experienced engine problems. Because of a failure to complete required training, Colonel Alkine was relieved of command and replaced by Colonel Howard M. Turner.

On 1 May, the 100th BG's air echelon, consisting of forty B-17s and their aircrews, took off for Wendover, Utah for twenty days of advanced training: bombing, navigation, formation flying, and gunnery, along with combined defensive gunfire at aerial towed target sleeves. From Wendover, flying in formation, twelve B-17s flew to nearby Ogden for combat modifications. The modifications took mechanics one week to complete. Back at Kearney, practice missions continued to be flown 20-21 May. Colonel Turner took off with the 349th and 350th BS on 25 May, the aircraft landing at Selfridge Field, Michigan or Syracuse, New York for refueling while en route to Atlantic coast staging bases for overseas flights across the North Atlantic to England. The 351st and 418th BS departed Kearney on 26 May, flying to

Active runway at Kearney. (Author)

Fort Wayne, Indiana. The B-17s then landed at Bangor, Maine, the last stop before flying over the North Atlantic to England and the Eighth Air Force. The ground echelon departed Kearney by Union Pacific train on 2 May to Camp Williams, Wisconsin for one week of infantry training. On 9 May, they boarded another train for Camp Kilmer, New Jersey, their overseas embarkation port. On 26 May, they boarded the *Queen Elizabeth*, departing for England the next day.[247]

Kearney AB was a training and processing base responsible for training cadres for AAF bomb groups. Ground crews were stationed at Kearney with

B-17 named *5 Grand*, the 5,000th Boeing-produced B-17 Flying Fortress, photographed while at Kearney for overseas combat modifications. The bomber carried signatures of the Boeing employees who built the bomber. Courtesy of Kearney Army Air Base Reunion Committee

Large B-29 hangar at Kearney. The shop facility is at the back of the hangar. In 1991, the roof was in bad shape, with siding sections coming off the hangar. The size of the hangar is immense, allowing the large B-29 to be towed inside and worked on, regardless of inclement or cold weather. (Author)

aircrews at McCook, Grand Island, and Harvard as instructors. B-17s were modified at Cheyenne, Wyoming, with additional work done at Kearney for specific Theaters of Operations. In May, the Processing Unit moved from Kearney and the base turned into a training center for replacement aircrews. Kearney did second and third stage aircrew training until December 1943, when its training function transferred to Sioux City, Iowa. Kearney then became a bombardment unit processing center for B-17s and B-29s.[248]

One of the many historic events at Kearney AB was the arrival of the first B-17G in July 1944. By April, Kearney's personnel trained 388 B-17 crews each month. Considerable publicity was given to the appearance of the 5,000th Boeing-produced B-17. It was processed at Kearney for overseas combat after completing a war bond sales promotion tour in the United States, raising money for the war effort. The B-17 survived WWII combat, flew back to the United States, and went into storage at Longman, Arizona; it was eventually scrapped.[249]

The municipal airport terminal and resurfaced aircraft parking apron at Kearney in 1991. (Author)

The Kearney AB chapel being moved into Kearney. Courtesy of Kearney Air Base Reunion Committee

By October 1944, the first B-29 arrived at Kearney AB for overseas processing. By January 1945, 544 B-29s had been processed through the base for Pacific combat operations, assigned to the 20th AF, Marianas Islands. By May, eighty-four B-29 crews were being processed each month, requiring a ninety-three day training cycle.

With the end of the war in Europe, Kearney AB switched over to preparing aircrews for Pacific combat. After Japan's surrender on 15 August 1945, the number of military personnel on base declined until 1 March 1946, when it was downgraded to housekeeping status for remaining personnel. In December 1946, the base was reactivated as an Air Transport air base, becoming Kearney Air Force Base in January 1948. However, its status as an active base ended on 15 March 1949.[250]

Many of the former WWII air base's buildings took on a new life after military operations ended. The chapel was moved into Kearney and used by the Family of Christ Lutheran Church. Sections of the base hospital were renovated and used by Newark Lions Club, Lexington Care Home, Walter's Duplex, Wilcox Drilling in Lexington, and the Fort Kearney Museum.

Barracks were moved from the base for various commercial businesses in and around Kearney. The Officer's Club was moved into Kearney as a youth center. Four-plex officer housing units were moved into Kearney, renovated, and upgraded for rental housing.[251] This was common throughout Nebraska after the end of the war as its once busy military bases became non-essential to the United States military. It is remarkable that even though these buildings were hastily built they withstood

One of the wood, two-story officers' quarters moved from the former WWII air base into Kearney. Courtesy of Kearney Air Base Reunion Committee

jacking up on to prime movers and surviving the slow tow to new locations.

From 3-5 June 1988, the former WWII air base again was the scene of activity by former personnel. A B-17 owned by Dave Tallichet of California landed on the main runway, the first such aircraft to do so since the end of WWII. This B-17 never flew in combat; it was used during the Korean War as a transport for general officers. The aircraft became a hurricane tracker aircraft and was then finally modified into a forest fire chemical and water bomber. The Flying Fortress was sold, restored, and flew at air shows throughout the United States. This reunion was sponsored by the Kearney Area Chamber of Commerce and Buffalo County Historical Society.[252]

CHAPTER TEN

POW CAMPS

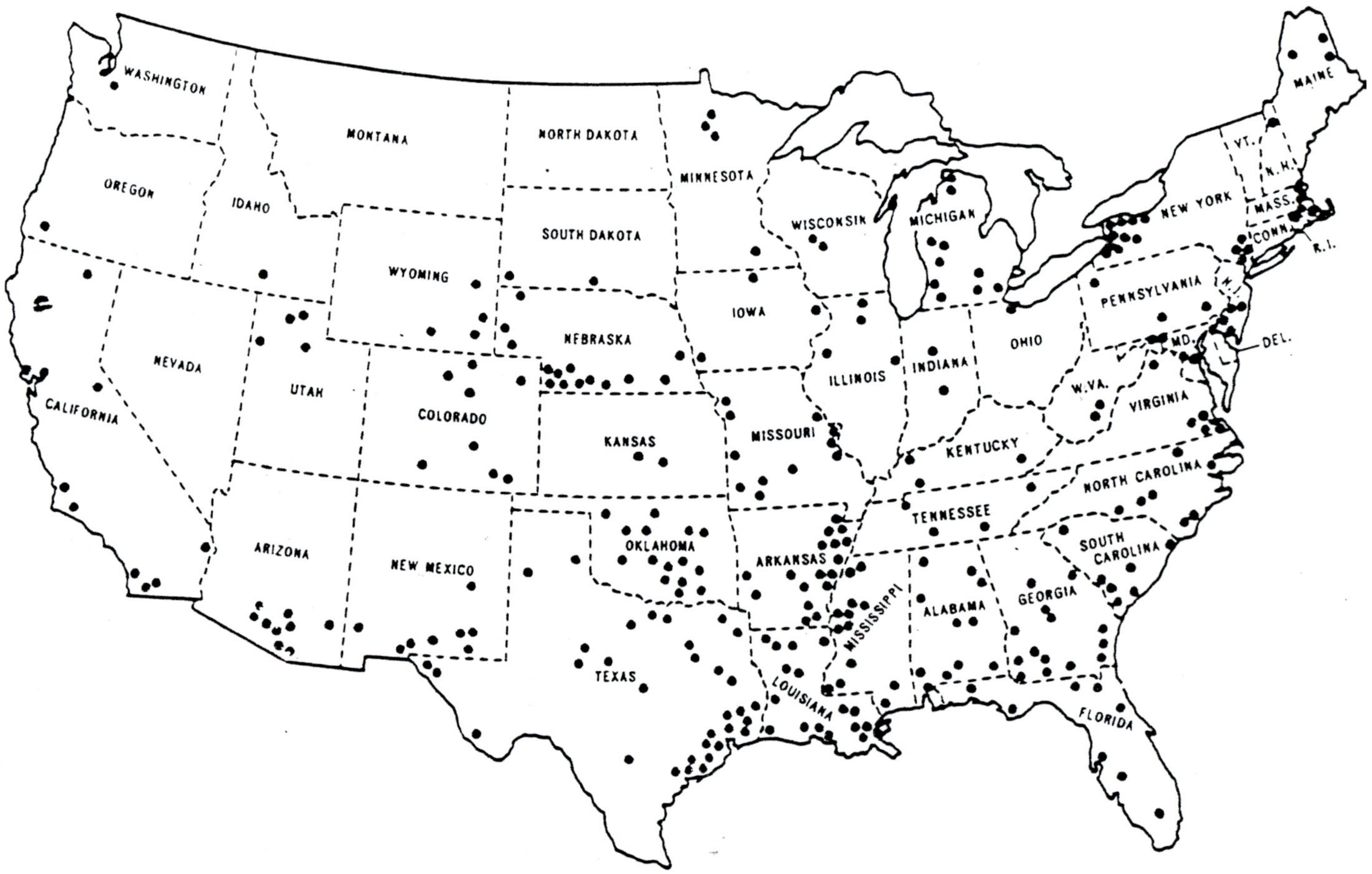

Distribution of POW camps established in the United States to handle large numbers of captured German, followed by Italian and smaller numbers of Japanese military personnel. Courtesy of United States Army, *The Military Engineer*, February 1946.

With the passage of time, most Americans do not know the United States was temporary home to thousands of German, Italian, and a few thousand Japanese POWs. The physical remains of these camps are all but gone at these former WWII POW camps.[253] The first U.S. captured Axis POW was an Imperial Japanese Navy man from a two-man midget submarine that washed on the beach outside the entrance to Pearl Harbor, Hawaii on 7 December 1941. He was actually captured and taken into custody prior to the formal declaration of war by President Roosevelt the next day during a speech before a joint session of the U.S. Congress in Washington, D.C. By the end of WWII, America's POW camps held 371,683 German, 50,273 Italian, and 3,915 Japanese.[254] In 1942, President Roosevelt agreed to take custody of large numbers of Axis troops captured in North Africa, Sicily, and Italy, later to include German troops captured in Europe after the D-day landing of 6 June 1944. It took until the middle of 1943 for the first American POW camps to be converted from existing military facilities or new construction.[255]

The Geneva Convention of 27 July 1929, signed by the majority of the world's nations, is specific on how POWs are to be treated. Even though the Empire of Japan signed the Convention's agreements, it did not follow the rules for housing, feeding, clothing, and medical and humanitarian treatment of POWs. After WWII, Japanese POW commanders and security troops were apprehended and tried for war crimes. The signers of the Geneva Convention agreed: "in the extreme case of war, it will be the duty of every power (country) to diminish, so far as possible, the unavoidable rigors to thereof, and to mitigate the fate of Prisoners of War."[256] These rules were guidelines for the security and care of POWs.[257]

Under Title II of the Geneva Convention: "POWs may be interned in enclosed camps, but may not be confined or imprisoned except as an indispensable measure of safety or sanitation. POW camp installations shall provide housing which will afford all possible guarantees of hygiene and healthfulness, adequate heating, lighting and fire protection. Also, space allowances and other housing

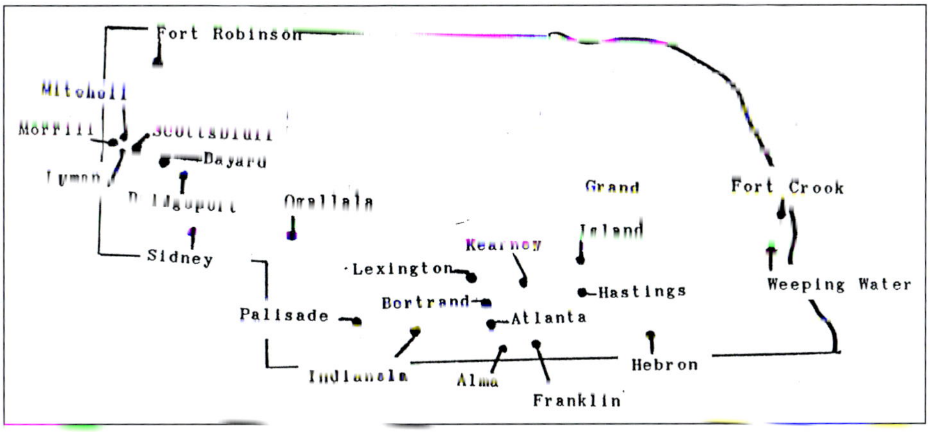

Locations of POW camps in Nebraska during WWII. (Author)

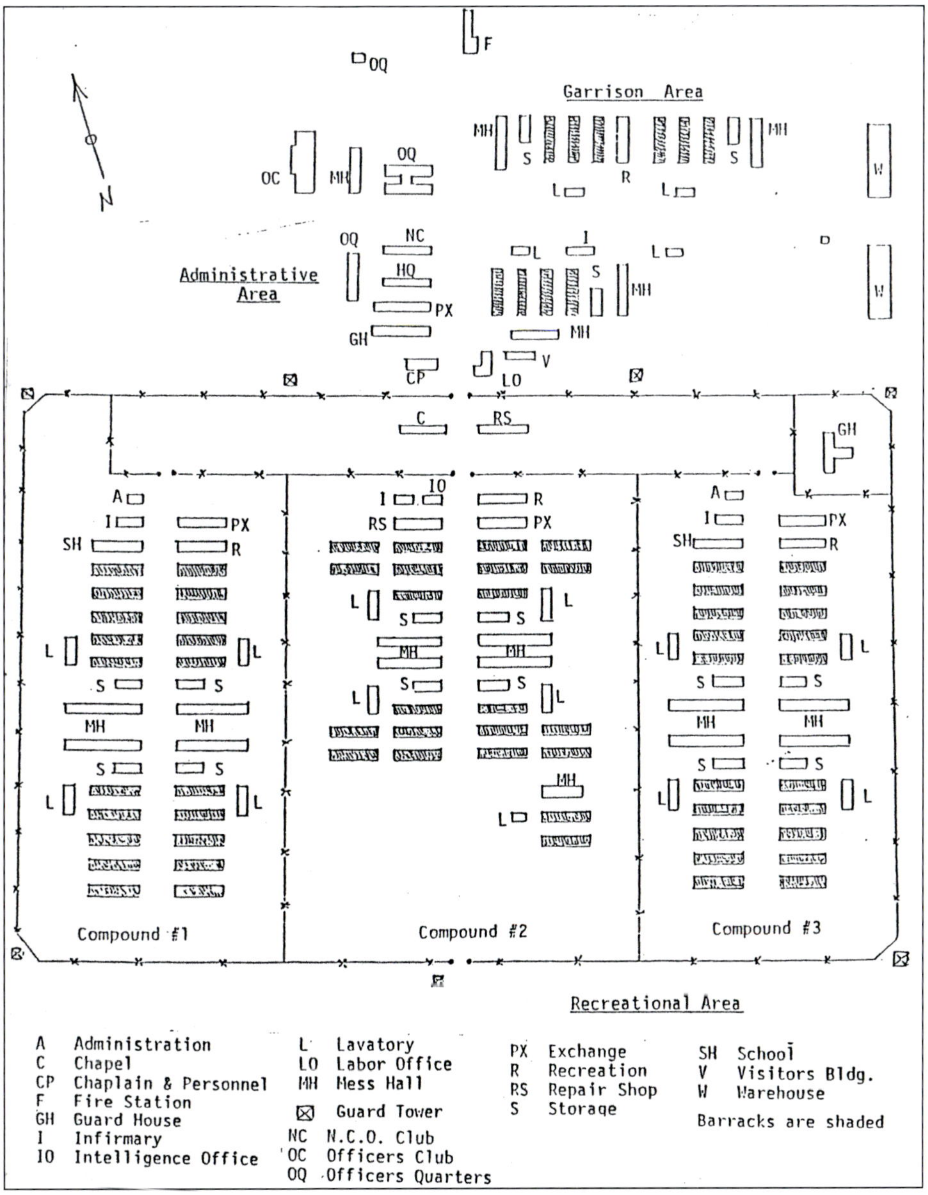

Standard POW camp layout. Courtesy of *The Military Engineer*, February 1946.

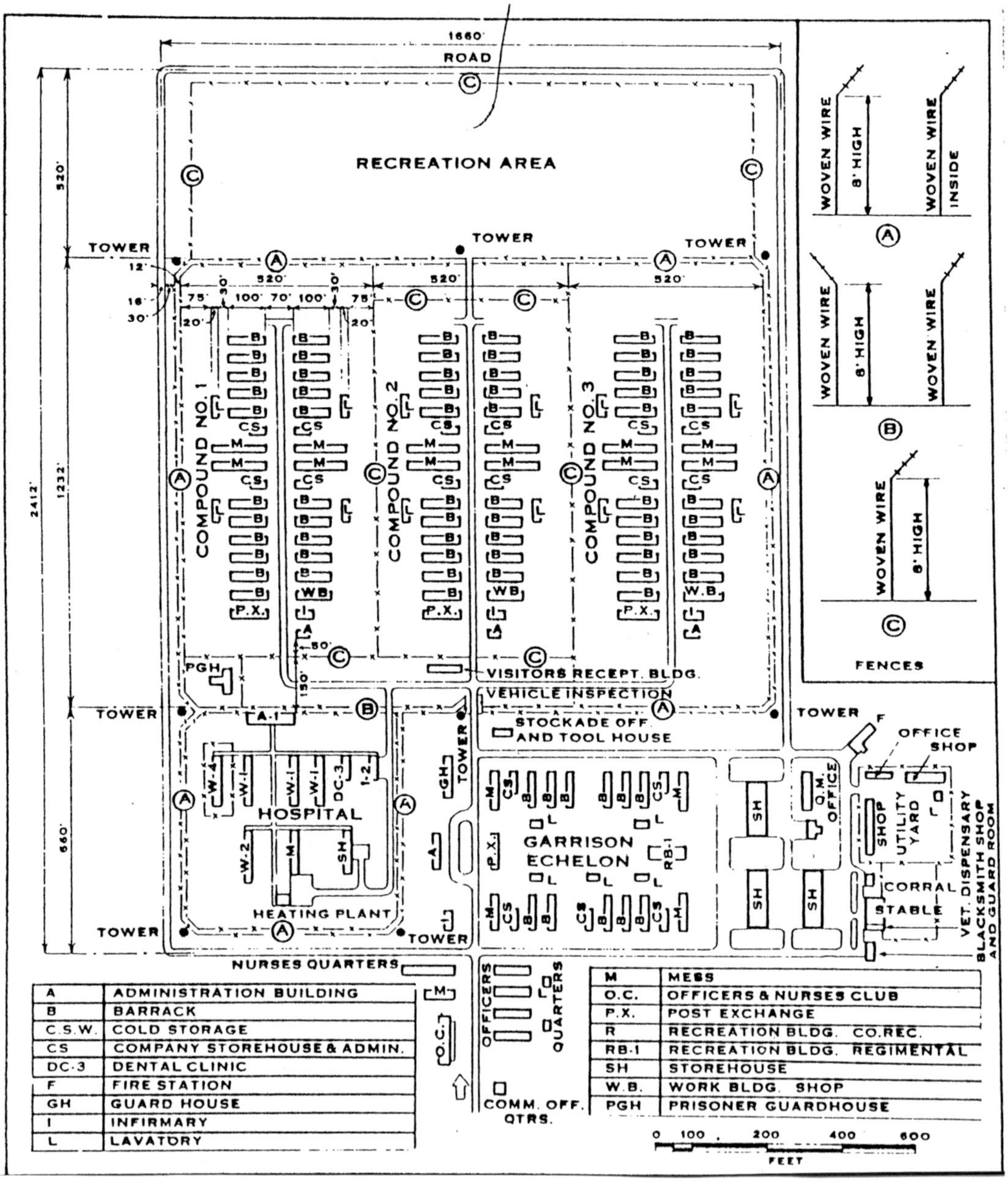

Standard layout of a camp for 5,000 POWs. *The Military Engineer*, February 1946.

conditions must conform to the facilities, which are provided troops at base camps of the detaining power."[258]

In the United States, POW camps were built at isolated locations away from declared blackout areas, designated 150 miles from the Mexico or Canada borders and 75 miles from the coast, shipyards, or war plants. This positioned two-thirds of U.S. POW camps in the south, southwest, and western part of the country. Select camps were built in agricultural areas critically short of farm and ranch workers due to men joining or being drafted into the military, working in war plants, or building military installations and war plants throughout the country.

The standard American-constructed POW camp allowed for a design with one or more compound configurations surrounded by perimeter security fencing, with each compound separated from the other by another security fence. A compound was designed to secure up to four POW companies (250 men per company, 1,000 men. Within each POW company, 50 men were assigned to each barracks, serviced by a latrine, mess hall, and administration building. POWs were granted access to a recreation building, infirmary, worship (church or chapel), canteen, and hospital.[259]

The camp's three compound configurations provided the facilities to secure 3,000 POWs. Each enlisted POW was authorized 40 square feet of barracks space and officers 120 square feet. Smaller 1,800-man POW camps were built as temporary facilities to meet an increasing need to accommodate POWs arriving

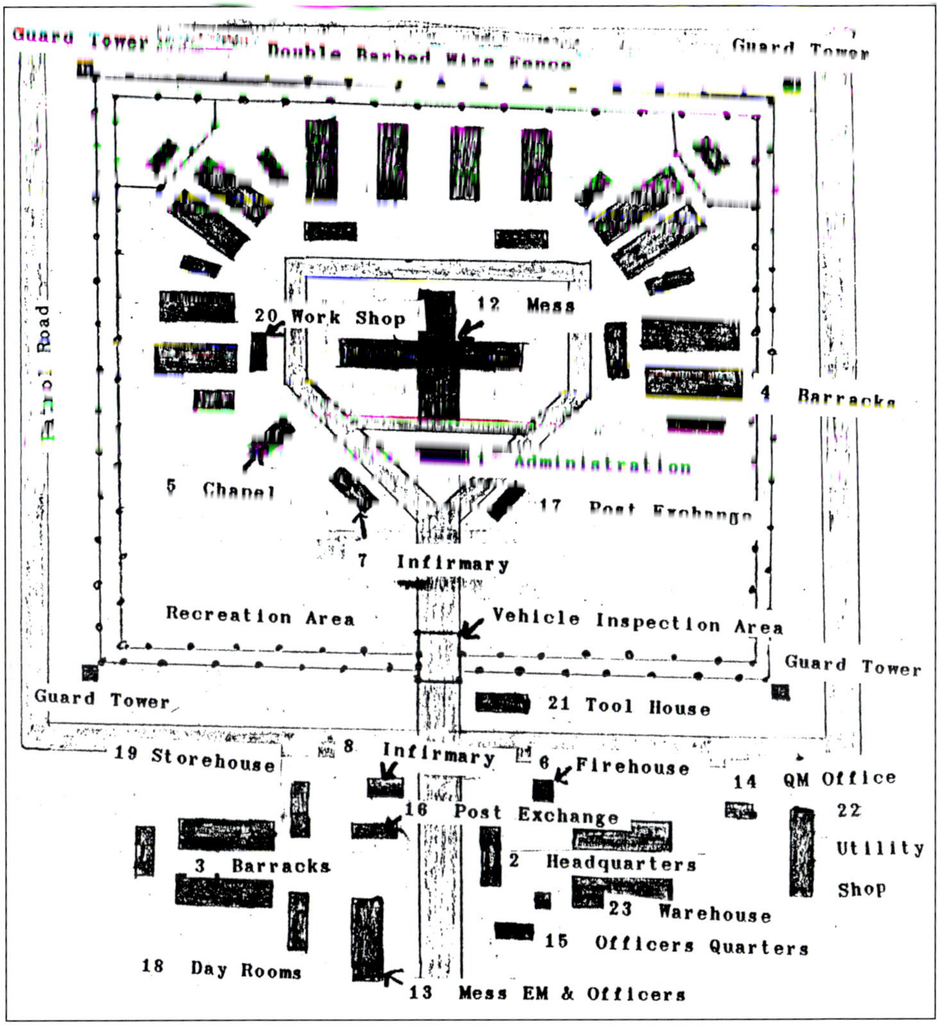

Drawing of a smaller branch, 250-man POW camp. (Author)

from overseas combat zones, as well as solving labor shortages in agriculture, farming, and ranching. These temporary camps were equipped with 150-man barracks, along with a consolidated mess hall, combined post exchange and recreation building, and miscellaneous support buildings. This required less space and construction time located in labor-short areas of the United States. Branch labor camps were designed to hold 250-750 POWs, although other side camps held 1,800 POWs. These POW camps required less security than main POW camps, primarily because POWs assigned were heavily screened and considered less of an escape risk than hard core politically vocal Nazi POWs.[260] Many of the first branch POW camps were converted from existing New Deal Civilian Conservation Corps (CCC) facilities, which had been positioned near agricultural areas and conservation projects to complete the Great Depression era work projects. These camps were pressed into service to provide labor to replace American men drafted or enlisting into the U.S. military, as well as those hired to work in vital war industries.

Under the rules of the Geneva Convention, POWs could volunteer to work in non-war jobs on military installations, private industry, agriculture, or farming. By the end of WWII, over 200,000 POWs labored outside main POW camps estimated in 1945 dollars—at a value of $22,000,000. An additional $5,000,000 of POW labor was in U.S. military installations.[261]

Interestingly, a non-military organization (the War Manpower Commission, WMC) was given the responsibility for determining and setting policy and procedures to use POW labor under the guidelines provided by the Geneva Convention.[262]

Each POW received a salary of ten cents a day while in U.S. custody to pay for necessities at the POW camp, with a higher wage of 80-90 cents per day for each POW who volunteered to work outside the camp. Most of the money was kept by camp authorities until the war ended and POWs were released from custody, at which time vouchers could be spent in the camp's PX to take home—more on this later when German POWs left the United States. While in the POW camp, only paper canteen coupons were issued as work payment to prevent collection of U.S. currency to provide potential escapees money to purchase civilian clothing, food, and transportation to reach the nearest border, possibly back to Germany (very long odds). Canteen coupons were printed in various denominations for purchases, such as candy bar (.05), shaving cream (.35), and pipe and Tobacco (.50). The U.S. Army Quartermaster Corps provided each POW with one raincoat, summer and winter clothing, underwear, wool cap, belt, denim work clothes, work gloves, white socks, and Government Issue (GI) military shoes. The standard POW uniform was dark blue in color with distinctive white lettering (POW): six-inch lettering on the shirt and coat back, four-inch on the arm front between the elbow and shoulder, four-inch on the pants seat, and four-inch above the knees.[263]

Nebraska was selected to receive German and Italian POWs. The state's borders were far enough from the Mexico and Canada borders, Pacific and Atlantic Oceans, and Gulf of Mexico to provide great enough distance for possible escapees' path back to Germany or Italy. There were still escapes from U.S. POW camps, although unknown to the American public so as not to create panic among the population. There was concern that escaped German and Italian POWs would seek out fellow immigrants for assistance to somehow get back to Germany and Italy. Out of the 425,000 POWs detained in the United States, there were 2,903 escapes. The majority of those

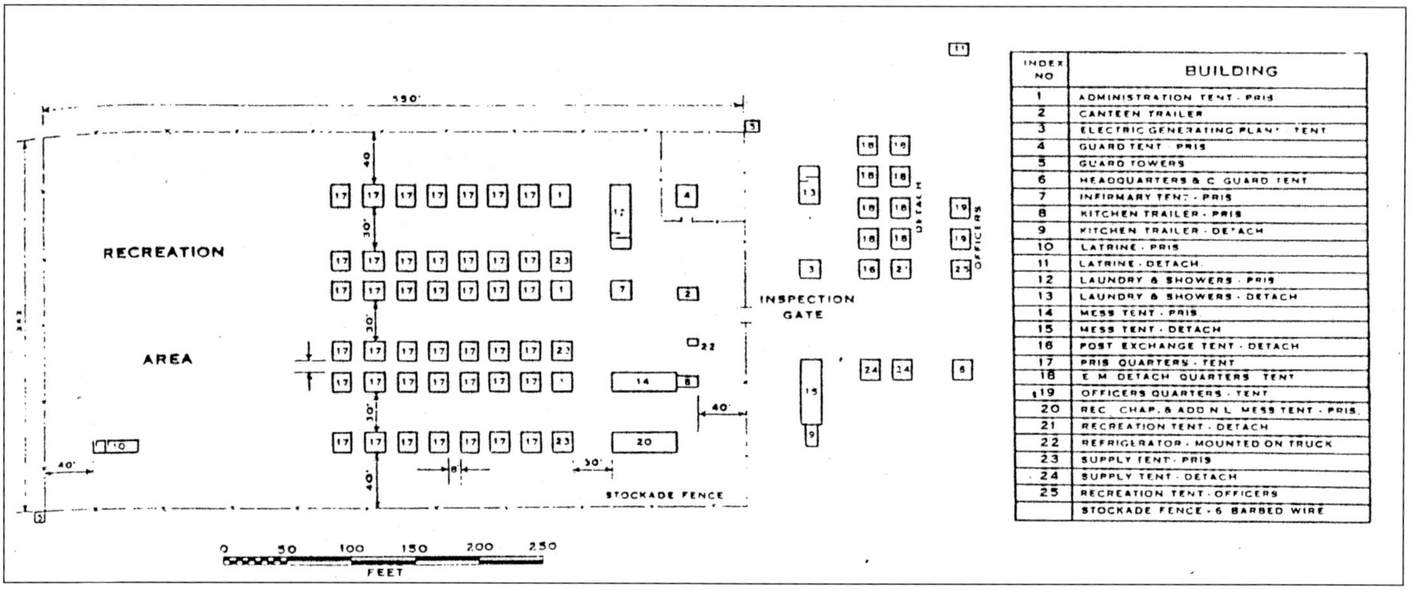

INDEX NO	BUILDING
1	ADMINISTRATION TENT - PRIS
2	CANTEEN TRAILER
3	ELECTRIC GENERATING PLANT TENT
4	GUARD TENT PRIS
5	GUARD TOWERS
6	HEADQUARTERS & C GUARD TENT
7	INFIRMARY TENT - PRIS
8	KITCHEN TRAILER - PRIS
9	KITCHEN TRAILER - DETACH
10	LATRINE - PRIS
11	LATRINE - DETACH
12	LAUNDRY & SHOWERS - PRIS
13	LAUNDRY & SHOWERS - DETACH
14	MESS TENT - PRIS
15	MESS TENT - DETACH
16	POST EXCHANGE TENT - DETACH
17	PRIS QUARTERS - TENT
18	E M DETACH QUARTERS TENT
19	OFFICERS QUARTERS - TENT
20	REC CHAP. & ADD N L MESS TENT - PRIS.
21	RECREATION TENT - DETACH
22	REFRIGERATOR - MOUNTED ON TRUCK
23	SUPPLY TENT - PRIS
24	SUPPLY TENT - DETACH
25	RECREATION TENT - OFFICERS
	STOCKADE FENCE - 6 BARBED WIRE

Layout for 250-man (mobile) POW camp. Drawing: United States Army, *The Military Engineer*, February 1946.

who escaped were returned to custody in one day. By October 1946, twenty-four POWs remained free somewhere in the United States. During these escapes, fifty-six were intercepted before making it through the POW camp security fencing, of which thirty-four were shot by guards. Statistics showed a .45 percent escape rate. This compared to the federal prison system's escape rate of .45 percent. For the U.S. Army, it was still troubling that enemy military men escaped and were roaming or hiding among the American public. POW camp site locations were part of the consideration when factoring in the critical movement of U.S. military personnel and war material overseas, so as not to be impacted by the inbound transportation of Axis POWs to the detention camps. The majority of POWs were transported in passenger railroad cars, heavily guarded with blinds pulled during the day to prevent memorization of the land route from the east coast ports to the POW camps. When near the POW camp, they were unloaded under guard and marched to the POW camp.[264]

In Nebraska, there were four main POW camps: Fort Robinson, Camp Scotts Bluff, Camp Indianola, and Camp

The security fencing around the POW camp at Fort Robinson. Courtesy of Fort Robinson Museum.

1991 photo of the upper POW compound at Fort Robinson. The middle and lower compounds look almost identical. The POW camp compounds were built in a relatively flat area. This allowed better security, in that without changes in elevation there was no terrain for POWs to hide in when trying to approach the fence, cut through, and then escape. The open country around the camp allowed a clear view from the guard towers. There was always a concern that somehow a POW would escape. (Author)

Simple wood sign that marked the entrance to Fort Robinson POW camp; entering German and Italian POWs passed it when marching into the camp. Courtesy of Fort Robinson Museum.

Atlanta.[265] Located at the site of the former Red Cloud Indian Agency southeast of the Army post's main administration area, Fort Robinson's POW camp was built in Nebraska's panhandle to hold 3,000 German and Italian POWs. It was ready to accept Axis POWs fifteen months after Pearl Harbor. The camp consisted of three compounds, each holding a maximum of 1,000, with one barracks per 50 men. This was a standard layout for a main POW camp in the United States.

POWs at Fort Robinson were provided a shower and latrine building, recreational hall, and canteen. Barbed wire and hog-wire fencing surrounded the camp with visual security provided by six guard and surveillance towers.[266]

Camp Scotts Bluff was the first POW camp to be completed in Nebraska. It was built at the site of a former CCC camp five miles east and one and one-half miles south of Scotts Bluff. Each of the three compounds held four POW companies serviced by six barracks, a shower and latrine building, one kitchen and mess hall, one workshop, and one officer building. Initially, the camp served as a

The area where Camp Scotts Bluff was built. (Author)

temporary internment camp for Japanese American citizens until they were moved to another facility; then the camp served Axis POWs.[267] Camp Scotts Bluff supported seven branch camps: Bayard, Bridgeport, Lyman, Mitchell, Morrill, and Sidney. Temporary branch camps were also supported at Sterling, Colorado (closed on 11 February 1944).[268]

Camp Atlanta was a one-of-a-kind POW camp in Nebraska. At peak occupancy, it was the largest in the state. It consisted of four compounds, 70 buildings, and seven miles of service/access roads staffed by 600 military and 300 local civilian employees to intern and care for 3,000 POWs.[269] It was the number and location of branch POW camps that set Atlanta apart from the other main POW camps in Nebraska, including Alama, Bennelman, Betrand, Elwood, Fort Crook, Franklin, Grand Island, Hastings, Hebron, Kearney, Lexington, Ogallala, Palisade, and Weeping Water.[270]

In 1991, this is all that remained of Camp Atlanta (German and Italian POW camp). The photo shows the outline of one of the 50-man barracks. (Author)

The remains of concrete from the wash, shower, and latrine building at Camp Atlanta in the process of being torn up for sale. (Author)

The interior of one of the 50-man, POW barracks at Fort Robinson. Two U.S. Army enlisted men pose in the barracks. The wood floor, walls, and ceiling barracks were heated by three wood stoves (one at each end and another in the middle). Each POW had a wood bed with mattress and bedding and a wood footlocker, along with hooks on the wall to hang clothes. There were upright storage lockers at each end of the barracks for clothes. The front bed has two pair of shoes underneath the bed, lined up in military order. Army personnel inspected the barracks constantly to detect illegal items and any actions or preparations under way not permitted by camp rules. Courtesy of Fort Robinson Museum.

Camp Indianola in 1991. The primary access road remains visible. (Author)

Camp Indianola in 1991. Only the concrete floor and wall footing remains of the wash, shower, and latrine facility. (Author)

Camp Indianola was designed to hold 3,000 POWs and was staffed by 350 military and 125 civilian employees. One part of the state's involvement in securing Axis POWs was not well publicized. The Army brought in cleared Japanese American soldiers from the internment camps to guard German and Italian POWs. This freed combat-qualified Army personnel for overseas duty. The POW camp was built at Atlanta to provide labor in building the Medicine Valley Water Project. After the water project construction ended, the POW camp was closed, as it was no longer needed.[271]

As main POW camps were built in Nebraska, and in other parts of the United States, the Army and War Department decided not to publicly announce the construction of these secure enclosures as German and Italian POW camps until 5 July 1943, referring to them as "special

William Oberdieck at his home in Nebraska City, Nebraska, in 1991. (Author)

U.S. Army installations."[272] It cost approximately two and one-half million dollars to build each main POW camp, with reduced costs for smaller and branch camps.[273] Most of the main POW camps were located within five miles of a railroad line, preferably near a railroad depot to provide off-loading of POWs from passenger cars, large open areas for security, and an access road directly into the camp. Rail transportation was the easiest, fastest, and most secure means to move large numbers of POWs into the U.S. heartland from coastal ports.[274]

By the middle of 1943, the Army was able to complete the conversion of enough former CCC facilities or finished the construction of new camps to house and secure the initial arrivals of Axis POWs shipped to the United States. I had the opportunity to interview William Oberdieck, former German military enlisted man, about his capture, shipment to the United States and Nebraska, camp life, his return home (a very difficult experience), and return back to the United States for a new postwar life in eastern Nebraska. He spoke openly of all his wartime experiences and his treatment while interned in the United States. The story of his return to Europe is one of the untold stories about the treatment of former WWII German POWs returned from the United States, transiting through France on their way home to Germany. This was not one of the best examples of treatment of former German soldiers by a U.S. military ally.

William recalls: "I was assigned to Field Marshall Erwin Rommel's intelligence staff. I was one of the first group of German POWs to be shipped to the United States. While I was in school in Germany I learned to speak English, with a working knowledge of French and Spanish. My job was to listen to British Army radio communications, locate the location of the transmitting units by radio triangulation, and plot their location on a chart for my commanders. I tried to escape from Tunisia, but I was captured by U.S. Army troops in Constantine, Algeria. From Constantine, Algeria, I and other POWs were transported by truck to Oran, Algeria for transfer to an Allied freighter for a seven-day sea voyage to Glasgow, Scotland. My fellow POWs and I moved into a temporary German POW holding camp near Comrie, Scotland for six weeks. The British issued us WWI British Army wool uniforms, dyed maroon with fabric sewn on the knees (front and back) and a cap marked with a large yellow half moon. This gave British Army camp guards a readily identifiable target if we attempted an escape. The uniforms were hot,

Mannequin dressed as a POW on his bunk in one of the barracks at Fort Robinson POW camp. On display at the Fort Robinson Museum. (Author)

scratchy, and uncomfortable. The Allies did not want to keep Axis POWs in the British Isles any longer than necessary because of the planned D-Day invasion preparations. From Comrie, Scotland, I and other German POWs were trucked to Glasgow, Scotland, then loaded into the *Queen Mary* for shipment to New York.

Once at New York, we were loaded into a sealed train for the railroad passage to a POW camp at Concordia, Kansas. The railroad trip took three days and two nights, during which I and other POWs had to remain on our assigned wood bench in the passenger car. Once at Concordia, the town's residents lined the streets to watch us arrive and march from the railroad depot to the camp. I was assigned to a POW company in compound one. One day at the camp, a group of my barracks mates were playing catch behind the barracks when the ball was missed and rolled under the one-foot high single warning wire positioned ten feet in front of the primary security fence separating compound one from compound two. We were repeatedly told and warned by sign and verbally not to step over the marking/warning wire and that guards were told to shoot to kill any POWs stepping over the warning wire! One of my fellow POWs who missed catching the ball looked at and made deliberate eye-to-eye contact with the nearest U.S. Army guard at the elevated guard tower at the intersection of compound one and two. He slowly moved deliberately towards the warning wire. The guard and he continued to maintain eye-to-eye contact as he lifted one foot over the warning wire, followed by the trailing foot. As soon as he placed both feet inside the warning wire, still maintaining eye-to-eye contact with the guard, the guard raised a rifle, firing one shot to the forehead and killing my barracks mate. The guard was in the right to shoot a POW inside the warning wire. I want to point out my barracks mate and the tower guard recognized visual contact, as it would not be with a guard aiming/pointing a rifle directly at him in broad daylight. More importantly, one of my fellow POWs would not try to escape by breaking through a fence separating two compounds. Any escape attempt would be through the main security fence at night, moreover with overcast weather conditions and evaporating into the darkness. We held a large and vocal demonstration that evening for the unprovoked killing."[275]

This is a drawing by a German POW at Fort Robinson depicting their hot work on some farm outside the main POW compound. Drawing on display at the Fort Robinson museum. (Author)

Work details were permitted for those who volunteered, Monday through Saturday. The majority of the work was agricultural. During WWII, POW labor in the United States amounted to [illegible] man hours on military installations performing non-war military-related jobs, with another 10,181,275 man hours assigned to contract employers, of which 50 percent was on farms or ranches. By the end of fighting in WWII, approximately 91 percent of non-officer Axis POWs—excluding a few thousand Japanese interned in the United States—only the most hard core and vocal Nazis were prohibited from working outside the main POW camps. They were sent home in accordance with the Geneva Convention, supposedly to assist in the reconstruction of their war-torn economies. For Nebraska, President Harry Truman authorized withholding or delaying the departure of German and Italian POWs so farmers could complete harvesting the Fall sugar beet crop for three months before being shipped home.[276]

Oberdieck remained at Camp Concordia until 25 December 1943. At this time, additional German POWs were being shipped to the United States. At Camp Concordia, 250 German POWs volunteered to be transferred to Camp Atlanta. He continues: "I volunteered, believing the Atlanta mentioned was Atlanta, Georgia, but it turned out to be Atlanta, Nebraska. We were assigned to occupy a newly-constructed POW camp. My fellow POWs and I actually helped build the ten-foot high camp security fencing and remove construction debris, especially nails and metal pieces that might provide us material to fabricate weapons and other prohibited items. We were constantly searched to make certain we were not hiding any of these possible weapon-making materials. The first trainload of POWs arrived almost as soon as we completed final cleanup. One of these arrivals was an eighty-year-old captured by U.S. troops advancing on an ammunition depot in France."[277]

Afrika Korps (Africa Corps) uniform worn by Dietrich Kohl while a POW at Fort Robinson from November 1943 to May 1944. In May 1944, he was transferred to Camp Grant, Illinois. POWs were allowed to keep their uniforms, but were also issued GI work clothes distinctively marked with a *PW* by the Army Quartermaster Corps. Uniform and photo on display at the Fort Robinson museum. (Author)

By March 1944, over 2,000 German POWs arrived at Camp Atlanta. Most of these Germans were between 22-24 years old and recovering from combat wounds and not in very good condition.[278] After POWs were allowed to settle into their assigned compound and barracks, Army officers announced they could volunteer for work, and after security interviews and clearance could work on local farms and ranches. There were conditions for a farmer to be eligible to acquire POW labor, supporting or accepting a minimum of fifteen POWs and one Army guard.[279]

Oberdieck continues: "Area residents around Camp Atlanta often stopped their cars and trucks—pulling to one side of the road along Highway 6, parallel to the camp's recreational compound— to watch us playing soccer to the cheers of hundreds or more of fellow POWs. Besides sports, we often fooled around to pass time while interned. Bets were often made that one of us could not hide during mandatory morning roll call and daily barracks inspection. One of my fellow POWs hid in the barracks ceiling with his absence not noticed at the morning's roll call, earning him a round of beers by us that evening."[280]

U.S. Army internment camp guards at Camp Atlanta often became complacent, expecting each day's POW count to always agree and not noticing the absence of the POW from Oberdieck's barracks. The fact that the POW hid in the ceiling was not lost on them, increasing possible escape scenarios. The low quality of Army enlisted personnel— not classified as front line or combat qualified troops—assigned to guard POW camps was very evident at Camp Atlanta.

On 12 November 1944, a tower guard started firing his rifle through barracks windows. He then shifted his rife fire toward other camp guards and those in nearby towers. Other camp guards had no option other than to fire on the guard, only stopping his wild firing when killed. This could not be tolerated in a POW camp, where the lives of prisoners were under the protection of the U.S. Army under the rules of the Geneva Convention. Unfortunately, many Army guards selected and assigned to POW camps often mistreated those they were sworn to guard and protect. This again was not permitted under any circumstances. It took time to identify these poorly disciplined troops and remove them under Army regulations. These violations had to be reported to the International Red Cross with results of the broken rules and corrective action. At the same time, Germany, Italy, and Japan did not follow such rules. Fortunately, Germany did not treat Allied POWs as those sent to concentration camps. It should be pointed out that toward the end of the war, when prisoners were moved away from advancing Russian Army troops, American POWs did end up in these concentration camps and discipline broke down and conditions in POW camps deteriorated.[281]

Drawing by a German POW at Fort Robinson of Germans playing soccer in the sports compound. Sports were very popular as a way to pass time in the camp, with competition keen between POW teams. Photo on display at the Fort Robinson museum. (Author)

Oberdieck continues: "Most of Camp Atlanta German POWs openly discussed various means and methods of possible escape. POWs knew about the Rocky Mountains from watching Hollywood films in the 1930s in Germany before the war. Hollywood films were popular in German movie theaters, especially those shown in the camp. One man in my barracks took these discussions seriously, planning an escape to the Rocky Mountains, living off the land,

Drawing of the morning count at Fort Robinson, on display at the Fort Robinson museum. (Author)

hiding in the forest and mountains until the war ended, only then surrendering to U.S. authorities for shipment home to Germany. At one morning's roll call, he was not on the barracks count, but again, as noted before, the short count was not detected. The guards did not properly make the count, not following their own procedures to properly account for all 50 men assigned to the barracks. It was summer, with temperatures over 90 degrees. The escapee realized he could not make it to the mountains, turned around, and headed toward the nearest road to flag down a car or truck and ride back to Camp Atlanta. A local farmer and his wife stopped and picked him up, driving on to Camp Atlanta. The POW camp's day work detail had already returned when the escapee walked to the main gate. Now, there followed a strange turn of events. The gate guard commented '...so the work detail left you behind and the farmer brought you back.' The guard admitted the escapee into the correct compound. The farmer at the front gate recognized something did not make sense and commented to the guard 'I think it is very strange you let a German POW out of the camp without a guard, thumbing a ride along the highway!' By this time the returning POW could not be identified. The next morning, the POW Army commander brought the farmer into the compound to witness the morning's role call to identify the escapee. The escapee wore a pair of reading glasses, making it impossible for the farmer to be certain which one of the fifty men he picked up. U.S. Army officers were extremely puzzled as to what happened. After an intense examination of the camp's perimeter security fence, guards identified a mended spot where it appeared someone had dug out, but the prisoner count was correct. Therefore, no one had escaped! This did not take into account the farmer's passenger delivered to the main gate and the guard's admitting him into a POW compound. Atlanta POW camp official records reported 'an unidentified POW had escaped from Camp Atlanta and later turned himself into camp authorities.'"[282]

This was a rare example of a surviving WWII POW building at a small branch camp located at Weeping Water, Nebraska. It has been turned into a duplex rental unit but retains its original shape. Its siding remains, although broken along the bottom edge near the ground. (Author)

German and Italian POWs were allowed to write one letter a week while in US custody, which were only mailed after an Army censor reviewed the letters. Letters then could be mailed to friends or relatives in the United States, or to family back home in Germany or Italy. POW officers were allowed to write five letters a month. POWs could receive any letters addressed to them. During the war, mail from Axis and Allied POWS continued to be delivered between Germany and Italy and the United States because of the efforts of the International Red Cross, which chartered five ships sailing the route between Philadelphia, Pennsylvania and the German-controlled port of Marseilles, France. These ships were distinctively marked, with German Luftwaffe aircraft and U-boats carrying silhouettes of these ships and standing orders not to attack. Ships were under the control of the International Red Cross and considered neutral vessels, even though they docked in combatant ports. This allowed U.S. held Axis prisoners to write home and receive letters, with the same for Allied POWs held in Germany and Italy.[283]

Oberdieck goes on: "I volunteered to work at the Weeping Water branch camp as a replacement for a sick POW at the camp. Camp Atlanta's operating procedures for we POWS allowed that if a POW was sick for three consecutive days, he went back to the main camp, replaced by another POW, and once healthy was allowed to return to the available labor pool."[284]

The Weeping Water camp area was set up in early 1936, part of a chain of camps to provide unemployed city men an opportunity and means to work and earn money to support themselves, as well as send money home to their families.[285]

Oberdieck continues: "I arrived at Weeping Water Branch Camp in April 1944, and was immediately assigned to picking cherries, tomatoes, corn, digging irrigation ditches, pitching hay, cutting rocks in the limestone quarry, and other jobs. I was at Weeping Water when Germany surrendered on 8 May

1945 to the Allied Military Powers Europe. Captain Junewicz, the U.S. Army officer in charge of Weeping Water, walked up to me saying Germany had surrendered, ending the war in Europe. The Weeping Water guards wanted to celebrate Germany's surrender that evening, requesting we, whose status was automatically changed and upgraded to that of detained troops, to guard ourselves for the evening.

"Suddenly, we noticed a change in U.S. Army attitude toward us and our provided care. Because the U.S. Army no longer had to be concerned about reciprocal treatment of American POWs held in Germany, rations at the branch camp were reduced, with only the evening meal for those returning after the day's work detail. It was now expected the farmers we worked for would provide us breakfast and lunch. These farmers had to feed us as well as the Army guard to get their work done, without camp support. Most of us were detained an additional three months after the end of the war to bring in the Fall harvest.

"In late October 1945, I and other German detained troops at Weeping Water were loaded into a passenger train for the trip to the U.S. Gulf Coast, boarding a Liberty ship for Bremerhaven, Germany. At this point in my story it gets ugly, with politics interfering. The Liberty ship was diverted to LeHarve, France. After disembarkation, we were told the next stop would be Frankfort, Germany. We were loaded into a passenger train for the rail trip across France. However, French troops stopped the train, supposedly to allow us to cross a weakened railroad bridge to a waiting train around the bend of the far railroad tracks. But once off the train we realized there was no damaged bridge, only a dirt road leading through a series of hills! French troops kept us marching through the night. We were used to living in the United States and unaccustomed to long marches. We each carried a U.S. Army duffel bag containing blankets, shoes, uniforms, radio, books, food, and other personal items. We purchased these items with our canteen coupons prior to leaving the United States. French troops forced some of us to drop the duffel bags along the side of the road, supposedly saying a French Army truck would pick them up and transport the duffel bags to a temporary camp. I knew better than to trust the French troops, keeping my duffel bag. When I marched away and looked back over my shoulder, French citizens were running out of the wood, grabbing the duffel bags and disappearing back into the woods. Those of us who kept our duffel bags had them forcibly taken by U.S. Army troops who joined the French troops at the designated temporary detention camp. All these actions violated the release of former prisoners of war during transshipment back to their home country under the rules of the Geneva Convention.

"Blankets taken from us were stacked in the open, radios were smashed by French troops, and looting of anything of value. I was in the rear of the column and stuffed food, clothes, and valuables in socks, throwing them over the wire fence to previously arrived Germans, and U.S. Army troops pushed us back and threatened us by saying 'The next German that throws anything over the fence will be shot!' After we were searched, we were segregated into groups of 50 and assigned to a crude shelter dug into the ground, covered with a U.S. Army field tent. The only way for us to sleep was for all of us to lay down in the same direction. We were not allowed to eat with knives or forks, only spoons. Food was served only after dark. At one evening meal, each tent was issued one wooden keg of salted herring. It was impossible to open the wooden kegs with a spoon, so we slammed it on the ground, breaking it open so we could share the herring. Other meals sometimes consisted of boiled potatoes. U.S. troops indicated we would be given white bread for Christmas evening meal. The U.S. troops were purposely mean. They wanted to go home, not baby sit Germans now that the war in Europe had ended.

"Our daily ration of coffee was served cold. We were issued powdered coffee mixed in a tin cup with cold water. Needless to say, for us held at Attichy, France, we were not cared for under strict accordance with rules set down under the Geneva Convention. We could not understand why we were being treated with disrespect after release from confinement in the United States. There was a separate group of Germans, consisting of intellectuals and Nazi Party members, who had to wear a special uniform marked with a white strip painted on the uniform's back. It should be pointed out that in Germany during Adolf Hitler's reign of terror, Nazi Party membership was essential to obtain a job, keep an existing job, earn or be selected for a promotion, find a place to live, and everything else during that time period in Germany. Most Nazis decreed knowing or taking part in the "Final Solution." The main reason the French wanted to detain us was for revenge and forced labor in the Attichy coal mines. I volunteered to work in the mines to get out of the camp. My legs became badly swollen, growing to twice normal size, keeping me in camp. The French Army only wanted able-bodied men who could perform hard, physically demanding work in the coal mines.

"Finally, on 28 February 1946, I made it home to Germany. At the time of my release, I was given one loaf of bread and told to walk home to Germany. At first, we were not allowed to mix with U.S. Occupation Forces in Germany, or any contacts made while in U.S. Army run POW camps in the United States. By June 1946, I began writing letters to an American family I worked for while at Weeping Water by the name of Wagner, in an effort to arrange for an American sponsor so I could return to the United States. All Germans sending mail out of the country had to leave envelopes unsealed, writing on the envelope in the language of the letter inside. This allowed U.S. Army censors to read letters prior to sealing and mailing. After writing a series of such letters, I received a sponsorship from an American family. The Kimmel family of Nebraska City, Nebraska agreed to sponsor me, along with my family. Even with a sponsor, it took four years for me and my family to leave Germany for the United States. The delay was stated as necessary to clear me of any Nazi ties or membership in the Nazi Party and involvement in the 'Final Solution' and to be issued a U.S. Visa for my family and myself. We arrived at the Kimmel Orchard on 22 February 1950, starting work at 6:30 a.m. the next morning."[286]

Italian troops were also captured in North Africa. One of the POW camps in Nebraska held Italian POWs. This was the Sioux Ordnance Depot POW compound, officially referred to as Side Camp Number Nine, located ten miles northwest of

In 1991, the former WWII Weeping Water passenger depot. It was at this passenger depot that Oberdieck arrived and departed Weeping Water in 1945. (Author)

Sidney, Nebraska, under the direction of Camp Scotts Bluff. The Sioux Ordnance Depot POW compound held 300 Italian and 300 German POWs. The Sioux Ordnance Depot POW camp was converted from part of the depot's barracks area secured by a barbed wire stockade. John Underwood, a Purchase and Supply Officer at Sioux Ordnance Depot noted: "The compound contained plain GI barracks, like the type provided to U.S. Army personnel. The Italian POWs had a small post exchange where they could go on a regular basis."[287]

Italian POWs worked in non-related support functions at the Sioux Ordnance Depot as common laborers, engineers, automotive mechanics, typists, tractor operators, hospital attendants, post exchange cooks, and other positions. Many of these Italian POWs assisted in loading and unloading railroad boxcars at the depot, as well as cargo trucks.[288] On 1 May 1944, the U.S. Army created the 70th Italian Quartermaster Service Company. Italy surrendered to the Allies on 8 September 1943, switching to the Ally side, even though the German Army occupied the northern two-thirds of the country. Four U.S. Army officers commanded the Italian Service Company.[289] By the fall of 1942, Italian prisoners who were members of the Italian Service Company could volunteer for any part of the Allied war effort at the Sioux Ordnance Plant. Most of the Italians at the depot after WWII did not want to be return to Italy. However, they were not given that option.[290]

Communities in Nebraska, and those in other states where POW camps were located, became directly involved in the American war effort. During the war, America sent their men and women to fight overseas. At the same time, for a select group of Americans living near Axis POW camps, the enemy was visible on a daily basis, a close up of the faces of war against which the country was fighting. This included Japanese POWs held in my home state, Iowa. POWs in Nebraska provided badly needed agricultural labor and worked in non-war related jobs. With the end of WWII, the release of POWs, and the passage of time, these camps became part of the unknown stories of the war.

CHAPTER ELEVEN

LINCOLN AIR BASE

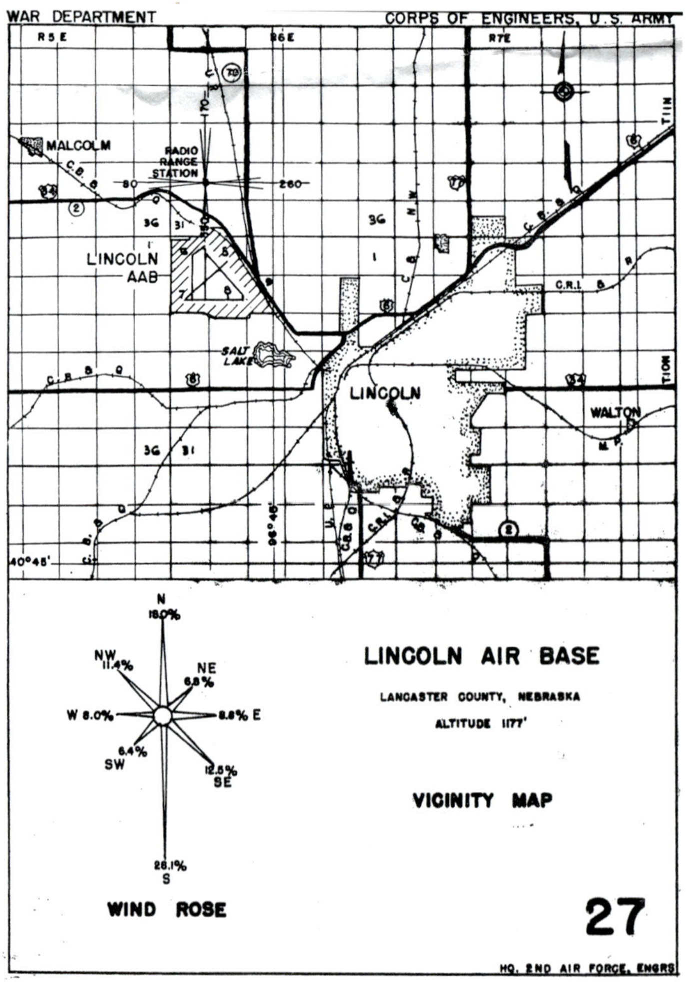

Lincoln Air Base vicinity map. (Author)

The history of Lincoln Municipal Airport began in April, 1928, after voters approved a $100,000 bond issue to acquire and develop a municipal airport. In June, after citizens raised a challenge to the passed bond issue, the City Council went ahead and approved the bond election. In August, 160 acres of land were purchased for the construction of the airport. The airport project started with the field area graded and seeded, construction of asphalt runways, a lighting system, on-site house remodeled into the airport's office, a waiting room, and a service road built to the main highway. On 12 June 1930, the Lincoln Municipal Airport was dedicated. Improvements were made in 1931, with a hangar built by the Lincoln Flying School. An administration building was added in 1932. In November 1940, voters approved another bond issue for $300,000 to expand the airport. The City of Lincoln began acquiring land in preparation to build a 600-acre airport containing a paved runway 5,000 feet long.

In February 1941, the City of Lincoln applied to the WPA for approval of an airport as part of the National Defense Program. In August 1941, the federal government requested permission to use the Lincoln Municipal Airport. In October 1941, the City of Lincoln was offered $292,000 in federal funds available from the Civil Aeronautics Administration. At this time, the Army Corps of Engineers Survey Board inspected Lincoln Municipal Airport about the prospect of building an AAF air base. On 1 May 1941, the Lincoln Chamber of Commerce distributed to various federal agencies in Washington, D.C. a survey of the area, pointing out the unique benefits for an AAF air base. On 3 June, the Lincoln Chamber of Commerce traveled to Washington, D.C. to talk to the responsible federal agencies to lobby for a military airfield or base near Lincoln, Nebraska.

In March 1942, because of on-site inspections and lobby efforts by the city of Lincoln, the Army authorized the construction of an AAF Mechanics School. In return, the City of Lincoln provided 2,750 acres of land for the large military

Aerial photo of Lincoln Air Base after its completion in June 1942.
Courtesy of NSHS

installation, along with necessary water and electric service for the installation. The City of Lincoln spent $395,698 to purchase the land and the Lincoln Flying School hangar. It allocated $191,793 from the Lincoln Water Department to extend a primary water main line to the airfield site. Another $36,251 was spent by Lincoln's City Commercial Light Department setting up an electrical substation and transmission line from Lincoln.[291]

Not everyone welcomed the construction of a military air base near Lincoln, especially those whose land was condemned. One landowner by the name of Zoe Zellar was contacted by federal officials offering him $125 per acre for 110 acres of land for the air base construction. He contested the offering price as below fair market value, indicating the land was actually valued at $300 per acre. The open dispute only ended when the City of Lincoln's Construction Board set the price of the land at $125 per acre.[292]

Those landowners who had to sell their land for the military airport on the central sections on which to build runways, taxiways, and support buildings were given fifteen days to either sell or remove their personal property from the condemned land. The landowners of less critical sections were permitted forty to sixty days.[293]

On 31 March 1942, the City of Lincoln accepted sealed bids from contractors on the first four buildings to be used to train U.S. Army Air Force aviation mechanics until the completed facility was taken over by the AAF.[294] Lincoln had to finish building the main water extension line to the air base site by 1 July 1942.[295] The airfield began to take on its military character on 7 April, when U.S. Army Colonel Early Duncan was transferred from Lowry Field, Denver, Colorado to Lincoln, Nebraska as the base's first commander, AAF Technical School.[296]

On 8 April 1942, a construction contract was signed for the first group of 59 buildings to be completed within 47 days or by 1 May. The first group of buildings consisted of warehouses, utility shops, motor park, prison stockade, two 2,000-man mess halls, and headquarters and support facilities.[297] Construction work began on the base's light, gas, and sewage systems, as well as roads and housing units. Most of the housing units were classified as temporary wood structures that could be built rapidly to meet wartime operations. This construction required the work of 5,000-6,000 construction specialists.[298]

Basloam and Raugh Company of Salina, Kansas constructed 198 barracks located west of the hangar area, each 100 feet long and 20 feet wide, to house base support personnel and trainees.[299]

A view for FAA control of the Lincoln Municipal Airport, 1991. (Author)

Construction work on the base built 1,070 buildings.[300] The training air base when completed was 1 1/3 miles wide at the north, two miles long along its north-south axis, and 2 3/4 miles long at its east-west axis. By 15 June 1942, 5,000 troops were expected to occupy the training air base, with the number of military personnel increasing to 15,000.[301]

On 20 April, the City of Lincoln signed a twenty-five year lease with the AAF for an annual fee of one dollar, with the lease renewed each year as required by the War Department. Under the terms of the lease, Lincoln's airport passed to the control of the federal government. The city assured the federal government that the airport would be large enough to accommodate commercial aircraft in cross-country routes and for private and commercial airline operations.[302] By May, construction of the large training base was 25 percent complete, with 300-400 buildings in various stages of construction slowed by shortages of lumber and other building materials.[303] Construction workers maintained an intense pace, erecting one barracks each day.[304] Lincoln's airport was incorporated into the air base. By the end of construction, the airfield's flight operations consisted of three 5,000 foot long and 150 foot wide concrete runways and one 6,000 foot long and 150 foot wide concrete runway. Poured concrete covered twenty-five percent of the air base's six hundred acres. The four runways were built thick and wide to support the weight of the heaviest AAF bomber, up to that of the new B-29. Runways were oriented to take advantage of the area's prevailing winds. With the four operational runways, aircraft could take off into the wind regardless from which direction the wind blew.[305]

The air base had a large hospital complex consisting of thirty-two buildings. Construction work continued on the remaining sections of the air base, including the main chapel's concrete foundation. Construction work continued on the aircraft hangars with one completed each day, completing all

A view of the military section of Lincoln Airport in 1991. The Nebraska Air National Guard, 155th Tactical Reconnaissance Group flew the McDonnell Douglas F-4 Phantom. They transitioned to the Boeing KC-135 Stratotanker and were assigned to the 155th Air Refueling Wing. (Author)

The commercial side of Lincoln Airport in 1991. (Author)

WWII two-story barracks and current Air Force Security Police headquarters in the background in the single story wood building. Many WWII buildings were modernized and continued to be used to support military operations. (Author)

nine days ahead of schedule. At this time, the officer's mess was 75 percent complete.[306]

On 16 June, 450 AAF personnel—one-half of a class—arrived from Jefferson Barracks. Nine hundred Airmen were scheduled to arrive every day to start training. To equip the air base, twenty-six railroad boxcars carrying this equipment arrived each day. Even with this large delivery of equipment each day, it was difficult to stock every piece of training equipment to adequately conduct the air base's training mission. By taking in one half of a class at the start of training operations, after Airmen advanced to mock up and follow-on training they moved into full classes containing the equipment required to complete their training.[307]

Air Mechanics classes reached full tempo on 9 July 1942, with the instruction part of the eleven-phase course on a six-day period from 6 a.m. to 2 p.m. each day. This allowed the first class to graduate in November 1942.[308]

Air Mechanics Course of Instruction

Airplane Division Classes	
Phase	Title of Instruction
1	Airplane maintenance & fundamentals
2	Airplane structures
3	Hydraulic systems
4	Airplane propellers
5	Airplane instruments
Engine Division Classes	
6	Airplane engine
7	Electrical systems
8	Fuel systems
9	Engine operations
Inspection Division Classes	
Phase	Title of Instruction
10	Inspection
11	Inspection[308]

A WWII hangar at the Nebraska Air National Guard at Lincoln in 1991. Today, the ANG has transitioned from the F-4 to KC-135s (updated to KC-135Rs), Air National Guard, 155th Air Refueling Wing, Air Mobility Command. (Author)

George W. O'Kelley was assigned to Lincoln AB: "I was sworn into the Army Air Forces in December 1942, and was put into the reserve to await training as an aviation cadet. In February 1943, I along with several hundred other cadet selectees was ordered to San Francisco, California to board a train to Lincoln, Nebraska. When we stepped off the train at Lincoln AB on 3 March 1943, the temperature was around 19 degrees and there was not an overcoat in the entire California contingent. We were then informed we were to take basic training: close order drill, manual of arms, and other training. During this time, we were given tests and from these results we were assigned to classes at different universities. I was sent to the University of Nebraska at Lincoln, near the air base. In Lincoln, white attending classes our barracks was the Love Memorial Library. I was in the third class to leave in late June 1943. I remember the 4th of July sitting on a railroad siding in Needles, California. I did successfully complete training as a pilot and was assigned to the Eleventh Air Force flying B-25s. We were considered special because we were to be officers and mechanics."[309]

Approximately 30,000 fighter mechanics graduated from Lincoln AB's Air Mechanics School by July 1943. It took seven ground men to keep one fighter operational. Although fighter mechanics are a little known part of the American war effort, for a commander of a fighter unit combat aircraft that cannot fly are useless, requiring sufficient ground crews for their proper maintenance. To train personnel in aircraft maintenance, the base's Technical School operated 24-hours a day. Classrooms and aircraft hangars were in operation around the clock, seven days a week. During the five-month training program, fighter mechanics studied every phase of fighter aircraft. The final part of the mechanic's training was a simulated combat environment at the Test Division at Ashland, Nebraska.

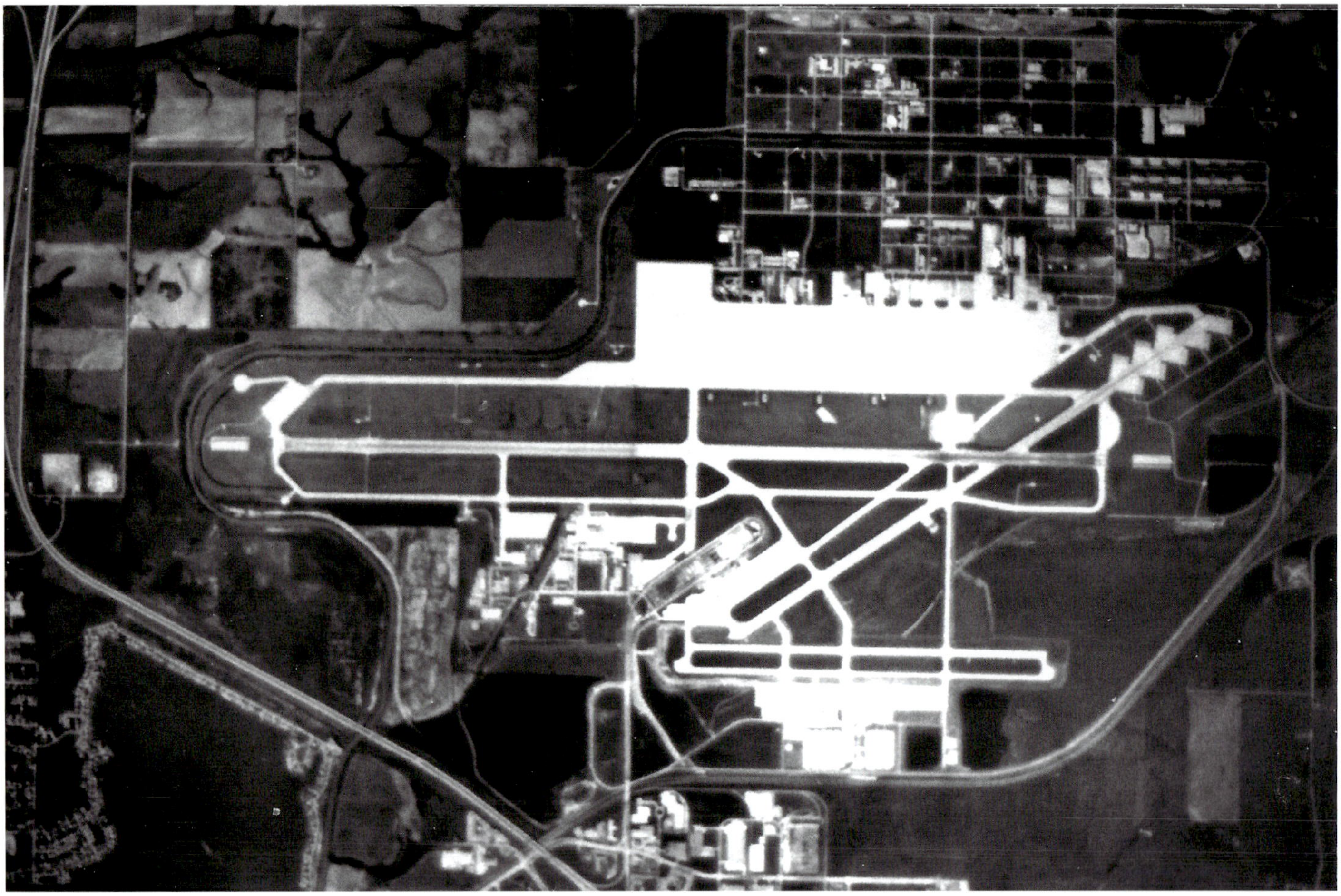

Aerial photo of Lincoln airport. Courtesy of Federal Aviation Agency

WWII supply building at Ashland modernized and now used by the Nebraska Army Guard. (Author)

Grass airstrip for light liaison aircraft at Ashland. It also supports Nebraska Army Guard helicopter training operations. (Author)

On 9 June 1952, the Lincoln Chamber of Commerce offered $225,000 for the construction of buildings, taxiways, and other required facilities. The City of Lincoln accepted joint use of the airport with the USAF. On 7 April 1943, the airport lease was approved by Lincoln voters. The federal government acquired a simple title to certain airport property as a result of two condemnation procedures in U.S. District Court to build housing units.[312] Currently, Lincoln Airport is a dual use facility between the municipal airport and Air Mobility Command, 155th Air Refueling Wing flying the KC-135R.

CHAPTER TWELVE

MCCOOK AIR BASE

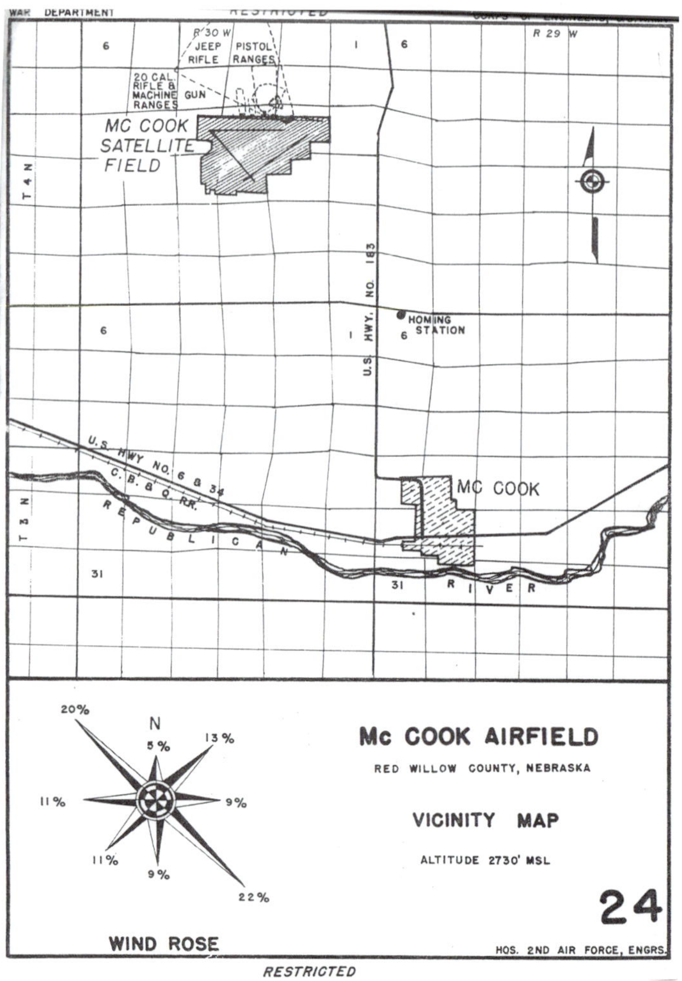

McCook Airfield vicinity map. (Author)

McCook was selected as a site for an AAF heavy bombardment training base. Work began on McCook AB nine miles north of the city on 23 September 1942, scheduled to be completed by 1 December.[313] Under the supervision of an on-site or work project assigned Corps of Engineers officer work progressed, as well as ordering changes received from the AAF. Construction activity on the flat plateau (elevation 2,750 feet) consisted of two 7,525 foot long and 150 foot wide concrete runways and one 7,454 foot long and 150 foot wide concrete runway. These were set up in the shape of an isosceles triangle with two runways on one side and the third on the other, with a concrete taxiway connecting them at the base. Concrete was seven inches thick and stressed to support an aircraft wheel load weight of 60,000 pounds and corresponding tire load pressure of 75.5 pounds per square inch to accommodate B-24s and later, B-29s. However, no allowance was made for the impact of these bombers' landing gear and tires making repeated lading cycles. These bombers produced a tremendous footprint impact pressure on landing, cracking and furrowing runways. The damage done to runways was similar to that created by heavily loaded eighteen-wheel trucks on U.S. secondary roads not stressed to current U.S. Interstate Highway specifications. When growing up in Altoona, Iowa, in the early 1960s, heavily-loaded semi-trucks turned off Interstate 80 to bypass a state run weigh station. Highway 6 through the town developed deep furrows from these overweight trucks. The road was eventually upgraded to stressed concrete to support these load weights.[314]

On site, construction was directed by the Corps of Engineers' Captain William E. Grubb with a support staff of 75 Army personnel.[315] On base housing facilities were built at the edge of the northeast-southeast runway. One could obtain a spectacular and unobstructed view of that area of the state from almost any point on the air base. On base facilities were built to house 260 officers and 752 enlisted. Due to a lack of

1943 aerial view of McCook AB. Courtesy of USAF Historical Research Center, Maxwell AFB, Alabama

construction bidders with sufficient equipment and financial assets/resources to assume responsibility for the entire base construction project, work had to be divided into six sections, making it possible for smaller contractors to bid on the project. This change in construction procedures worked well, except for concrete paving; the primary contractor did not have enough equipment to complete the project. The lack of construction equipment delayed completion by thirty-two days.

McCook's satellite airfield status changed to an independent airfield when additional work was authorized by the AAF and War Department on 29 January 1943. McCook AB was expanded to a Type C heavy bombardment airfield with additional aircraft hangars, mess facilities, utility buildings, hospital, aircraft parking apron, wider taxiways, extension to the utility system, and acquisition of 174 acres to increase the air base's boundary. The air base's final size was one and three quarter miles wide on the north-south axis and two and one half miles wide on the east-west axis. Increased facilities allowed the air base to handle 384 officers and 2,508 enlisted. The bottleneck on base was the mess facilities, which could only handle 360 officers and 1,340 enlisted at one time, requiring mess shift schedule breaks to feed all personnel throughout the day and night.

The base hospital was staffed by 41 officers (doctors and nurses) and one hundred enlisted. The hospital's mess could feed up to 118 assigned staff as well as patients at one time. Construction started on the Type C base expansion project on 26 February 1943 and was completed by 1 July. At this time, construction projects neglected training facilities because of a shortage of workers and lack of War Department approved funding.

After an OTU detachment arrived in October 1942, the bombing range was operational but lacked lighting. One pistol range had been set up in a gully adjacent to the air base, including

Aerial view of the air base to provide a perspective of the runways, hangar, and support areas. Courtesy of USAF Historical Research Center

a skeet range for gunner training. Complicating training operations was a legal problem, in that the air base had not properly negotiated right of operations for air-to-ground or air-to-air gunnery training sites with local residents through proper federal agencies. Construction work continued while federal agencies continued to obtain the proper access rights for these two training ranges. Classroom equipment was inadequate, with required training charts and publications available in limited quantities to meet posted training objectives. Base directed control tower operations and airborne flight control was not available and the radio range facilities were too far from McCook AB to provide bad weather landing assistance or guidance.

The air base construction plan specified four hangars: three 202 feet wide and 115 feet deep, each with 25-foot high doors. The fourth hangar was 220 feet wide and 202 feet deep with 25-foot high doors. Later, a fifth and larger hangar was added to the air base.

The base was organized into three divisions: 520th Base Headquarters and Air Base Squadron, bomb groups assigned to the base, and various detachments (23rd Medical and 23rd Airways Communications Squadron). The 520th Base Headquarters was the administrative section at McCook AB activated on 1 April 1943, initially with 20 percent of its personnel transferred from Kearney AB.

Because of McCook AB's relative isolated geographic location, especially its distance from large towns, the 520th could never locate and hire sufficient personnel from the local area to fully staff the base, forcing Base Headquarters unit to take out help wanted advertisements in newspapers in towns around McCook. The personnel shortage was partially corrected by

Large hangar under construction showing the wood arch supports and wood cross bracing sections. Wood was readily available and did not take away from steel needed for military equipment, especially ship building. Courtesy of United States Historical Research Center

hiring officer wives for clerical work and men hired through the Federal Service Employment program. Further compounding the personnel problem was transportation to and from McCook.

Supplies for the air base were trucked from Kearney AB, with shortages the norm, not the exception. These shortages continued even after the 520th started its own quartermaster sub-depot supply operations because transportation to and from McCook was difficult. The eleven-mile road was dusty in the summer, turned to mud when it rained, and was slick during winter ice and snow storms.

In April 1943, McCook AB was assaulted and captured by an airborne training assault force from Alliance AB that arrived in gliders and parachuted from C-47s.[316] Mildred L. Zink was a Registered Nurse working in the base hospital at the time: "During construction work on the base we had a varied lot of

One of the squadron building's concrete foundations surviving from WWII along hangar row in the support area of the air base. (Author)

Two-vault Norden bombsight building at McCook AB. (Author)

A squadron parts and supply building along hangar row. (Author)

injuries, from cement dermatitis to foreign bodies in the eyes and fractures from falls. Our emergency room and supplies were adequate for that time, but of course nothing like they are equipped with today. One afternoon, I looked out the hospital window and saw many parachutes coming down and men landing. It was a surprise mock attack staged from Alliance AB. It was conducted and carried out well and was a success."[317]

Bomb Groups Trained at McCook Air Base

Bomb Group	Bomb Squadron	Date Assigned
454th	736th	31 July to 1 October 1943
(B-24)	737th	
	738th	
	739th	
486th	832nd	28 September to 1 November 1943
(B-24)	833rd	
	834th	
	835th	
465th	780th	5 October 1943 to 1 February 1944
(B-24)	781st	
	782nd	
	783rd	
9th	1st	12 May to 18 November 1944
(B-29)	5th	
	99th	
	430th	
331st	334th	22 November 1944 to 8 April 1945
(B-29)	355th	
	356th	
	357th	
98th	343rd	26 June to 10 November 1945
(B-29)	344th	
	345th	
	415th	
448th	713th	8 September to 1 December 1945
(B-29)	714th	
	715th[318]	

Interior of a large wood warehouse at McCook AB. In 1991, the wood building was intact, although the roof leaked and there was water on the concrete floor. I was able to wander through the former air base with no restrictions, which has greatly changed, as many of the WWII buildings have been torn down. There was an ongoing effort to repair this former WWII warehouse. Note the rolls of tarpaper roofing stacked on end against the back wall of the warehouse. (Author)

Concrete foundation of the WWII Celestial Navigation Training building. (Author)

McCookAB was controlled by the host bomb group commander until August 1943, when the OTU arrived. On 24 August 1943, the air echelon of the 454th BG arrived with its B-24s to begin training. By 30 September, the group was partially into phase two of its training. When the 486th BG arrived on 7 December 1943 (two years after Pearl Harbor), its training schedule was rigidly controlled by the War Department and Second AF as it transited through the training program. Two more B-24 bomb groups (465th and 493rd) trained at the base as well.

To keep training on schedule for transition into B-29s in April 1944, construction added a Camouflage building, B-29 Turret Trainer, and Gunner Film Evaluation buildings. Other training facilities included a Celestial Navigation Training and Photographic building, as well as a base fire station. On 29 April, seventy aircraft were at McCook AB, but only fifty-two were operational. Ground training picked up the slack from the lack of operational aircraft with instruction conducted on engineering, bombing, navigation, communications, gunnery, physical fitness, general subjects, Link Trainer, and precision radar. Flying training focused on air-to-air gunnery, formation, completion of the one thousand mile celestial navigation mission, pilot instrument checks, camera bombing scoring, and bomb release techniques. On 31 May 1944, seven B-17s were flown to McCook AB to keep transition on line for B-29 aircrews preparing for Pacific combat duty. The 9th BG was the first at McCook AB to fly B-24s, moving directly into transitioning aircraft. More facilities had to be built to support B-29 training.[319]

The 9th BG's training at McCook AB provides a good look at B-29 training. During its first five days of training, combat crews flew a total of 659 hours (509 in B-17s and 150 in B-29s). The group only had nine B-29s when it began training operations; this was not considered a great problem because the group only had five complete B-29 aircrews. There was a shortage of aerial gunners (MOS 611) and flight engineers (MOS 3750 enlisted and MOS 1028 officers). With the arrival of forty gunners from Lincoln AB and an increase in availability

The WWII water tower built at McCook AB was brick, with the distinctive black and white checkerboard paint scheme at the top to make it visible to low flying aircraft. Its position in the middle of an empty field gives an indication of the many wartime buildings no longer remaining. (Author)

of flight engineers, an additional ten complete B-29 combat crews were created. It was not until 20 June 1944, that all 64 crew allotments were filled to authorized strength. A shortage remained in radar mechanics (MOS 685) and ordnance (MOS 511 and 901). The shortage of ordnance personnel was corrected by on-the-job training within the bomb group. Another problem was shortage of radar trained personnel. Although each B-29 combat crew was to have a radar trained and qualified navigator and bombardier, only one officer had been completely trained. The 9th BG had navigators with radar training, but none of the bombardiers or enlisted personnel had completed radar training; technical training only covered familiarization radar training for bombardiers. This was not an acceptable situation for the bomb group commander, who constantly faced shortages of trained personnel in the middle of combat preparations for Pacific duty in the Marianas Islands.

The 9th BG operated with twenty-three B-17s and nine B-29s to conduct required aircrew training. This one bomb group was not an isolated occurrence, because B-29 production had not reached maximum capacity to meet equipping operational bomb groups, combat replacements, accident replacements, and providing aircraft for newly formed B-29 bomb groups at stateside training bases. B-29 shortages greatly affected bomb group training schedules. Each B-29 crew had to complete one hundred hours of flight and combat training over a three-month period at McCook AB to meet AAF minimum training requirements. To be fully equipped, the bomb group needed a complement of twenty-seven B-29s. Getting ready for combat at a stateside air base was still stressful and the pace relentless. With inadequate numbers of B-29s, it required crews to fly in B-17s to complete their missing training: formation flying at altitudes above 25,000 feet, bomb releases above 25,000 feet, and copilot instrument hours under the hood while airborne. By the end of the seventh week, the group had only completed one-third of its B-29 flying hours. This was a serious shortfall resulting from the group having such limited flying hours in B-29s. The group did complete 55 percent of its required ground training, including small arms qualification.[320]

A view of the large aircraft parking apron at McCook AB. It was slowly being taken over by grass and partial salvage operations to remove the concrete for fill material. (Author)

The Second AF directed all B-29 training to be conducted on a precise schedule. There was a problem obtaining enough B-29 gunners for the aircrews. Beginning in August 1944, B-29 aircrew flying training consisted of sixteen days flying in a B-17— a total of 1,807 hours for the bomb group—with 425 hours in the available B-29s on base. This broke down to a per crew average of 282 hours in B-17s and 6.6 hours in B-29s.[321] B-29 crews completed a standardized training course prior to being shipped to the Pacific. Initial B-29 flight crew training was conducted at Alamogordo, New Mexico. Air echelon training was held at the AAF School of Applied Tactics at Orlando, Florida. Ground training covered three sections completed at each individual bombardment training base location.

Ground Training at McCook Air Base

Section One: basic echelon training consisting of Army orientation, bomb reconnaissance and dispersal, gunnery, and camouflage.
Section Two: consisted of technical training, unit ordnance, photographic procedures, armament, and communications.
Section Three: on-the-job training covering supply, engineering, and communications maintenance.

B-29 aircrews also trained at Lincoln AB on the effects of high-altitude explosive decompression in the base's altitude chamber. Crewmembers also attended special courses at Boeing Aircraft, Renton, Washington; R-3350 Engine Course at Amarillo, Texas; Flexgate Compass and Air Position Indicator Course at Chanute Filed, Illinois; Turbo-supercharger Course at West Lynn, Massachusetts; and an Automatic Pilot Course at Honeywell Corporation in Minneapolis, Minnesota.[322]

Andrew Gordon, 331st BG, remembers: "I became Operations Officer at McCook AB. The busy time of forming and training crews went fast. We had a mix of Flight Engineers; some were old B-17 and B-24 flight crew chiefs, while some

View along the access road of a large hangar at McCook AB. In 1991, siding was coming loose and falling off the hangar and the doors were shut. The tail aircraft cut out is visible above the center of the hangar doors. To the left front is one of the WWII maintenance supply warehouses. (Author)

were not delighted at the prospect of riding in a B-29 sitting backwards. The former perhaps presented the difference in pay for similar duties. In late winter, we learned to our dismay that waist gunners were now scanners, as we had the Central Fire Control System. Not long after this we lost them too; we would have to rely on the tail gunner only. Our practice in radar bombing increased as we learned the intricacies of the AN/APQ-7 Eagle system. This would aid us in mine laying operations around Japan."[323]

Robert Griffin, 331st BG, noted: "We trained in B-29s at McCook AB, Nebraska, using aircraft with full armament: two revolving turrets in front and two revolving turrets in back, in addition to the tail guns. However, just before departing overseas, we learned that our group was to be equipped with a new variant of the B-29 with all revolving gun turrets removed, leaving only the two .50 caliber machine guns and one 20mm cannon in the tail. The theory was that we could bomb by the new radar from altitudes of 30,000-33,000 feet, where the air would be too thin for an enemy fighter to maneuver to maintain a firing lead without washing out directly into our tail zone. Our tail gunner could pick off the fighters. These planes were to be equipped with the new APQ-7 radar that scanned a plus and minus 35-degree sweep along our flight path. Synchronization of the radar scan with the bombsight cross hairs was claimed to give a greater pinpoint accuracy that could be relied upon in cloudy weather."[324]

Larry McCarthy, 331st BG: "During transition training at McCook AB, Nebraska, some of us worked nights on aircraft maintenance. One night, a radio technician was called to service or check a problem with a radio in one of the planes. Although the radio technician was not supposed to use a jeep, there was one parked nearby, so he thought why the one-quarter mile or so walk to the plane? He was not familiar with the light switch location, so when he got out of the lighted area he was concentrating on

The McCook Air Base Historical Society built a concrete outline of the WWII air base's runways and taxiways, setting three flag poles inside for special ceremonies and activities. (Author)

looking for the switch while heading toward one of the B-29s that had its number one engine running at about 1,100RPM. The first propeller blade to strike the jeep hit its radiator, splitting the radiator's core. The propeller blade struck the middle of the jeep's engine block. The third propeller blade struck the clutch and nicked his ankle. The fourth propeller blade split the back of the seat. He considered himself quite lucky until charged with the destruction of government property and unauthorized use. Of course, the engine and propeller on the plane had to be changed, creating more maintenance work and down time."[325]

When more than one bomb group was stationed at McCook AB training problems increased. During November 1944, the 331st and 9th BGs were on base at the same time, if only for a brief time. No B-29s were initially available for the 331st and only a few B-17s that had to be flown so many hours, causing maintenance headaches to meet Second AAF training requirements.[326] To increase maintenance a new aircraft supply warehouse was built and stocked to improve availability of spare parts. A new ordnance warehouse improved support for B-17 flight training operations. Construction of six large wood aircraft maintenance docks allowed B-29s to be worked over on the flight line in cold and bad weather, assisting aircraft maintenance personnel and increasing daily aircraft availability for training flights.[327]

There were frequent aircraft training mishaps. In December 1944, a B-29 flying over Dickens, Nebraska had its crew mistake the town for McCook AB's bombing range, releasing seven practice bombs on the town. One bomb struck and destroyed a foreman's wood building inside a lumber yard, with the other six exploding in unoccupied areas of the town with no one injured.[328]

In December 1944, the 331st BG was unable to complete any B-29 aircraft sorties because the B-29s were allocated to

Another B-29 capable hangar at McCook AB. It is testimony to those who built the wood hangar that it remained standing after so long. (Author)

the 9th BG.[329] On 1 January 1945, the 331st BG flew its first B-29 sorties after receiving twelve B-29s, which was increased to seventeen by the end of the month. This allowed a planned five daily B-29 training sorties, but with a commission rate of 76 percent that impacted training, the actual number available was reduced to four.[330]

In January 1945, B-29 training program adjustment was initiated by Second AF. These changes consisted of instruction on autopilot circuits for factory representatives; on-the-job installation and calibration of gun sights and stabilizers; loading 500, 1,000, and 2,000 pound bombs; use of hoisting equipment, shackles, and controls; A-2 and A-4 release mechanisms; pre-flight and trouble shooting of bomb racks; Central Fire Control operations and maintenance; instructions to bombardiers on pre-flight, loading bombs, and fuse settings; and instructions on emergency procedures to drop bombs and internal bomb bay fuel tanks. The auxiliary fuel tanks could be installed for extended range, but on the down side reduced available bomb loads.

McCook AB was one of the U.S. air bases that stripped factory-installed equipment under directives from Second AF determined unnecessary for combat missions against Japan. There modifications were directed after a special study conducted at Alamogordo, New Mexico, under specific guidelines developed to prepare the 509th CG to drop atomic bombs on Japan. The tests indicated a stripped B-29 carrying a 20,000-pound bomb load (estimating the maximum weight of the atomic bombs under development) could reach the Japanese home islands at 30,000 feet for the bomb run and return. More importantly, stripped down B-29s could carry 20,000 pounds of incendiary bombs, bombing at night and at low level and creating maximum destruction to Japanese war

During WWII, this large warehouse was built to provide spare parts for maintenance personnel at McCook. (Author)

industries set up in home industries around the main factories. This combined change in tactics made the low-level night flying B-29 a difficult target for Japanese fighters to locate and intercept, as well for anti-aircraft to counter large numbers of B-29s passing over the target. B-29s fitted with APQ-7 navigation and bombing radar provided the bombardier with accurate bombing releases up to 35,000 feet, even with the effects of the Jet Stream winds over the Japanese home islands. The bombardier also had the capability for visual target recognition at night, during periods of low visibility, and warning of attacking Japanese fighters in the aircraft's tail cone.[331]

The 98th BG, which was also equipped with the B-29, trained at McCook AB, arriving in June 1945. It went through Ground Training School, consisting of 36 hours of instruction on various military subjects over nine days: chemical warfare, camouflage, booby traps and explosives, small arms qualifications, intelligence, medical lectures and first aid, and aircraft recognition.[332] The bomb group did not start flying training sorties until 2 July 1945, with staff pilots flying these missions. Practice briefings simulating Pacific combat missions were conducted by the staff pilots and instructors.[333] In August 1945, after the unconditional surrender of the Japanese Empire, the bomb group's training became disorganized due to rapidly changing postwar priorities, demobilization orders, and war contract terminations. By December 1945, the War Department, through Headquarters AAF, announced McCook AB would close, since it was no longer needed. Military personnel on the base were transferred to other active AAF bases by the third week of January 1946. At this time, remaining civilian employees received termination notices, affecting McCook's postwar local economy. Federal officials held surplus government equipment sales to get rid of items consisting of office furniture and equipment and military

In 1991, the process of destroying WWII history was well underway at McCook. Heavy construction machinery moved in to tear up the unused runways, taxiways, and aircraft parking aprons. The concrete was dug up and trucked to concrete crushers for resale as concrete fill material. This was one of the primary reasons the author wanted to cover these former WWII airbases before they disappeared and became a chapter lost in America's Greatest Generation. (Author)

exchange stocks, along with other items determined to be sold rather than shipped to other bases. Military vehicles were loaded onto railroad flatbed cars for shipment to Denver, Colorado for reconditioning, then were distributed to stateside military bases or offered for sale at federal surplus auctions. Other bases received shipments of priority equipment removed from closed bases for use or storage. Approximately 15,000 military and 5,000 civilians trained or worked at McCook AB from 1 April 1943 to 31 December 1945, excluding those who worked on building the base.[334]

CHAPTER THIRTEEN

FORT ROBINSON WAR DOGS, K-9 CORPS

The first use of dogs in war can be traced to the Greek armies. During the Seven Years War (1756-1763), dogs were used as messengers by the Prussian King Frederick the Great's army. During WWI, the German Army fielded 30,000 dogs. The French Army used dogs on the Western Front, losing 3,500 and 1,500 missing in the trenches and in no-man's warfare. To a lesser number, the British and Russian armies used dogs.

United States Army interest in the use of military dogs began in June 1940. In the 1930s, the German Army trained thousands of dogs for guard and attack roles. POW camps, forced labor camps, extermination camps, military installations, war plants, and front lines of combat were patrolled by sentry or attack dogs. The Germany Army used dogs as an integral part of its combat units. What spurred the U.S. Army's interest in war dogs was intelligence confirmation the Japanese army was trying to obtain large numbers of these dogs from Germany. After Pearl Harbor, the U.S. Army Quartermaster Corps looked into the concept of using guard dogs to protect its depots from possible enemy agent sabotage. American dog owners donated their pets so the federal government did not have to purchase these dogs and the Army began the program by accepting thirty-two dogs for the Military War Dog Training Program.

Army war dogs were between one to five years old, in good health, at least 20 inches high, and weighed over 50 pounds. For every forty-five dogs volunteered to the Army twenty met Army requirements. Between 1942 and 1945, the Army accepted 20,000 dogs. The Army first called this the War Army Guard Service (WAGS), but the name was too close to that of the Army's Women's Army Corps (WACs) and needed to be changed. The name was shorted to K-9 Corps. The Army Quartermaster Corps was responsible for receiving, conditioning, training, and issuing military dogs because of its experience in managing the Army's Horse Remount Branch. The Army created a new classification for military facilities to train dog handlers and their dogs. The Army advertised, interviewed, and hired professional civilian dog handlers and trainers to supervise the startup of the War Dog Field Training Program. Army enlisted personnel with aptitude and experience in handling dogs were trained by these civilian instructors to become war dog instructors, readied to meet the expected war dog's program strength.[335]

The War Department decided to set up war dog reception and training facilities at two Army Quartermaster remount depots: Fort Royal, Virginia (the first to begin operation) and Fort Robinson, Nebraska. The remount depots had a ready source of food for the dogs—meat from condemned cavalry horses. Each dog consumed two and three-quarter pounds of cooked horse meat, corn meal or oatmeal, and a commercial dry dog food mix. The dogs' feeding was done at 4 p.m. to lessen each dog's excitement and cumulative noise. As noted in Chapter 10, Fort Robinson was also the site of a large German and Italian POW camp located over the hill from the war dog kennel area. Prisoners could hear the noise from the daily dog feeding cycle.

The Army recognized it needed specialized war dog schools to meet its commitment for worldwide combat. In September 1942, a sled and pack dog school was established at Rimini, Montana. Another war dog facility was established on Cat Island, near Gulf Port, Mississippi. Cat Island had a jungle facility to train dogs and their handlers for the Pacific and CBI combat.[336]

Sgt. Gen M. Campbell began dog training at Fort Royal: "In June 1943, I and forty other dog/handler teams arrived on Cat Island to assist in making an Army war dog training film on beach combat. We temporarily camped on the island for six weeks while the training film was shot on location. We were later assigned to Cat Island's main K-9 training facility."[337]

As reports filtered back from North Africa, Sicily and Italy on deployed war dog units, it was apparent more dog and personnel training facilities were needed. In January 1944, the 135th United States Naval Construction Battalion (USNCB or

In 1991, the only remains of the WWII War Dog Reception and Training Center at Fort Robinson was this sign erected by the Nebraska State Historical Society. (Author)

During winter operations at the War Dog Training Center as Army enlisted personnel feed dogs inside the kennel area. A double horse team was used to pull the food pans for each dog to lessen the noise from trucks and keep the dogs calm. This was a large effort to feed all the dogs and frequently was not completed until after dark during winter months. Some dogs mounted the top of their kennels, anticipating the arrival of the horses and their food as the wagon moved between the rows of kennels. Photo on display at the Fort Robinson Museum, Fort Robinson, Nebraska. (Author)

The War Dog kennel compound was fenced, including its primary training area, and set on a great pictorial scene, with the hills of the western panhandle visible. The tall tower allowed the commander to review training below and throughout the kennel area. Dogs are visible on top of their kennels and alongside. Photo on display at the Fort Robinson Museum. (Author)

Seabees) worked on Horn Island, a secret Army experimental training base near Gulfport. At the request of the Army War Dog Facility Command on Horn Island, the 135th surveyed and built a simulated mine field for war dog training.[338]

The fourth War Dog Reception and Training facility was established at San Carlos, California. By October 1943, San Carlos was renamed the Army Casual Dog Detachment, War Dog Replacement and Training Center. The center trained one hundred man and dog teams in attack, sentry, interior guard, and scouting (reconnaissance). The planning, construction, and operation of the Fort Robinson War Dog Reception and Training facility was typical of how the Army undertook creating a new military training program. Fort Robinson's dog facility was initially designed to accommodate 500 dogs on a 500-acre site.[339]

Construction of the war dog training facility began in September 1942, consisting of a K-9 veterinary hospital 250 feet long and 20 feet wide; 80 kennels with outside exercise runs; examination and operating rooms; offices; and a ten-kennel isolation and conditioning building with 96 outside kennels. Administration offices and K-9 headquarters were set up on the second floor of Fort Robinson's post headquarters until permanent structures were completed. Other facilities consisted of a classroom building, a large agitator training area, carpenter shop, and support buildings, all enclosed inside a ten-foot high chain link security fence. A large kennel complex was built north and east of the K-9 buildings. The War Dog Reception and Training Center's capacity increased from 500 to 1,800 dogs. The dog kennels were constructed using fiberboard and were four by four and one-half feet long, two feet eight inches high at the front, and two feet four-inches high at the back, with a single opening facing south to shelter the kennel from Winter winds and snow. Each kennel's roof was hinged to permit easy

The first permanent K-9 training instructor detachment lived in pre-WWI (1908), two-story, brick barracks. (Author)

cleaning. The kennels were laid out in blocks of ninety-six, occupying one-third of the K-9 training area. At the rear of the kennel area, a 32 by 208 foot indoor training and drill building was constructed for inclement weather training.

As the number of students and trainees increased, in January 1943, temporary campaign type wood barracks were built to house 150 trainee handlers. The training center was activated on 23 October 1942, and by December, 1,070, dogs and 400 enlisted personnel were on site.

The K-9 induction process began on the dog's arrival, lasting ten days. A dog was issued a dog collar with its own identification number and was exercised and placed in observation quarantine to check for diseases. The dog was given a complete physical examination and required vaccinations by the center's veterinarian. Once the dog was declared physically fit, its permanent identification number was tattooed inside its left flank. The next processing step was the assignment of trainers. It was important K-9 handlers possessed a friendly attitude toward the dogs and patience. Each trainee dog handler received two weeks of training, learning to analyze a dog's temperament and care.[340]

In August 1942, Sgt. Richard J. Zika reported to Fort Robinson to begin war dog training: "Twenty-five of us that had been selected for the special unit were issued a string of four dogs. We would start training with these dogs, under the stipulation that after three weeks we would decide which one to keep as our partner. The other three dogs would be returned to the cadre pool for finish training and deployed to various installations around the country. Our dog strings were issued to us by lottery draw, but the final choice would be ours. The first week of training was devoted entirely to the dog's obedience and following simple commands: heel, sit, down, stay, and come

An enlisted dog handler/trainee and his instructor with a dog on top of a dog-shipping crate outside the initial dog processing kennel area. Photo on display at the Fort Robinson Museum. (Author)

when called, all designed to teach the dog to unhesitatingly obey his master's commands. Next, the dogs were trained to attack, but without adequate control, it would be too dangerous for all involved. One week is not sufficient to polish the process, but far enough along to advance the dog to agitation training. To those ignorant about war dog training, the term agitation brings on visions of brutalized conditions done in secret locations by club-carrying individuals. This is opposite of the actual truth! If the training was brutal, it would crush the dog's spirit and render it useless for military operations. At all times, the dog's confidence must be built up until it reaches a point of being fearless but controlled aggressiveness. This is what makes up dog agitation theory.

"To start agitation training, we would hold our dogs on a leash with an individual playing the role of agitator who would approach and make over the dog. He would talk soothingly, stroking the dog's back and ears. He would patiently wait until the dog was completely off guard, then suddenly reach out and tweak an ear or yank its tail or flank, while at the same time jumping away from the dog's slashing teeth. The dog, already screened for the instinct to stand up and protect itself, would lunge toward its tormentor while we would hold it back, just out of biting range, while at the same time praising and encouraging the dog. Once the dog's initial anger died down, the agitator would approach again, speaking soothingly to regain the dog's trust. If he succeeded, the process would begin over again. After tricking the dog several times with several different agitators, quickly the dogs learned only to trust their handler. Deception and agitation quickly becomes a two way street. Some dogs learned after the first or second approach and recognized what the name of the game had become. The dog saw no profit in being held back out of reach of the agitator. It quickly became the dog's turn to lull the agitator's defenses and when he came into reach, the agitator suddenly found himself under real attack. While the human agitator had no intention whatsoever of injuring the dog, the dog was not burdened with such inhibitions. Many agitators had to make trips to the medical station for stitches and first aid.

This rare surviving WWII War Dog wooden shipping crate was used to transport dogs from Fort Robinson after the handler and dog completed training. The crate had wire to reinforce the sides and metal corners to further strengthen it. Crate on display at the Fort Robinson Museum. (Author)

The Nebraska State Historical Society erected a marker on the site of Fort Robinson's WWII, K-9 training area. (Author)

At a Fort Robinson Open House, a dog climbs over a high wood wall with its trainer alongside to a large crowd watching the exhibition. The Open House provided local and area residents a view of the training for a unique aspect of the war against the Axis countries. Photo on display at the Fort Robinson Museum. (Author)

"From the beginning, agitation for the dog was conducted using the lunge, which was a twenty-five foot long leash designed to instill even greater confidence. The agitator would approach with a whip and using threatening gestures and the dog was alerted, ready to repel the attacker. Slowly the agitator would retreat as we slowly played out the line, keeping our dog just short of its goal to grab onto the attacker. Now at the end of the twenty-five foot leash, the dog felt he was driving off the intruder without having the handler immediately alongside. This process was a big step in building the dog's self confidence.

"At the same time, the dog was considered ready for line training, which was nothing more than a twenty-foot length of steel clothesline stretched between two six-foot high upright poles secured to the ground so they could not be pulled over. On this line rode a pulley attached to an eight-foot length of chain. The dog was snapped onto the end of a sturdy chain. The dog's handler would retreat out of sight behind a building. An agitator would now appear with a dummy whip, again making threatening gestures toward the dog, but this time it was up to the dog to fend off the enemy alone. Slowly, the human menace would goad the dog along the length of the line and back, keeping just out of the leaping and snarling dog's reach. Once back to the starting point, the agitator would suddenly give up and run away from the charging dog, leaving the animal victorious as its handler returned, giving great praise to the dog.

"The training had now reached the halfway point, the three-week decision point where we had to choose one of the three dogs to stay and which two to send back. Each handler weighed the pros and cons of which dog to choose. I selected a dog named Kayo. Now it was on to advanced training for six days and three evenings a week. This training developed greater obedience, navigating high hurdles and long jumps, more agitation, and night patrols where agitators concealed themselves in shrubbery or building mockups. The agitator would suddenly leap out of hiding and fire a pistol loaded with blanks toward the dog. The dog in turn would follow in hot

Dogs undergoing sled dog training for use in Alaska, where the threat from Japan seemed real. Photo on display at the Fort Robinson Museum. (Author)

pursuit through the building's door or window, or do whatever the situation called for."[341]

In scouting problems, decoys were hidden in the woods and fields, giving the dog and its handler the problem of finding them, much as a bird dog locates its game. The dogs were trained to wear muzzles and gas masks, become accustomed to gunfire, and ride in open Army trucks and jeeps. The student trainers worked with each dog for two hours a day. At the end of basic training, both dogs and trainers were tested on instructed materials and with specialized training assignments made. Most advanced training was conducted at San Carlos, California for those going to the Pacific. However, many going to the CBI departed from Virginia. Specialized training lasted eight to thirteen weeks. Dogs and handlers were trained for guard duty or tactical service. Sentry dogs were trained for eight weeks for guarding supply depots and military sensitive areas. Attack dog training lasted for thirteen weeks. Tactical and service training included different K-9 assignments, each requiring thirteen weeks. Messenger dogs were used instead of human runners in combat situations because they were faster and more difficult for enemy snipers to hit. Two handlers were required for each dog. Dogs had to travel specific distances, facing an assortment of diversions along the designated training route. Casualty dogs aided Army Medical Corps personnel in locating badly wounded men unable to communicate their location. Scout dogs provided silent warning of an approaching enemy. This was valuable in jungle combat on Pacific islands and in the CBI. Sled dog training was added to the curriculum at Fort Robinson in January 1944, after the Pimini Training Center closed. Sled dog training was set up at a former CCC camp west of Fort Robinson in an area referred to as Wood Reserve. Dog sled teams were trained and prepared for cold weather and arctic rescue of downed airmen.

During training, many dogs were classified as unsuitable for the rigorous requirements of guard or combat duty and returned to their civilian owners. After war dog training reached full capacity, training attrition was high. Between January and

At Fort Robinson, the surrounding open areas were ideal for gliders from Alliance AB. Dogs training at Fort Robinson were carried in gliders, adding to realism for combat in the CBI and later in the Philippines in the closing phases of war in the Pacific. Photo on display at the Fort Robinson Museum. (Author)

June 1943, the Army received 3,503 dogs at Fort Robinson, with 1,708 completing training and qualified for combat operations or sentry duty. The Army returned 520 dogs to their civilian owners, with 661 put down for various reasons. After completing training at San Carlos, many dogs and their handlers faced long sea voyages to the Pacific Combat Theater of Operations. The war dog training effort in Nebraska assisted in winning the Pacific war and was just as important as combat troops, aircraft, warships, and logistics. War Dogs served with the Marines and Army throughout the Pacific: Guadalcanal, New Guinea, New Britain, Saipan, Guam, Peleliu, Okinawa, and the Philippine Islands. However, it was in the CBI where War Dogs earned many combat accolades.[342]

Richard Zika recalled: "On 24 January 1944, we boarded the Liberty Ship *Benjamin Ide Wheeler* at Wilmington, Louisiana, assigned to a K-9 company of 100 enlisted men and two officers, plus four casual officers and 108 dogs."[343]

The Liberty ship was designed to allow U.S. shipyards to mass-produce a simple and inexpensive emergency cargo medium-sized transport.[344]

Zika notes: "None of us knew our final destination, but all of us had our sleeping quarters, galley, and dining area jammed into number three hold (forward of the engine room and pilothouse). Our 108 dogs were quartered in crates under the protection of two large temporary sheds on the port and starboard sides of the ship, just aft of the mid-ship house. When it came to shipboard housing, the dogs appeared to have the better accommodations for the next 72 days. Without escort, we zigzagged our way across the Pacific into the South Pacific waters. The food, which was abominable at the beginning, went downhill from this point, until we were subsisting on canned salmon that tasted like spoiled dry soda crackers, washed down with black unsweetened coffee. On the opposite, our officers dined with the Liberty Ship's officers, eating very well compared to what

Liberty ship SS *Benjamin Ide Wheeler*. Courtesy of National Parks Service, Washington, D.C. to author.

we had. The enlisted men's growing resentment of the quality of our food rations led to a miniature food riot, with the swill of the day being thrown all over our ship's cargo hold eating area. It brought the attention we wanted, but the only result was that we were promised fresh provisions when they became available. The fresh provisions could only be stocked at our first Pacific port of call—Freemantle, Australia. While this promise sounded good, it is hard to make a sandwich out of a promise between imaginary slices of bread. Therefore, the bad feelings among the enlisted men still ran high on the ship.

"It was in the Pacific that we had our first glimpse of the war up close. We suddenly plowed through floating debris that could have only come from a recently sunk ship. We eventually came upon an overturned, bullet-riddled, wooden lifeboat bearing the printed name of a Dutch freighter that left Wilmington 24 hours before our ship sailed. It was a sobering experience to many of us, forcing us to wonder what the odds were on seeing another sunrise. However, the Tasmanian Sea showed us the awesome power of nature. We ran into a typhoon that scared us to death, not only out of fear of our dogs' sheds being swept overboard, but also of the probability of the ship breaking apart. The three-day storm pushed us back the way we came so that it took five days steaming to return to the point where the storm first hit the ship. Remembering the size of those mountainous waves and damage done to the ship, there were many shaken men onboard, as well as very sick dogs. At 10:30 a.m. on 4 March 1944, we docked at

Freemantle, Australia for a two-day refueling and provisioning stop. Most important for us was the two days, which allowed us to gorge ourselves on fresh food and fruit, beer, and whatever else we could find before returning to the ship. On the evening of the second day in Australia, all of us returned to the ship carrying large bags of fruit and other food that we could buy in Freemantle. Although we had been promised improved onboard ship rations, Army promises do not always coincide with reality. Consequently, it was our belief that a separate personal commissary was simple prudence, given the circumstances of the previous trip across the Pacific. Surprisingly, the ship's food stocks had been restocked as promised; although it was nothing to get excited about, it was a great improvement over the swill we had suffered on the earlier part of the trip across the Pacific. Now, we wondered what was in store for us on the Liberty ship as we and our dogs headed north by west into the Indian Ocean. The closer we came to our destination, the hotter it became for all on the ship.

"The ocean turned out to be a 'bitch,' because the extreme heat and humidity forced us to quickly consume our personal stocks of fruit and food before it could spoil. The ship's decks became frying pans, blistering the pads of our dogs' feet and opening sores for infections. We tried making canvas foot booties for each dog, but the deck was still so hot it burned through the booties and burned the dogs' pads. The best we could do was keep the ship's decks in the area of the dog crates flushed with salt water from the onboard firehouses. However, the salt water used caused problems when the salt water evaporated, leaving a dried salt crust on the dogs' pads that had to be scraped off them, as well as from the ship's metal decking plates. The only thing we could do was keep the dogs under cover as much as possible and continue to check them for problems. Unfortunately, we lost two dogs because of heat related problems. While transiting the Indian Ocean, the Liberty ship's captain, D.J. Caughlin, informed us that this passage would be the most dangerous of the trip and the ship's lookouts were doubled. We eagerly assisted the ship's crew, searching the horizon for enemy planes or submarines.

"It was during this leg of the transit that we passed through wreckage of another ship, including machine-gunned life rafts. Again, we were unable to locate and rescue any survivors. We really became scared when our ship's engine stopped for thirty minutes just as the sun set, making us a sitting duck for any lurking Japanese submarine that might be near. The morning of 21 March 1944, we dropped anchor in the Bay of Colombo, Ceylon. We were not allowed to leave the ship during the four days we swung at anchor in the repressive, sweltering heat. We were greatly concerned about the condition of our dogs. It was also disconcerting to watch the ship's gun crews constantly hosing down the ammunition lockers to reduce the 100-degree plus temperatures inside the lockers and keep the ammunition from blowing up, taking us and the ship with the detonation. It was a relief to leave Colombo, Ceylon on 24 March 1944, but this time in a convoy of seventeen ships escorted by three corvettes and an occasional long-range B-24 patrol aircraft for the final leg of our trip through the Bay of Bengal, up the Hooghly River to the port of Calcutta, India. During this part of the trip, an older and smaller freighter dropped out of the convoy because of engine problems, limping along at slow speed. Later, we were told by our ship's officers that the freighter had been torpedoed and sunk by a Japanese submarine. For us, after traveling thousands of miles and weeks alone, we felt foolishly secure in the company of so many other ships and escorts. Our sea voyage ended at the King George Docks at Calcutta, India on 4 April 1944. We unloaded our dogs and trucked them to Kanchrapara, India, where we went through several weeks of frustration, giving working dog demonstrations to Indian, British, and American high-ranking officers."[345]

Army ordnance officer B.K. Kennedy traveled on the same Liberty ship as Zika. While waiting for a combat assignment, he was temporarily detailed as the War Dog Detachment's on-site commander while the detachment's commanding officer traveled forward, scouting combat locations to determine the best use for his dogs and their handlers: "In all my travels in the CBI, I encountered many different military units. However, I never met a more dedicated group of men. Despite their lack of rank and equipment, they performed their duties at a 100% plus level."[346]After the War Dog Detachment's commander returned in July, a group of forty-three handlers and their dogs went by train to Ramgarah, India, in company with the U.S. Army's 475th Infantry. The dog unit camped in a clearing carved out of heavy jungle near the ruins of an ancient overgrown temple. Bob Lischer was temporarily detached from this group to take a section of dogs to train with the 5307th Provisional Regiment, better known and referred to as Merrill's Marauders.[347]

Dogs and their handlers with the 475th Infantry departed for Burma. Staff Sergeant Carl M. Hutsell recalled: "On December 31, 1944 we left Tonkwa, traveling on a rough jeep road until it ended, then we marched through streambeds for eleven miles to a Chinese Army outpost at Khamot. On 1 January 1945, we walked eight miles and camped at the Nam Moa Chinese Army outpost. On 2 January, we hiked six miles and crossed the Shrui River on a pontoon bridge. On 3 January, we walked six miles through Palaurg N-Oeu village and bivouacked at Manhkat. On 4 January, we received a ration airdrop, then bivouacked on the side of a mountain. On 5 January, we reached To Pang and crossed a 4,600-foot mountain to a camp in Mong Wi Valley. On 6 January, it rained all day and night and we received another badly needed ration airdrop. On 7 January, a dog rescue team left for a reported C-47 crash on a mountainside approximately twelve miles from our camp. On 9 January, we were getting regular food rations, but nothing for our dogs, which was of great concern to us."[348]

Bob Lischer and dog handler teams that originally stayed behind departed with the 124th Cavalry for Mitikyina at the end of October 1944, training until December. The 475th and 124th Cavalry temporarily joined to create the Mars Task Force on 10 January 1945, supported by the 612th and 613th Artillery and pack mule outfits.[349] Hutsell noted: "On 13 January, the combined unit left Mong Wi, eventually bivouacking eleven miles distant at Nammo. On 16 January, the 475th Infantry was pulled out for rest. On 17 January, we crossed a stream 31 times during the day's march while fighting the Japanese in the afternoon. On 18 January, we bypassed the Japanese unit we had been fighting, then bivouacked at Nawhkam. The Japanese attacked in the evening and we continued to fight them all night. On 19 January, our constant artillery fire excited some of our dogs while others were not affected. The Nawhkam Battle was fought along and near the Burma Road, a vital supply line for both sides. On 20 January, the Japanese regrouped and continued their attack, with our artillery firing at them all night, supported by mortars. Japanese snipers fired into our positions all night. One of the L-5 light observation and utility aircraft sent to pick up some of our wounded crashed while attempting to land on the short and rough airstrip."[350]

Sgt. Earl O. Cullum recalled: "A Japanese soldier armed with a bag of grenades infiltrated our inner perimeter and by midnight had crawled as far as the unit's command post. Fortunately, he stumbled into one of our dogs chained near a foxhole occupied by his handler."

The following description of what happened closely mirrored the dog's training as conducted at Fort Robinson: "The dog waited until the Japanese soldier came very close, then lunged at and terribly chewed on the enemy soldier. The Japanese soldier was in such pain he grabbed a grenade out of his bag, pulled the pin, and held it close to his chest, blowing himself up. The explosion woke up the entire unit and earned the dog a well-desired amount of praise. While leading a patrol towards a fringe of woods, my dog gave indication that it contained a hidden force of Japanese troops greater than that of the patrol. We dropped back and called for supporting artillery fire. Later, it was discovered the Japanese numbered approximately 125, with only 30 yards separating the patrol's point from the prepared enemy trap from where the dog warned them of the danger."[351]

Rusty Mizner stated: "During another instance, a patrol knew there were two Japanese snipers in front, but could not flush the enemy into the open. My dog and I were sent to the patrol's front to sniff them out. My dog quickly alerted me to the Japanese location, concealed in thick brush. I emptied my Thompson sub-machine gun into the brush, killing one Japanese soldier and forcing the second out into the open. The patrol killed the fleeing Japanese soldier."[352]

Hutsell recalled: "The 124th Cavalry and its supporting war dogs received a badly needed food drop on January 23rd. On January 25th, there was an intense artillery duel with Japanese east of the Burma Road. On January 26th, artillery fire continued all day and night. The unit received a rare mail drop and welcomed C-rations. On January 27th, artillery fire continued. On January 28th, artillery fire was very heavy."[353]

During its tour in the CBI, the War Dog detachment consisted of 120 dogs. This included War Dogs killed in combat and replaced to keep the unit operating. It is estimated approximately 85 War Dogs from this unit survived combat. Forty-six dogs and their handlers were flown to Assam, China over the "hump." With dogs in combat in the CBI, the War Dog unit became officially referred to as the War Dog Detachment CBI.[354]

Campbell continues: "I was one of the handlers assigned to the 1337th Transport Command at Sookerting Air Base, Assam. The air base's personnel unloaded and serviced 'hump' transports, primarily C-46 transports. We guarded the base's supply warehouses, bomb and ammunition dumps, and fuel dumps that were dispersed into the jungle, adjacent to the air base. We also guarded the base's aircraft fuel storage and refueling positions, and would cover troops sent to investigate and recover downed crewmembers from crashed transports in the area. We would frequently guard the crash site of salvage operations where possible, since the supplies carried on the aircraft were very valuable and important to the China Front."[355]

Brewster: "To reduce the theft of supplies at the India storage depots on the 'hump' supply line into China, it was quickly found that patrolling guard dogs drastically cut down local pilfering of supplies. I, along with eleven other dogs and their handlers, was assigned to patrol Chabua Airport. We did sentry service, patrolled warehouses, and guarded radio beacons and radio stations out to a distance of 10-15 miles from the airport. These beacons and stations provided transport pilots radio directional beams and communications before going over the mountains or returning to India. Radio location was extremely important because of the bad weather the transports had to fly in and through, as well as providing warning of enemy fighter activity."[356]

As the war slowed in Europe emphasis shifted to the Pacific, changing War Dog training. Fort Robinson's War Dog Training Program K-9 strength dropped to 1,400 dogs from July to December 1944. Training shifted to reconnaissance operations. By August 1945, dog strength had increased to 1,800, taking up the slack from other closing War Dog training facilities. After V-E Day on 8 May 1945, the supply of War Dogs caught up to demand. At this point, many dogs were returned to their civilian owners rather than issued to combat units. By V-J Day (15 August 1945), the Army had completed training of 10,425 War Dogs, of which approximately 50 percent trained at Fort Robinson. Scout and sled dog training continued at Fort Robinson until June 1946, at which time the remaining seventeen on station dogs were sold. The temporary wood buildings, barracks, and dog training facilities were torn down by 1955. All that remains today is an empty grass area at Fort Robinson.[357]

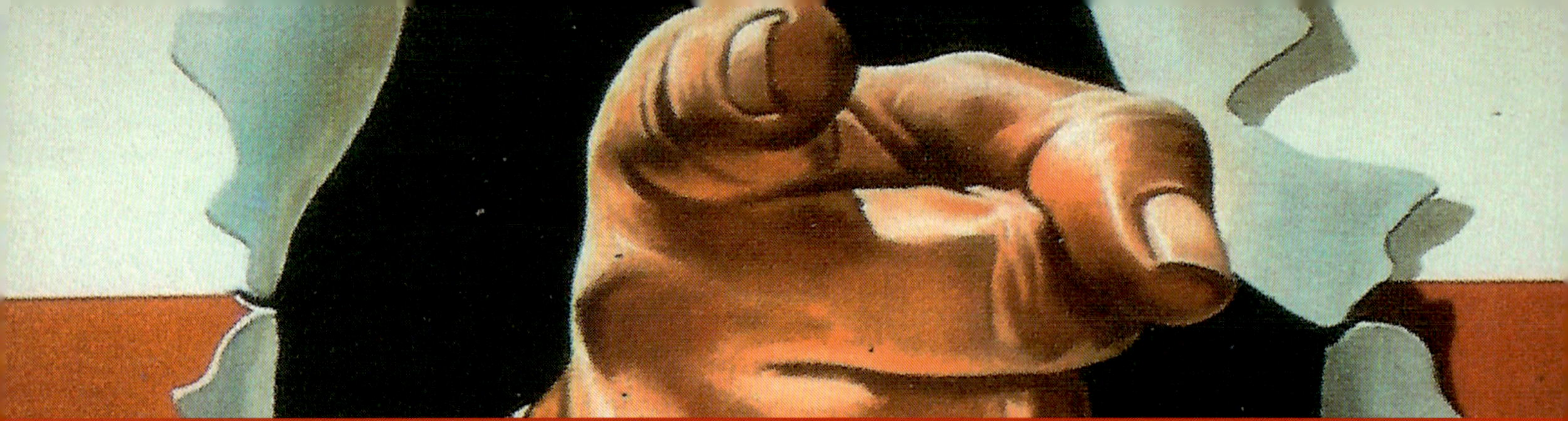

CHAPTER FOURTEEN

SCOTTS BLUFF AIR BASE

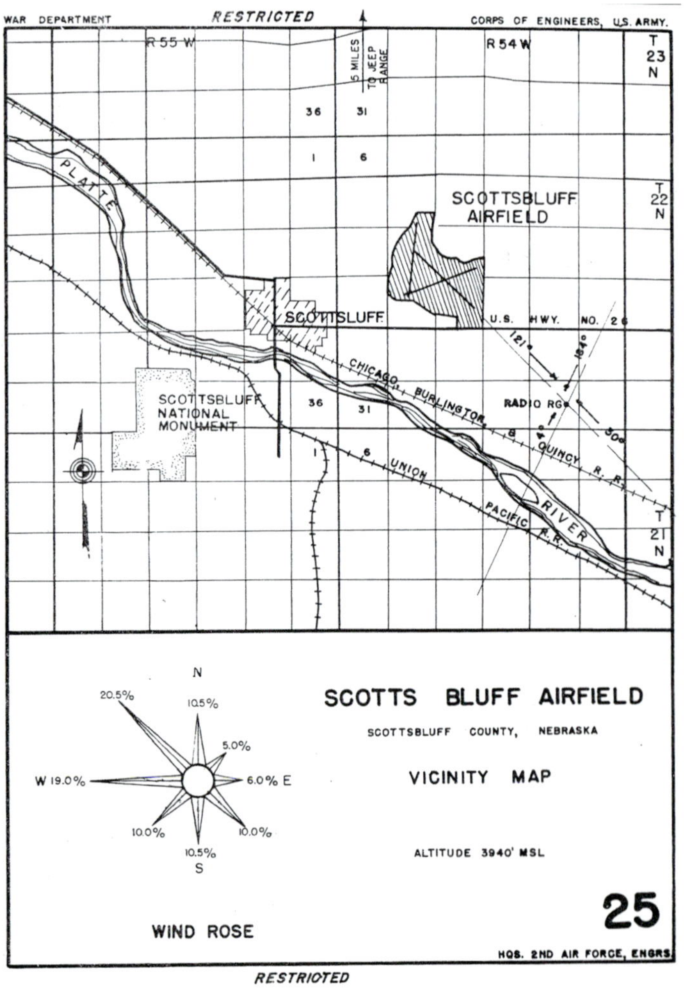

Scotts Bluff Airfield vicinity map. Author.

The Scotts Bluff County Airport was an important contributor in Nebraska's roll in assisting in winning WWII. On 5 September 1942, the War Department announced that Scotts Bluff had been selected as a site for an AAF satellite training air base, with the base to be built five miles outside the town. The air base would operate three primary runways: 12/30-8,200 feet long and 150 feet wide; 5/23-8,000 feet long and 150 feet wide; and 17/35-8,087 feet long and 150 feet wide.

The estimated cost of the air base was $2,000,000. Construction of the training air base required the acquisition of twenty-eight local farms. Most of the landowners, as at other base construction sites in Nebraska, protested condemnation of their land by the federal government, filing lawsuits because they were to be paid for the land only and nothing for value of improvements or crops lost from non-harvest. Farm and landowners lost their legal challenges and were ordered to vacate immediately. At this time, Scotts Bluff Municipal Airport closed because Army regulations prohibited the operation of a private civilian airport's operations within six miles of a military air base so as not to endanger flight and training activities. [358] The closed airport was converted into a POW camp for German and Italian soldiers, airmen, and sailors.[359]

Air base construction began on 7 December 1942, concentrating on offices and barracks. Seven hundred construction workers were employed on the site by 16 September, increasing to 2,500 by 1 October. As with other war construction projects in Nebraska, the rapid influx of workers created a severe housing shortage in and around Scotts Bluff. The new air base was along Nebraska State Highway 26, which was patrolled by Army Military Police who restricted vehicle traffic to a maximum speed of 25-35mph, with no parking allowed to watch construction workers on the air base site.

On 25 September, a $100,000-500,000 construction contract was awarded to Krammer, Fenson and Walker, of Des Moines

During WWII, this building served as the air base's primary fire station. It was modernized in the 1950s and used as a fire station. In 1991, the building was empty and scheduled to be torn down, after being replaced by a modern fire station complex at the airport. (Author)

and Iowa Falls, Iowa, to build the air base's drainage system. On this date, the first concrete was poured on the runways and taxiways, consisting of Portland cement eight inches thick. The concrete base fill material was dredged from the North Platte River, east of Scotts Bluff. Large pumps sucked gravel from the river's bottom that was loaded into railroad hopper cars and delivered to the construction site via a temporary railroad spur line. Dredged gravel is normally screened to produce uniform size fill material, however, because of the requirement to pour concrete as soon as possible the dredged gravel was not screened. Work crews poured concrete 24 hours a day to meet construction deadlines. J.A. Terteling and Sons of Boise, Idaho was the primary concrete contractor. On 11 October 1942, the Army authorized on-site construction workers to occupy completed barracks to ease the local housing shortage as at other military facilities built in Nebraska before starting operations. On 8 November, the last of the concrete was poured one week ahead of schedule. Construction workers moved one million cubic yards of earth, pouring 600,000 cubic yards of concrete in 45 days. Final edge grading continued on the runways, taxiways, and parking aprons. This was remarkable, because the harvest season was in progress around Scotts Bluff. Many construction workers labored on the air base part time after their normal jobs, earning extra income and helping reduce labor shortages on the air base project. There was never enough labor to meet all contractor needs on the air base. On 10 October, Scotts Bluff residents petitioned the Army to name the new air base Osborne Brown Field in honor of the town's first AAF death in the war, but this was turned down.

On 30 November, the seeding contract was awarded to a Scotts Bluff company. The contract was worth $65,000 to seed the construction-disturbed areas to prevent prevailing winds from kicking up dirt, creating hazardous dust clouds that could endanger safe aircraft operations. Dust clouds could reduce

WWII camouflage training building modernized and used for vehicle repair and an office building for the city's landfill operations. (Author)

visibility, damaging piston aircraft engines. Thirty workers using nine tractors spread a variety of grass seed over 150 acres.[360]

Bernice Wilson worked on the project: "I worked for the U.S. Army Corps of Engineers as a telephone operator chief during construction of the POW internment camp at the former Scotts Bluff Municipal Airport, as well as Sidney, Nebraska during the construction of the Sioux Ordnance Depot. When these internees were being received here I transferred home to Alliance, taking a job at Alliance AB, which was in operation at that time. While in Scotts Bluff, I lived in a home where some of the airmen's wives had rooms but not kitchen privileges as I did. Our landlady had one aircrew for dinner one evening."[361]

The Sioux Ordnance Depot was located ten miles northwest of Sidney, Nebraska, where 300 Italian POWs were housed in temporary barracks near the depot's entrance, secured by barbed wire. Later, 300 German POWs were transferred to the depot in Spring 1944. German and Italian POWs in the camp had volunteered as laborers, engineers, carpenters, automotive mechanics, typists, tractor operators, hospital attendants, cooks, and various other jobs. Those POWs without specialized training unloaded trucks or railroad boxcars. When Italy surrendered to the Allies on 1 May 1944, Italian troops at the depot became the 70th Italian Quartermaster Service Company, eligible for any job except assignment to combat.[362]

Scotts Bluff AB was a satellite air base of Casper AB, Wyoming. The first contingent of sixteen AAF troops arrived from Casper AB at Scotts Bluff on 4 December 1942. Scotts Bluff AB was tasked to provide first phase combat training. Part of this training included B-17 night landings under minimal lighting conditions. Aircrews went through aircraft and radio maintenance training. Because of a lack of radio equipment, local Scotts Bluff businesses and citizens bought commercial radio sets for classroom instruction use. The Army modified its original plans for Scotts Bluff AB, awarding a construction contract to widen the taxiways from 50-75 feet to support possible B-29 training operations. Construction work stopped training operations from 1 March to 24 April 1944.[363] Aircrews flew simulated combat missions, briefed on and conducted aircraft inspections, bombardier installation of the top-secret Norden bombsight, and coordination from IP to target as soon as taxiways could support their aircraft.[264]

The Second Air Force's Heavy Bombardment Training Program was updated on 5 March 1943. The new training requirements were used by all heavy bombardment training groups. This provides a good look at war training conducted throughout the United States to prepare and fight a global air war, including training in Nebraska. The new requirements stated:

> 1. Pursuant to instructions contained in Section II of Secret letters, AAF, January 15, 1943, subject: Saturation Point of the Second Air Force to accomplish its part of the assigned mission in the 1943 Army Air Forces Expansion and Training Program.
>
> 2. The program provides for the expansion of the Heavy Bombardment Training Program of the Second Air Force and plans for its operation were established by the Director of Bombardment in his memorandum to the Assistant Chief of Air Staff, dated January 7, 1943: Subject: "Expansion Program for the Army Air Forces," and required facilities included "Table C," to the letter of January 15th, referred to in Paragraph 1, above. This plan provided for the activation of two additional Heavy Bombardment Parent Groups in the OTU system and one B-29 Very Heavy Group as a Parent OTU for B-29 units, together with the establishment of nine additional bases to handle the three cycles of OTU training as projected.
>
> 3. After a study of the expanded program had been made, a counter-proposal was made whereby the organization of the additional Heavy Bombardment Groups required in the 1943 Army Air Forces Expansion Training Program will be organized and trained in the existing OTU system of the Second Air Force. This action was taken in as much as the accelerated program of six groups per month extends over a period of but a few months during the latter part of 1943. It was therefore believed expedient to accomplish the mission in this manner to obviate the necessity for the establishment of nine new bases as proposed by the Director of Bombardment.
>
> 4. It was further established that the RTU Program was to be expanded from the existing program peak of 384 crews per month to 511 crews per month. At the present time (March 1943), the Second Air Force has three cycles for RTU training. Under the existing three cycles for RTU training, it would necessitate the training of 174 crews at each of the stations in the training cycle. Experience in the operation of the Heavy Bombardment RTU Program has shown that it is impracticable to operate in excess of 50 airplanes and itwas therefore proposed that the Second Air Force establish an additional RTU cycle to distribute the load. In as much as the Army Air Forces will not provide any additional fixed units for the operation of the Second Air Force Program, it was determined that the three additional Parent Units authorized for the Extended Program be utilized as such, and that a fourth RTU cycle can be established. In the organization of the new cycle, it was found necessary to secure the transfer of two bases to the Second Air Force, and the Army Air Base at Dalhart, Texas and Dyersburg, Tennessee were transferred to our jurisdiction. The 46th Bombardment Wing has been organized with the 19th Bombardment Group at Pyote, Texas as the Parent Unit; the 333rd Bombardment Group transferred from Topeka, Kansas as a Second Phase RTU Group at Dalhart; and the 346th Bombardment Group, formerly as Salina, Kansas, transferred to Dyersburg, Tennessee as a Third Phase RTU Group.
>
> 5. The original Air Force program contemplated the utilization of the Army air bases and their satellites at Salina, Kansas; Topeka, Kansas; and Kearney, Nebraska as Third Phase stations of the Second Air Force OTU and RTU Program. Subsequent to the inauguration of the original program, the Second Air Force was required to take over the activities in connection with the final processing of crews and aircraft, prior to delivery overseas, formerly handled by the First Concentration Command. The 21st Bombardment Wing was organized at Salina, Kansas, utilizing the stations enumerated above and fixed bombardment groups for the accomplishment of this particular mission.
>
> 6. Due to the expansion of the Heavy Bombardment OTU and RTU Programs, paragraphs 2 and 4 above, the fact that Army Air Forces would not acquiesce to the activation of any additional fixed groups for the operation of the 21st Bombardment Wing, a reorganization of the activities of the Wing was required. The 333rd Bombardment Group and 346th Bombardment Group were transferred to the 46th Bombardment Wing to establish the additional RTU cycle as indicated in paragraph 4, above. The personnel of the 333rd Bombardment Group and 346th Bombardment Group were utilized to organize the five Airdrome Squadrons at Topeka and Salina to permit continuity of operations at those stations. The two units were transferred at cadre strength to the new stations, where they will be built in place.
>
> 7. To provide the personnel and facilities required for the operation of the activities of the 21st Bombardment Wing the following actions were taken:
>
> A. The Director of Program Planning indicated that the Second Air Force would be called upon to activate and train airdrome squadrons for eventual shipment overseas and that during the period of their organization and training, these airdrome squadrons could be utilized to perform the functions formerly performed by fixed bombardment groups in

Remains of the concrete foundation for the air base's WWII hospital. (Author)

This poured slab concrete aircraft parking apron was the only WWII-era poured concrete remaining at the municipal airport. The civil/light commercial aircraft flight operations building is located across the concrete parking apron. (Author)

At the top center of the photograph, in front of the trees along the horizon, are three surviving WWII small caliber ammunition earth-covered bunkers still intact; it was remarkable the three bunkers survived into the present. I talked to a small group of local residents in a downtown Scotts Bluff restaurant about the former WWII air base that had no idea these bunkers remained nor anything about the former AAF training base. (Author)

the 21st Wing bases. In this connection, a request was made for the activation of airdrome squadrons to insure maintenance of an inventory of 63 airdrome squadrons at all times, to be utilized at the station of the 21st Wing as indicated. In as much as the organization of the airdrome squadron is essentially that of a heavy bombardment squadron, plus certain overhead personnel, to permit its independent operation in the field, it was established that each squadron should be able to maintain 12 heavy bombardment air planes and all computations for the utilization of airdrome squadrons were based on this factor of 12 airplanes per squadron. It is essential to the success of this substitute method that thus headquarters be notified of the number of airdrome squadrons which will be required for shipment overseas each month so that additional activations can be effected in sufficient time to permit the maintenance of 63 fully manned units in the bases of the 21st Wing at all times.

B. Because of the physical restrictions on a number of heavy bombardment aircraft that can be efficiently operated from one base and, in view of the requirements of the expanded program, it is necessary that the satellites of the three main bases of Salina and Topeka, Kansas; and Kearney, Nebraska expanded to approximate group size and that the use of certain facilities at Oklahoma City be made available.[365]

For example, to meet the new Second Air Force program at Kearney AB, training facilities were built to accommodate two squadrons, but were inadequate. Under the reset training program of January 1943, it became designated a Parent 21st Wing base to hold sixty airplanes and their crews at all times. Housing was required for 1,235 men at an estimated cost of $722,500; construction of an addition to the sub-depot at a cost of $240,000; addition to aircraft parking apron; one additional aircraft hangar at a cost of $570,000; and an upgrade to the base hospital. This construction was necessary because aircrew training was expected to peak in late 1943.[366]

All that remains of the WWII site of the air base's barracks is an empty field; even the concrete blocks used for foundations are gone. (Author)

The Second Air Force Heavy Bombardment Training Program (B) continues:

> In addition, it is necessary that bases for the conduct of over water navigation checks be established on the Gulf of Mexico, and a request was made for the use of facilities at Gulf Port, Mississippi, and the establishment of bases at Alexandria, Louisiana and Galveston, Texas. The number of airdrome squadrons to be based at each of the base of the 21st Wing and the number of airplanes that is contemplated operating for each base.
>
> C. To provide the necessary supervisory personnel to insure the efficient performance of the functions of the 21st Wing in the processing of aircraft and final checking of crews prior to departure overseas, it was determined that a group or sub-wing headquarters was necessary. However, because of the restrictions of the Army Air Forces on the activation of any additional group or wing headquarters under the Stabilization Program, a special technical order was prepared by representatives of Second Air Force for a Heavy Bombardment Processing Headquarters. This technical order provides certain key personnel required to accomplish the dual function of a group headquarters for the several airdrome squadrons at each base and as a sub-wing headquarters of the 21st Bombardment Wing in the conduct of its assigned mission. This table was prepared based on providing only such key personnel as were not available in the airdrome squadron or base organization. All other personnel required for the processing of aircraft and crews to be withdrawn from personnel available in the airdrome squadrons and base activities where the Processing Headquarters are established. This headquarters has made a request for the activation of 13 Heavy Bombardment Processing Headquarters, which had been approved.

8. As stated above, certain airbases with the 21st Wing were required to be expanded to full group bases and request was made for the activation of Base Headquarters and Air Base Squadrons and Guard [illegible] necessary in the operation of these bases.

9. The Concentration Program, which has been approved and is now underway, will provide the needed housing facilities at 21st Wing bases. Any additional construction, which may be found necessary, will be of a minor nature or for repairs and improvements. On First, Second and Third Phase bases and their satellites, adequate facilities now exist for the execution of plans. In certain instances, facilities exist over and above for those immediately required for the program, but these will be utilized for Air Service Command units training with bombardment groups, and, at times, to provide an over strength in certain bases to adjust training and flying operations necessitated by weather conditions.

10. The requirements for personnel to implement this program are already established in the request for activation of the units and should be furnished in accordance with existing policy of the Army Air Forces for furnishing personnel upon activation of units and prior to commencement of operational training. However, it is essential to the success of the program that provisions be made to provide a flow of experience both from active theaters and from other commands, to provide the nucleus about which to build new organizations in the OTU Program and to provide the necessary staff and supervisory personnel for the effective training of units by this Air Force.

11. At the time that the program was presented to the representatives of the Second Air Force, they were informed that the units and stations of the II Air Support Command were transferred from the jurisdiction of the Second Air Force. This action clears all stations and facilities not required in the operation of the Heavy Bombardment Program from the Second Air Force and [illegible] to other activities.

12. This plan requires flexibility in operation accomplishment of mission assigned to the Second Air Force, which necessities the conversion of certain Parent Units and cycles to take care of the changes in type of aircraft set up in the Army Air Forces Plan.[367]

Scotts Bluff AB was transferred from the Second Air Force to the First Troop Carrier Command on 29 May 1944, for use as a satellite of Alliance AB. Scotts Bluff AB was used for maneuvers, air operations, routine training flights, and glider operations. C-47s were the primary aircraft seen at the air base. After the war ended in the Pacific on 15 August 1945, operations declined. On 6 January 1945, the Scotts Bluff City Council signed papers agreeing to the federal government's provisions for use of a landing strip and associated facilities. The contract transferred the air base and associated equipment, exclusive of the containment area with barracks, administration buildings, and warehouse to the City of Scotts Bluff. Any excessive supplies and equipment were sold by the Federal Reconstruction and Finance Corporation. The air base's transfer to the city did not include 98 buildings. Some sixty buildings were under control of the Federal Housing Administration and operated by the City of Scotts Bluff as emergency housing. Thirty-eight buildings were bought by the city for $8,900. These included the air base's 50-foot high flagpole, four remaining farmhouses not torn down during base construction and training operations, a twenty-six bed hospital, a windmill for pumping water, and assorted structures. Most of the acquired buildings were sold by the city, with most moved into town to ease postwar housing shortages for returning servicemen.

CHAPTER FIFTEEN

SCRIBNER AIR BASE

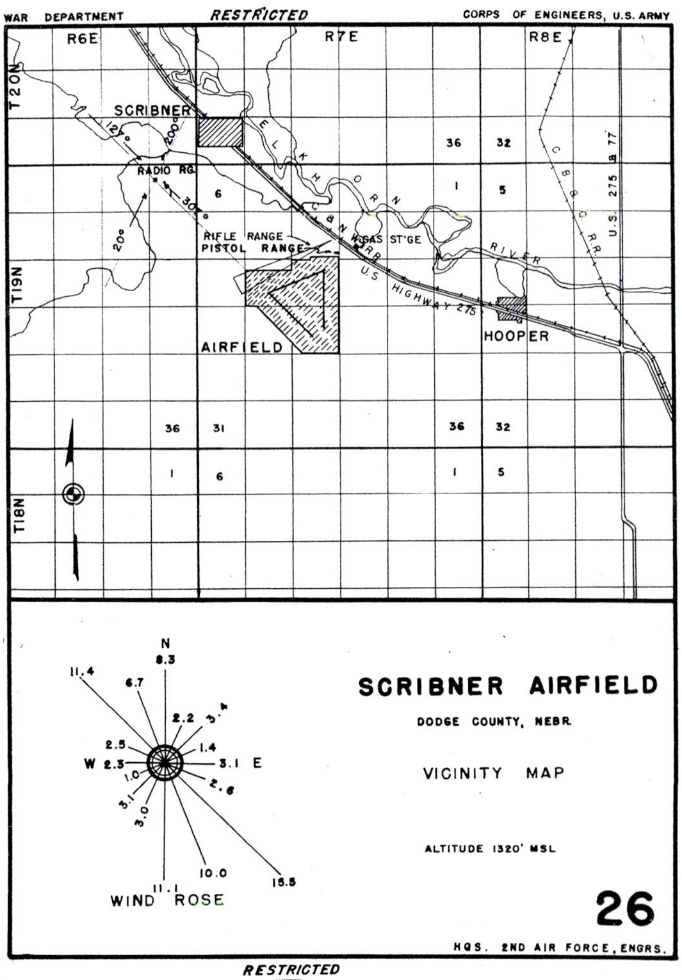

Scribner Airfield vicinity map. (Author)

Beginning in August, 1942, land sections 16-17 and 20-21, located in Everett Township, Scribner, Nebraska, were surveyed by personnel assigned to the U.S. Army Corps of Engineers as a possible site for an AAF base. After the survey, federal government officials made no official announcement or indication if a military airfield complex would be built near Scribner. On 1 October 1942, funds to build an air base at Scribner were authorized by the War Department with an estimated cost of $2,000,000. A construction contract was awarded to Fox Valley Construction Company, of Appleton, Wisconsin. Farmers on land to be taken for the air base began harvesting immature corn for cattle feed, rather than letting it remain and rot in the fields. Farmers reported an average yield of 70 bushels of corn per acre. On 15 October 1942, most of the farm owners on the airfield construction site were served official federal condemnation and evacuation notices to leave the property immediately. The Army Corps of Engineers appraised the condemned land for payment, although farmers argued it was below market value and did not include property improvements and losses from premature crop harvesting. At the same time, the Army Corps of Engineers published a requirement to hire 350 workers, offering a wage of 62 cents per hour.

Scribner officials indicated an immediate need to prepare a trailer camp at the Scribner Fair Grounds, to provide a place for workers starting to arrive to work on the air base to live, but it was never set up. Many workers drove from Omaha or Lincoln, Nebraska to work on the air base and did not require living quarters in town. However, after construction started, the Scribner Women's Club and local newspapers listed available rooms for rent, filling up every empty space in town. All of a sudden, all services and businesses in town were quickly overburdened by the influx of construction workers.

The airfield was built on 2,060 acres of land near the town. On 26 November 1942, two concrete runways were finished

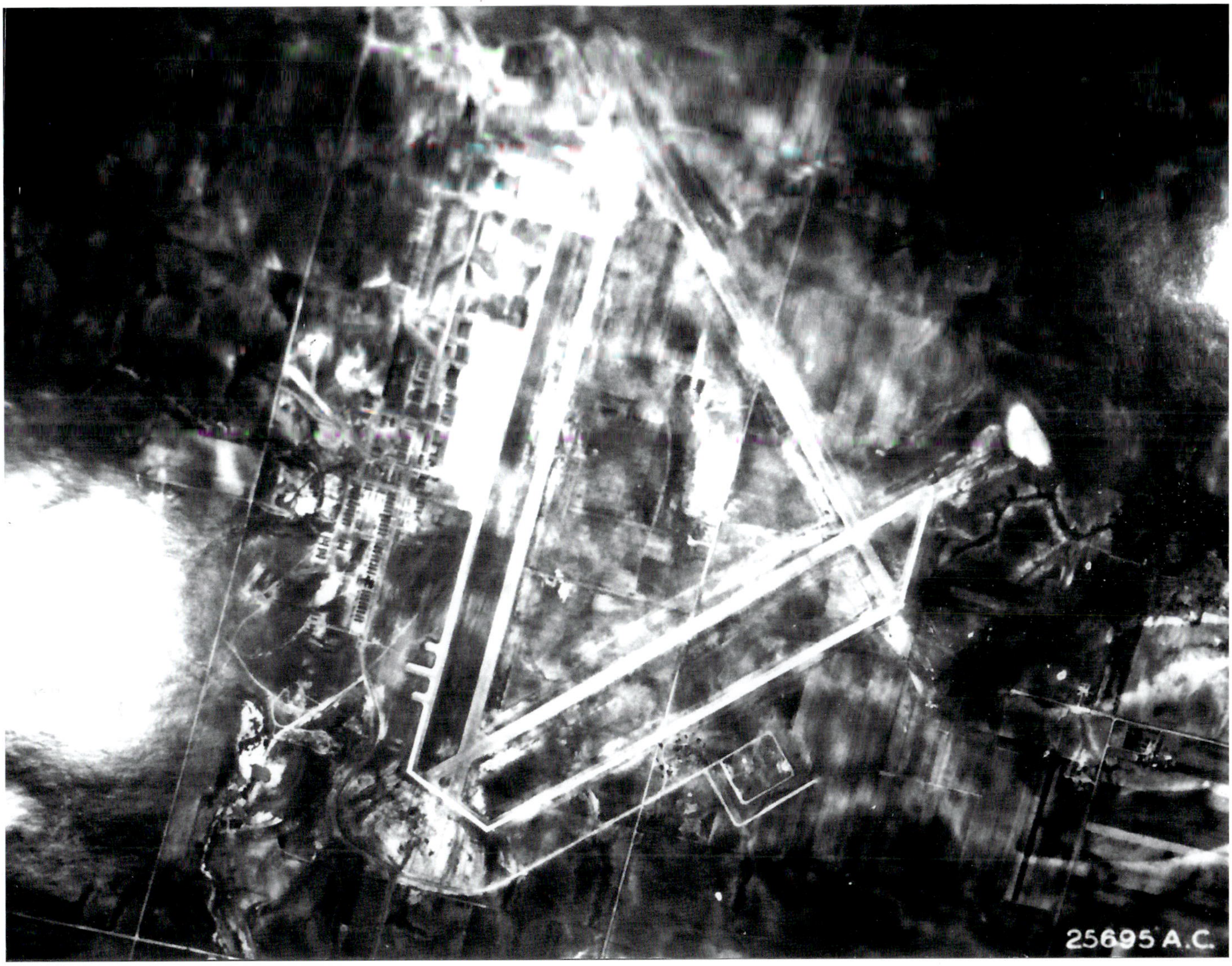

Aerial view of Scribner Air Base in 1943. Courtesy of Nebraska State Historical Society

with a third under construction: 12/30-3,199 feet long and 60 feet wide; 17/35-4,200 feet long and 75 feet wide; and the third connected the above two, with a base leg 4,200 feet long and 75 feet wide.

Air base facilities consisted of one large hangar, fifteen barracks, officers' quarters, a Post Exchange, and a hospital annex. Scribner was controlled by Sioux City AB, Iowa.[368]

In January 1943, hastily constructed tarpaper-sided barracks became a temporary home to airmen training at the air base. B-17s and B-24s frequently deployed to the air base for training. Their crews found the barracks not very pleasant after a full and hard day's training; it was fitted with rows of double bunk beds, portable free-stranding clothes closets, a wood or coal stove to heat the barracks, bare electric light bulbs, and not much else.[369] Many Scribner residents helped to brighten these spartan barracks with loans they negotiated themselves to provide more comfortable furnishings. Scribner bankers issued these loans at no interest; the terms specified the loans to be repaid from local company funds and Officer and Enlisted Club dues. The funds received allowed citizens to purchase and donate furnishings to make the barracks comfortable and livable.[370]

During WWII, Chris Blumm, a Scribner resident, helped maintain morale on the air base by taking his local dance band to the base to perform on special entertainment nights. In addition, the band played each time a group of aircraft arrived for training and when they departed. The band played every Saturday and Sunday night. Blumm played the accordion and was hired by a Fremont, Nebraska, music promoter, and booked for base appearances with the band. Blumm sometimes went solo into the barracks in an effort to brighten up the lives of off duty enlisted personnel.

All that remains of the WWII wooden barracks is a few concrete slab foundations. The long structure in the background is a light civil aircraft hangar. Many concrete foundations at other Nebraska air base sites have been dug up, crushed, and sold for construction fill material. (Author)

A surviving WWII taxiway that remained operational in 1991 and was used for light civil aircraft operations at the airport. (Author)

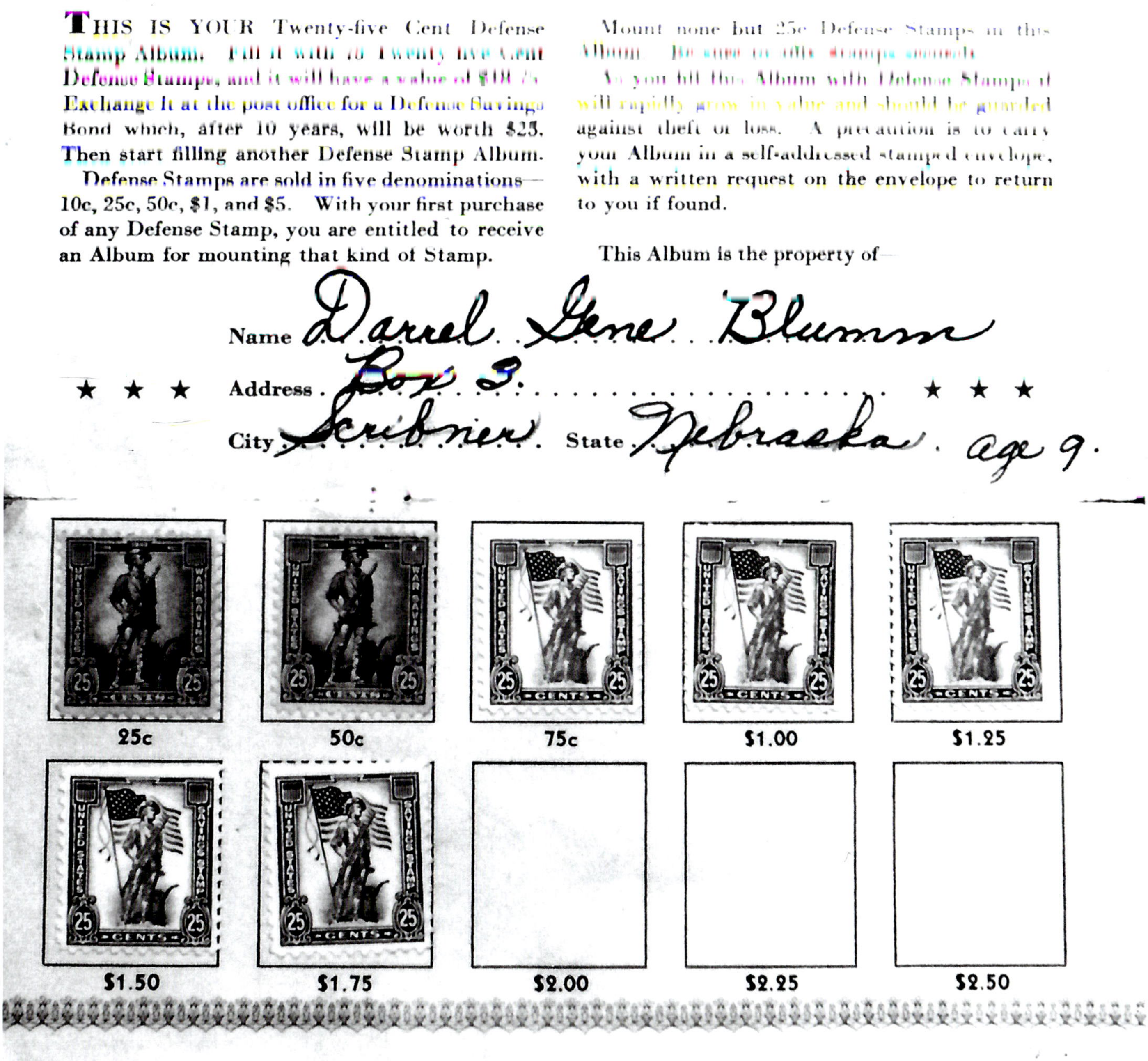

THIS IS YOUR Twenty-five Cent Defense Stamp Album. Fill it with 75 Twenty-five Cent Defense Stamps, and it will have a value of $18.75. Exchange it at the post office for a Defense Savings Bond which, after 10 years, will be worth $25. Then start filling another Defense Stamp Album.

Defense Stamps are sold in five denominations—10c, 25c, 50c, $1, and $5. With your first purchase of any Defense Stamp, you are entitled to receive an Album for mounting that kind of Stamp.

Mount none but 25c Defense Stamps in this Album. Be sure to affix stamps securely.

As you fill this Album with Defense Stamps it will rapidly grow in value and should be guarded against theft or loss. A precaution is to carry your Album in a self-addressed stamped envelope, with a written request on the envelope to return to you if found.

This Album is the property of—

Name Darel Gene Blumm

Address Box 3.

City Scribner State Nebraska. age 9.

25c 50c 75c $1.00 $1.25

$1.50 $1.75 $2.00 $2.25 $2.50

A copy of a WWII Defense Stamp Album to hold stamps toward a United States Defense Savings Bond. The book is in the name of Darel Gene Blumm, nine years old, of Scribner, Nebraska. Most bond books were turned in after the war. Some families kept them as memorabilia of their contributions to the war effort. Courtesy of Chris Blumm.

Frequently, those whom Chris Blumm entertained in the barracks dropped coins and paper money onto a bunk's blanket, where the musician sat playing for them, in appreciation for the music. When back home, Blumm's wife collected the money, dropping it into a glass Mason jar. Their son, Darel, took money out of the Mason jar to purchase War Bond Stamps at his school. From the coins acquired from his dad's music playing in the barracks, Darel bought enough War Bond stamps to pay for his college education in full. This is an important example of residents earning money and giving the funds to pay for the war effort against the Axis powers. Everyone wanted to contribute to winning the war. The country was behind its military and wanted to do something, regardless of its size.

During WWII, not only did Americans purchase War Bonds, but they were also issued United States of America, Office of Price Administration War Ration Books. These were numbered from their date of issue and usage. The books had stamps to be used for different purchases. It is rare to find these books, including a complete set of stamps not used. They reflect part of civilian life on the home front and show citizens were equally important as those fighting and supporting active combat operations. War Ration Books and stamps are shown courtesy of the Kandaras family of Aberdeen, South Dakota.

Army officers who drove to Scribner would bring local girls back to the base for advertised and supervised Saturday night dances at the USO and Officers' Club. The air base commander was very careful, using only screened and selected escorts to drive Army trucks to Scribner and surrounding small communities to transport these girls to and from the air base. Every effort was made to maintain guidelines of decorum for Army personnel.

Chris Blumm played at most of the air base dances, purchasing candy and gum during break periods at the Post Exchange, a privilege given to him and members of his band for their unpaid music service. His son, Darel, became popular

Certificate of Registrar

Stamps must not be detached except in the presence of the retailer, his employee, or person authorized by him to make delivery.

The Stamps contained in this Book are valid only after the lawful holder of this Book has signed the certificate below, and are void if detached contrary to the Regulations. (A father, mother, or guardian may sign the name of a person under 18.) In case of questions, difficulties, or complaints, consult your local Ration Board.

Certificate of Book Holder

I, the undersigned, do hereby certify that I have observed all the conditions and regulations governing the issuance of this War Ration Book; that the "Description of Book Holder" contained herein is correct; that an application for issuance of this book has been duly made by me or on my behalf; and that the statements contained in said application are true to the best of my knowledge and belief.

Any person signing on behalf of Book Holder must sign his or her own name below and indicate relationship to Book Holder

OPA Form No. R-302

UNITED STATES OF AMERICA

War Ration Book One

WARNING

1 Punishments ranging as high as Ten Years' Imprisonment or $10,000 Fine, or Both, may be imposed under United States Statutes for violations thereof arising out of infractions of Rationing Orders and Regulations.
2 This book must not be transferred. It must be held and used only by or on behalf of the person to whom it has been issued, and anyone presenting it thereby represents to the Office of Price Administration, an agency of the United States Government, that it is being so held and so used. For any misuse of this book it may be taken from the holder by the Office of Price Administration.
3 In the event either of the departure from the United States of the person to whom this book is issued, or his or her death, the book must be surrendered in accordance with the Regulations.
4 Any person finding a lost book must deliver it promptly to the nearest Ration Board.

OFFICE OF PRICE ADMINISTRATION

No 173625

68964 CU UNITED STATES OF AMERICA OFFICE OF PRICE ADMINISTRATION

WAR RATION BOOK TWO

IDENTIFICATION

68963 CU UNITED STATES OF AMERICA OFFICE OF PRICE ADMINISTRATION

WAR RATION BOOK TWO

IDENTIFICATION

WARNING

1 This book is the property of the United States Government. It is unlawful to sell or give it to any other person or to use it or permit anyone else to use it, except to obtain rationed goods for the person to whom it was issued.
2 This book must be returned to the War Price and Rationing Board which issued it, if the person to whom it was issued is inducted into the armed services of the United States, or leaves the country for more than 30 days, or dies. The address of the Board appears above.
3 A person who finds a lost War Ration Book must return it to the War Price and Rationing Board which issued it.
4 Persons Who Violate Rationing Regulations Are Subject to $10,000 Fine or Imprisonment, or Both.

OPA Form No. R-121

War Ration Book courtesy of the Kandaras family of Aberdeen, South Dakota, to Author.

at school, sharing highly rationed items with his classmates and friends. When Chris Blumm and the band played on base, each musician had to sign in and out with Military Police at the main gate. The band became popular on the base and were given special treatment. When they played at the Officers' Club, they could order a steak dinner during break between music sessions at no charge, which was a great treat, given the rationing of this high grade cut of meat in the local economy and how much beef was raised in Nebraska. Blumm drove his Model "A" Ford to and from the base. With the end of civilian car production during the war, and after the effects of the Great Depression ended, from 1940 to the end of 1945, there were no new cars to purchase. He often picked up servicemen hitchhiking to and from the air base, sometimes making four round trips in the evening hours. He did this to help the enlisted men, even considering the difficulties in purchasing rationed gasoline. His neighbors pitched in, helping him purchase gasoline for these shuttle trips. His Model "A" kept on running when many other modern cars were up on blocks for lack of spare parts. Blumm was able to tinker and keep his Ford running, patching tires and locating parts in neighbors' garages.

One Saturday evening, Blumm was playing at a small town of Hooper, south of Scribner, instead of his regular weekend appearance on the air base, when an Army Lieutenant went crazy at the bar, striking the band's piano player. The Lieutenant ran into a storage room containing empty glass soda and beer bottles in wood crates. The Lieutenant began throwing wood crates against the wall, breaking hundreds of glass bottles. He kept this up until the Military Police arrived from Scribner AB. The MPs quickly subdued the officer, pushing him into a jeep for the ride back to the base and punishment!

Training on the base sometimes disrupted the everyday lives of local residents. One farmer's house in Pierce was built on a top section of his land, with fields and grazing cattle below. B-17s flying from Scribner AB flew into the valley below the farmer's house, deliberately trying to spook the cattle as gunners fired their .50 caliber machine guns into the creek bed in the valley, which was against all published training procedures and rules. The farmer called the base, reporting the .50 caliber machine gun fire to the appropriate Squadron Commander. The commander got off the phone with the farmer, drove out to the flight line, and waited for the offending crew to land. This was not a pleasant encounter by that crew with their commander.

B-17s dropped one hundred pound inert practice bombs filled with flour into creek beds, to give bombardiers simulated, live ordnance training. Local farmers and ranchers watched these aircraft drop the flour bombs, riding horses or tractors to the creek beds and looking for intact flour sack bombs or partially intact flour bombs. They picked up this rationed item before their cattle could eat the flour, taking it back to their wives. They also picked up any metal from the split-open bombs, to prevent their cattle from digesting the metal when eating the flour. The farmers also cleaned up the flour to prevent any spoiled flour from sickening their cattle. However, sometimes they were unable to locate all the flour bombs and cattle got sick; many died from spoiled flour and internal injuries from metal fragments. Scribner AB's legal department was busy with farmers' claims of loss of cattle due to .50 caliber machine gun wounds or from being hit by ricocheting rounds; ingesting spoiled flour and metal bomb fragments; and broken legs from running when spooked by low flying aircraft and .50 caliber machine gun fire. Cattle were a valuable wartime resource needed to feed the U.S. military, its allies, and civil population. Farmers carried notebooks to write down tail numbers of the offending low flying bombers over their farms, documenting losses and damage to Scribner AB command authorities. The claims were paid, with aircrews fined to pay for damages. It did not take too long before these low-level offenses ended and crews quickly learned to use specified bombing and gunnery ranges.[371]

Operation runway at Scribner Airport. As a note on this and many of the photographs taken at Nebraska airports: in 1991, one could walk around these airports onto seldom used runways or up to fenced areas and take photographs without the sudden appearance of security officers asking what you were doing, which today is a part of airport operations after the combined terrorist attacks against the United States on September 1, 2001. After these attacks, the whole world changed and these photographs are part of an earlier history that is hard to come by with all the restrictions of today's airport security procedures. (Author)

A view of a remaining WWII asphalt service road on Scribner. In 1991, grass was growing up to the edges of the road and up through cracks in the roadway. (Author)

The AAF worked through the Army Corps of Engineers, Omaha District to assist in setting up a camouflage school on base. This was covered in the introduction.[372] There were two permanently assigned units on the air base: the 393rd BG and 22nd Fighter Squadron (FS). The 393rd BG consisted of the 580th, 581st, 582nd, and 583rd BS.

These four squadrons flew B-17s as an OTU until 1 August 1943. The 22nd FS operated from the air base from 26 November 1943 to March 1944, flying P-47s.[373] The P-47 was classified as a heavy, single-engine fighter. Beginning in January, 1944, Scribner's P-47s conducted aerial intercepts and a combination of escort and intercept training missions against B-29 groups

Aerial view of Scribner Air Base, 1943. Courtesy of Nebraska State Historical Society.

training in Nebraska. The P-47 performed similar to Japanese fighters defending the Japanese home islands. P-47 pilots completed Phase III training while at Scribner AB: air-to-ground gunnery, day and night navigation flights, instrument flying, and aerial and camera gunnery.[374]

As the war continued, the activity at Scribner AB never reached the levels of other Nebraska air bases. In June 1944, the Fremont Chamber of Commerce sent a letter to Lieutenant Colonel Delbert, Director, U.S. Army Corps of Engineers, Omaha District, requesting information on why Scribner AB was not being used to full capacity when millions of dollars were being spent on other U.S. training bases or to build additional air bases. The Fremont Chamber of Commerce asked if some of the land on the air base could be returned to the former owners who had never been satisfactorily compensated, according to the farmers and landowners, but were paid only for their land and not any improvements or loss of income for their land and destruction of property.[375]

On 15 November 1944, Scribner AB went into standby status, and on 22 November it was declared surplus federal property. In January 1946, the Department of War Assets Administration began selling buildings and equipment on the base. The Nebraska Department of Aeronautics took over management and responsibility for 2,400 acres of the air base.

In 1951, after the U.S. became involved in the war in Korea, rumors came from USAF officers in the Pentagon that Scribner was being considered as one of a series of locations for the USAF Academy campus. However, Colorado's Congressional members had more political clout and the academy was built at Colorado Springs, Colorado, with initial classes held at Lowry AFB in Denver.

In 1956, civilian light aircraft hangars were built on the parking apron at Scribner. From 1948-1956, local residents could rent barracks as private residences, for fifteen dollars a month plus utilities. The rent was based on accepting the buildings as they were, with renters responsible for any remodeling and adapting the barracks for civilian accommodation. In 1960, the USAF operated a communications facility there. In 1992, it became a receiver site.[376]

CHAPTER SIXTEEN
SIOUX CITY AIR BASE

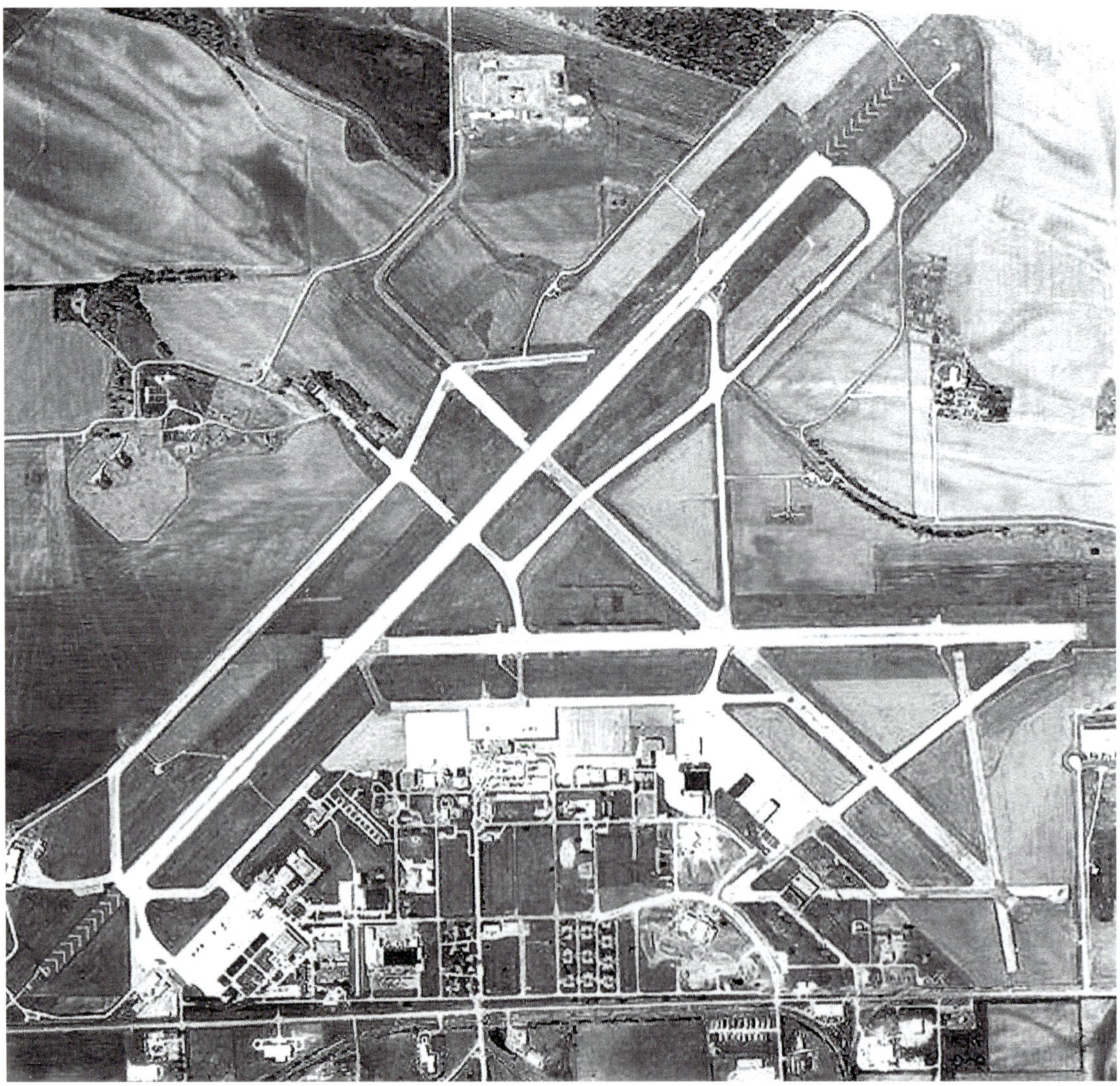

Sioux City, Iowa, Sioux Gateway Airport. Courtesy of United States Geological Survey

WWII fighter-size hangar with a modern FAA control tower visible behind the hangar (1991). (Author)

Air Base History

Scribner AB was controlled by Sioux City AB, in Sioux City, Iowa, located south of Sioux Falls, SD, and east of the northeast corner of Nebraska. Many of its WWII buildings survived long after their expected life span of five to seven years. The buildings on this base are representative of the temporary wooden buildings constructed throughout the great plains during the second world war.

Construction work started at Sioux City AB in March 1942. The base consisted of one concrete runway (13/31), 9,002 feet long and 150 feet wide, and one asphalt runway (17/35), 2,012 feet long and 150 feet wide. Construction was finished on the 2,460-acre air base 5 July 1942. The base trained B-17 and B-24 aircrews, and directed training activities at satellite air bases, such as Scribner in Nebraska. The host (or directing) unit at the air base was the 345th AAFB unit, supporting the 393rd Combat Training School, later becoming the 224th Combat Crew Training School in 1944. In October 1943, the air base supported 940 officers and enlisted personnel and provided training on aerial gunnery, navigation, formation flying, and advanced aircrew courses.

During 1943, training at the air base prepared a complete bomb group organization for overseas combat duty. As sufficient bomb groups trained for combat duty with the Eighth Air Force in England, training transitioned to preparing individual crews as replacements or additions to existing bomb

A large aircraft hangar at the Sioux City airport. The photograph from the back shows the administrative offices on the side of the hangar with repair shops along the back. The hangar was constructed with wooden framing covered by metal roofing and siding. The hangar survived many years after the end of WWII. (Author)

groups. B-17 aircrew training continued until May 1945; at this time, when B-29 aircrews began training. The base was controlled by the 17th Bombardment Training Wing for B-29 transition training. By June 1945, only ten B-29s were at the base and the war ended in the Pacific before the base could fully implement the B-29 aircrew training program. The base then became a processing center to discharge returning military personnel into civilian life. However, unlike many other air bases after WWII, the complex continued to support civilian and military operations. Today, the airport supports commercial and general aviation, along with the Iowa Air National Guard's 185th Air Refueling Wing, assigned to the Air Mobility Command, and flying the Boeing KC-135 Stratotanker.[377]

In 1991, the author was able to take a rare photograph of some of the remaining wreckage from United Airlines Flight 232. On July 19, 1989, a UAL DC-10 on a flight from Denver, Colorado to Philadelphia, with a stopover at Chicago, crashed at Sioux Gateway Airport while attempting to make an emergency landing when the aircraft suffered nearly total loss of control. The crash killed 112 passengers and one crewmember, with 184 passengers and 10 crewmembers surviving, including the pilot, Captain Al Haynes. (Author)

Many former WWII buildings on the air base completely changed roles. During the war, this building was the air base's hospital complex. After equipment was removed, the building remained vacant until being used to store furniture for a Sioux City furniture company. (Author)

One of the few buildings on the former WWII air base that did not change functions was the base chapel. It was painted and remodeled, and continues to serve as a house of worship. It was converted from a barracks floor plan with the door at one end and the addition of a steeple and windows on both sides of the building. (Author)

Former base headquarters building. (Author)

In 1991, this area of wood warehouses provided support for Army Quartermaster Corps personnel. (Author)

A WWII squadron aircraft parts storage building near the air base's hangar row. (Author)

A 1960s era diesel locomotive with USAF markings parked on a rail spur line behind one of the warehouses. The locomotive was used to supply USAF missile sites in the area, including those in Nebraska. (Author)

Shop and maintenance area on the air base. (Author)

Modernized fire station annex currently used to store fire equipment at Sioux Gateway Airport. (Author)

Warehouse area supported by rail spur lines behind each warehouse with a separate dock for unloading. (Author)

A two-story barracks building next to a single-story barracks. (Author)

CHAPTER SEVENTEEN

THE WAR EFFORT AND POSTERS

Posters such as *Battle Stations!* informed Americans how they could help shorten the war. The Fisher Body Division, General Motors Corporation, created the poster in 1942. Many posters directly tied home front production to success on the war front. These posters helped turn employees into "production soldiers" or "factory combatants." No longer were employees working just for their factory or company, they were now working for Uncle Sam. The poster is from "Produce for Victory, Posters on the American Home Front, 1941-1945," part of "Museum on Main Street," a partnership of the Smithsonian and State Humanities Councils nationwide in service of rural America. Posters on display at the South Dakota Air and Space Museum, Ellsworth AFB, July 4-August 8, 2003. Subsequent posters are from same source unless noted. (Author)

To train men and women for war and produce aircraft, munitions, and food for WWII, the AAF and War Department conducted a peaceful invasion and occupation of great plains communities, creating a booming wartime economy. These towns' economies slowed and for many citizens declined after the end of the war on 15 August 1945, slowly recovering from, but not returning to, the disaster of the 1930s.

During WWII, it is estimated that over 10,000 AAF flight personnel, 5,000 glider pilots, and 4,500 Air Transport Command aircrew members, along with thousands of airborne glider infantrymen and paratroopers, including mechanics, trained in the great plains. German and Italian POWs were here and the home front efforts of Nebraska helped fight and win the war against the Axis powers. The dropping of the atomic bombs on Hiroshima and Nagasaki, by modified B-29s assigned to the 509th CG flying from North Field, Tinian Island, helped

The demands of WWII required industry to shift from manufacturing consumer goods to producing war material. A fundamental change in workers' and managers' attitudes, from antagonism to cooperation, was required to produce the needed supply of armaments. The government launched a promotional campaign encouraging workers and managers to take personal responsibility and to make individual sacrifices to help win the war. Individual companies and labor units soon followed suit.

Come on, Gang! We're Building Arms For Victory! Poster created by Pontiac Motors Division, General Motors Corporation, 1943.

convince the Imperial Japanese military, cabinet members, and Emperor to accept the Allied terms of unconditional surrender.

The federal government had a large and far-reaching program to urge maximum efforts on the home front that was rapidly accepted by war industries, displayed in factories, and in virtually every town in America during the war. To bring back the history of patriotic posters during WWII, the Smithsonian Institution and State Humanities Councils sponsored a traveling exhibit of posters on the WWII effort, "Produce for Victory, Posters on the American Home Front, 1941-1945." WWII posters helped mobilize a nation that faced a long and terrible war on two fronts. They were inexpensive to produce and displayed everywhere. Posters were the perfect way to inform Americans how they could help their country and their soldiers overseas win the war. Federal agencies, businesses, and private organizations created poster images that linked the war "over there" to the home front, inspiring Americans of all ages to do their part. Every effort was made to produce more for the war. The United States, especially Nebraska, shifted efforts to switch to a full war economy. The

One objective of wartime poster art was to increase factory production by encouraging employees to work harder and faster. The Pontiac Motor Division used a poster of its prewar car production line to impress its workers that as they did producing civilian cars before the war, the transformation of assembly lines to war production was equally important. Consequently, war posters communicated this importance and much more. Production incentive posters enlarged people's view of their wartime responsibility, helped create a shared sense of sacrifice, and increased output. Uniting the powers of art and advertising, poster campaigns were the ideal medium to inform and persuade. Posters hung everywhere in war plants: production lines, lunchrooms, wash rooms, and on almost every blank wall space to increase war production to win the war.

Great Depression stressed their lives, setting up the sacrifices during the war years 1941-1945. The poster exhibit toured twenty-three states and 128 cities from September 1994 until April 10, 2007.

Even though the primary objective of wartime posters was to increase factory productivity by encouraging employees to work harder and faster, they also communicated much more. Production incentive posters encouraged workers and their families to commit to the war effort, highlighting their responsibilities and creating a shared sense of common sacrifice.

Uniting the powers of graphic art and color advertising, poster campaigns were the ideal print medium to inform and attempt to persuade Americans to work harder and make sacrifices for the war effort. Along with rationing, Nebraska's citizens were well educated and motivated to collect scrap metal for the war effort. The scrap metal collected was to be melted into ingots for use in weapons and equipment manufacturing for the war effort. Paper was recycled for packing material to prevent war-produced goods from being damaged. Even grease was saved from civilian homes and

Campfire girls in Omaha, Nebraska, collecting scrap metal for the war effort in September 1942. Courtesy of Nebraska State Historical Society

restaurants, collected, and shipped to munitions plants for explosives and synthetic rubber production.

Nothing was thrown away in America during the war. Repairmen were a vital part of the war effort, keeping old appliances running because new ones were unavailable, with newly produced appliances going to equip stateside military bases. Limited production made it difficult to equip these bases with minimal amounts of appliances. After the war, federal surplus auctions at former WWII military bases sold refrigerators, washers, stoves (cooking and heating), water heaters, coal and gas furnaces, lights, furniture, clothes, sheets and blankets, wood for building homes, and barracks and wood buildings that could be dismantled or moved for private homes and businesses. Four years of war restrictions and sacrifices for the war effort created a huge pent-up demand for consumer goods of all types, starting inflation after removal of price and wage controls. Americans had sacrificed to win the war and wanted a better life after living through the Great Depression and WWII.

Colorful posters attempted to show Americans how they could unite and pull together to win the war against Germany,

In 1943, as WWII continued, posters showing African-American airmen were printed as pilots entered combat. The Tuskegee Airmen quickly earned a reputation that when they escorted bomber formations in their P-51s, there were no bomber losses to attacking enemy fighters. The posters featuring African-American pilots showed that the pressures of war opened jobs, military service, and opportunity as never before.

Billboards, radio, and movies were prevalent means of communication in the 1940s, and wartime posters could reach many Americans. The U.S. Office of War Information (OWI) established a national network of volunteers to distribute posters to factories, offices, schools, community centers, post offices, railroad and bus stations, stores, restaurants, and hotel lobbies. Americans could buy war bonds everywhere and there were great efforts to fund the expensive war around the world. School children could buy stamps for war bonds in their schools, indicating that even the smallest amounts added to the war effort.

A scrap drive was run by Junior Commando Boy Scouts in Lincoln, Nebraska, during WWII. Courtesy of Nebraska State Historical Society.

Scrap drives were important to the war effort. Courtesy of Nebraska State Historical Society.

Italy, and Japan. Posters attempted to indicate home front war production activities as sources for winning the war. The terms coined were creating "Production Soldiers" and "factory combatants" to urge full production to maximize support for soldiers, airmen, Marines, and civilians in combat theaters around the world. This was a two-ocean war, covering areas involving millions of Americans and her Allies.

Before the bombing of Pearl Harbor, as the United States slowly moved to a war industrial base to support Lend Lease in the middle of 1941, the Museum of Modern Art advertised a National Defense Poster Competition to create a large pool of poster designs. The competition was designed to give local artists in communities throughout the United States a chance to showcase their creativity and ability to contribute to the United States' growing involvement to counter the military threat from the Axis powers.

Scrap drives were lifted to importance in boosting morale for the state, as well as providing essential products for the war effort. Citizens collected tin foil from chewing gum wrappers, making a tin foil ball until it reached a size large enough to be accepted at a collection site. Scrap paper was more easily collected and used to pack munitions and delicate production equipment, such as electronics, medicine, and blood. Grease was also collected and recycled into war production. The importance of scrap drives was one of civilian morale. In a 1942 scrap drive, the *Omaha World Herald* reported that the state reached 111 percent of its assigned quota, ranking Nebraska as 14th in the nation. Copper was withdrawn from the money supply, with pennies becoming zinc-coated steel by 1943.[379]

In 1943, a Works Progress Administration (WPA) handbook entitled *How to Make and Reproduce Posters* simplified the serial production of color posters and declared that "Anyone can make a poster." The made-by-all possibilities and seen-by-all accessibility of posters promoted the democratic ideals of a nation and reinforced America's war aims: why we fight and what we fight for. Posters encouraged all citizens to participate in the war effort in every possible way.

Hollywood filmmaker Frank Capra produced the *Why We Fight* movies, shown in movie theaters throughout the United States. Comments taken from posters advertising these movies follow:

Because of the military's priority on produced manufactured goods, there were home front shortages of most every essential item. Those living in the United States were urged to support the war effort by eating less at meals, collecting scrap metal that could be made into bombs, and by car pooling, thereby cutting the amount of gasoline consumed in the United States so that more fuel was available for defense.

Posters were displayed everywhere to create voluntary changes in personal lifestyles. With the official policy of government rationing, to provide maximum support for America's military and its Allies, it was important that posters made statements that everyone was equal in the war effort.

In federal patriotic phrasing, "The made-by-all possibilities and seen-by-all accessibility of posters promoted the democratic ideals of the United States, reinforcing the nation's war aims of why we fight and what we fight for."

War posters promoted workers to produce in order to give America's soldiers the weapons to fight the enemy.

The Nazi Strike. See Hitler's troops stomp Europe. Brutal enemy footage, captured after their conquests in Europe, reveals the atrocities of the Nazi war machine witnessed in the invasion and capture of Austria, Czechoslovakia, and Poland.

The Battle of Britain. Documents the brutal air attacks that England suffered. Incredible air combat scenes and a prologue for Winston Churchill makes this unforgettable.

Prelude to War. The events that lead to world to World War II present chaos in Germany and Europe. See Hitler and his Nazi Party take control of Germany. Witness the rise of Fascism and the takeover of Italy and Ethiopia. Incredible scenes of the Japanese invading Manchuria.

Divide and Conquer. The German conquest of Belgium, Holland, Denmark and Norway. Watch Germans invade France and occupy the country. The British are defeated at Dunkirk.

The Battle of Russia. The battle of Stalingrad is a turning point. Russians stop the Nazi onslaught in one of the most dramatic and bloody battles in history.

War Comes to America Shows why America got involved and our fight to first help our allies and then our ultimate fight for survival. An incredible conclusion to the series.

The great plains contributed to winning the war with its food production. Families who did not live in the rural part of the region—the area comprising most of the land—became committed and involved in hands on agriculture, part of the federal government's *Victory Garden* program. Citizens living in small towns and larger metropolitan areas were encouraged to plant gardens to make up for the loss of food to rationing.

In 1943, over 50 percent of the fresh vegetables grown and produced in the United States were picked from Victory Gardens. Many citizens canned food for use through non-growing months of cold weather and snow. This allowed home meals to be more varied and abundant, and supplemented ration purchased food items. Demand quickly resulted in a shortage of glass canning jars, metal caps, and rubber seals. Cellars, attics, garages, and warehouses were searched for this suddenly valuable commodity. Just as chopping

Americans greatly contributed to winning the war with their food production. Even families who did not live in the rural part of the country, comprising most of the land, became committed and involved in hands-on agriculture, as part of the federal government's *Victory Garden* program. Citizens living in small towns and larger metropolitan areas were encouraged to plant gardens to make up for the loss from food rationing.

The demands of WWII required industry to shift from manufacturing consumer goods to producing war material. This photograph is of steelworkers on break, with war posters nearby, outside Columbia Steel Company, United States Steel Corporation, in Pittsburg, California, in 1942.

wood was a chore for providing heat for homes, canning provided food.

For most Americans, their first sign of the war's impact was the implementation of rationing of more than twenty essential items. The first item to be rationed in the United States was sugar, followed by coffee and shoes. Many farmers switched to growing sugar beets, which could be processed into a reasonable tasting sugar substitute similar to granular sugar. Many farmers bartered homegrown sugar beets processed into sugar for scarce manufactured goods available in towns, but in short supply on farms and ranches. Residents were given ration books at their local schools. In combination with price controls, rationing was the government's attempt to distribute scarce food and manufactured goods as equally as possible, while controlling inflation and not hurting the war effort.

With the strikes and violent labor disputes of the 1930s still fresh in everyone's memory, manufacturers used the wartime changes in production as an opportunity to gain greater control over their workers. Factory managers called for employees to suspend union rules, take shorter breaks, and strive for perfect attendance. Posters that played on workers' guilt and their sense of duty blended traditional themes of workplace discipline with imagery of sacrifice and patriotism.

The demands of WWII required American industry to rapidly and painfully shift from manufacturing consumer goods to war materials. Because of the Japanese attack on Pearl Harbor and declaration of war against the Japanese Empire, followed by war being declared by Germany and Italy on the United States in support of Japan, long time labor management relations had to change. This was a fundamental change in industrial workers' and unions' combative attitude toward management and arguments over wages and safety limits to one of mutual cooperation to work long hours and jobs at fixed wages to ramp up production to meet expanding war requirements.

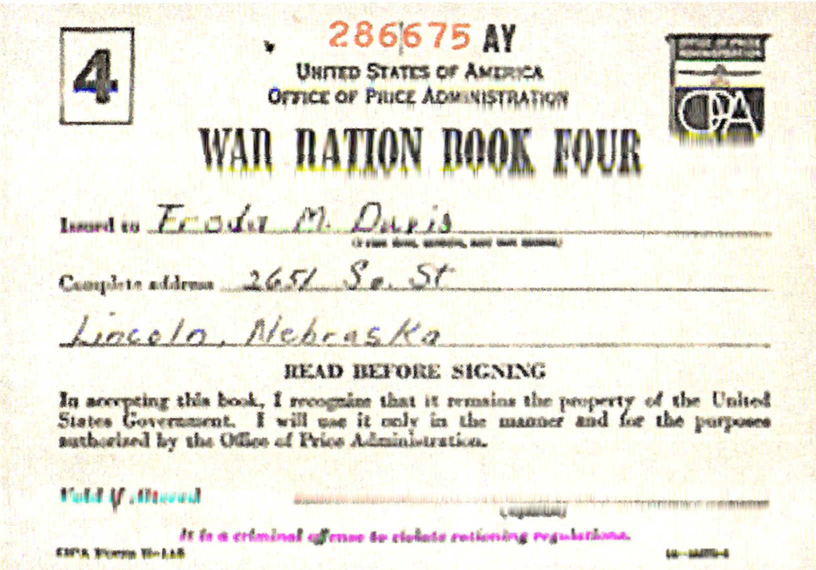

WWII ration book issued to Freda M. Davis, of Lincoln, Nebraska. Courtesy of Nebraska State Historical Society

It was every American's patriotic duty to support the wartime economy by buying responsibly, but posters advocating self sacrifice, conservation, and thrift often discouraged spending. Some retailers turned to posters of surrealistic fantasy to prompt their customers to spend in order to protect America from a grim future. Warning against inflation, the Office of Economic Stabilization encouraged homemakers to avoid paying black market prices for food and other items.

The Office of Price of Administration regulated prices to prevent businesses from gouging American consumers, already sacrificing to support the war effort. The Federal government [illegible] many products previously available in abundance, if they had money to purchase them, with many just starting to recover from the Great Depression, able to pay for some luxuries. Residents were issued ration books containing coupons that could only be redeemed when authorized to purchase available rationed items. Many times, even with ration coupons allowing purchase of an item, might not be available. This was a hardship throughout the war. Once you were out of ration coupons for a product, no more were issued until the next ration book period. Local ration boards were established in every community and staffed by volunteers from the community. These local boards decided who should receive items exceeding established federal allowance guidelines under unusual circumstances. The Office of Price Administration issued tokens, many of which were colored wood disks for purchase of rationed goods. The author found a metal can full of these wooden disks when taking care of his father during the last year of his life. Interestingly, it was up to the consumer to be honest when using coupons, wood disks, or points when purchasing rationed items. Most in Nebraska followed the rules, with few reported incidents of black marketing, although there was considerable bartering of goods, as previously shown with sugar.

With millions of men in the U.S. armed forces during the war, the burden picking up the resulting slack fell to women to take jobs of men in factories and workplaces not previously readily opened to women. Many labor short companies created colorful and imaginative posters to attract women to apply for their vacant war jobs. There was still a level of discrimination, in that women were not hired for managerial or supervisory positions. The Omaha-Martin bomber plant broke the glass

With so many men in the U.S. armed forces during the war, it fell to the women of America to fill the employment void in factories and other workplaces. Many companies' labor management committees created posters like We *Can Do It* that seemed to encourage and empower women. However, this empowerment was narrowly defined; women were encouraged to follow orders and work hard, but to defer decision making to male supervisors and managers.

ceiling, although only with a limited number of women hired and assigned to upper management positions.

The federal government created the U.S. Office of War Information (OWI), in 1942, to control the content and imagery of war messages and posters created to raise patriotism of America's workers and civilians. As with any new program, an open conflict arose as to how to best reach this goal. OWI artists and graphic designers wanted to use sophisticated, abstract, and highly stylized designs to convey the government's message for an all out war effort. On the opposite side, OWI advertising specialists opted for a more straightforward, positive, usually considered superficial look at the home front. The decision was made to follow the traditional approach, in that federal government posters followed period magazine type appearance. This was more familiar to the majority of Americans. OWI managers believed the artistic and stylized war posters could not be correctly interpreted by the average American citizen.

OWI advertising specialists opted for a straightforward, positive, usually considered superficial look at the home front. The decision was made to follow the traditional approach, in that federal government posters followed period magazine type appearance, This was more familiar to the majority of Americans. OWI managers believed the artistic and stylized war posters could not be correctly interpreted by the average American citizen.

By 1943, war posters looked more like advertisements appearing in *Life Magazine*. OWI took one more step, using posters tied to magazine, radio, and other paid print advertising. According to artists and media consultants, messages of American personal sacrifice and struggle were translated into posters of bright colors, smiling faces, and those depicting scenes of efficient victory homes. Every effort was made to use advertising to sell the importance of supporting the war.

Poster depictions of America's home front soldiers were carefully crafted. Designers used an average Joe to personify America workers in order to gain the common man's allegiance to wartime production goals. Women in the work place were shown as young, white, middle-class women with glamorous good looks. This fashion model image was chosen to assure women that they would not sacrifice their attractiveness for war work.

By 1943, war posters looked more like advertisements appearing in *Life Magazine*. OWI took one more step, using posters tied to magazine, radio, and other paid print advertising. According to artists and media consultants, messages of American personal sacrifice and struggle were translated into posters of bright colors, smiling faces, and those depicting scenes of efficient victory homes. Every effort was made to use advertising to sell the importance of supporting the war.

Gasoline rationing hit America hard, considering the large open spaces and travel distances in the state. Each motorist was issued a vehicle windshield sticker with the appropriate letter of priority from "A" to "C." Trucks received a special "T" sticker. Most of those living in the state were issued an "A" sticker, allowing them to purchase three to five gallons of gasoline per week. The government rationed gasoline in an effort to save gasoline and tires, because the Japanese conquests shut off supplies of raw rubber from the Far East. Speed limits were reduced to a maximum of 35mph, which reduced gasoline consumption and wear on tires. If a sticker holder was ticketed for speeding this affected future gasoline sticker issue. Farmers

Posters were designed to not only get the American worker to increase production, but to impress on them the prevailing period's social, economic, and political ideals. However, this had a central or centrist theme in imagery celebrating or depicting the white, middle-class home, the traditional nuclear family, and consumerism and the free enterprise American system. These propaganda posters offered or presented a look at American life expected in the postwar world with images of men and women that fit these assumptions.

Even with urgings by these posters, rationing had the greatest impact on America's citizens. Windshield stickers were used to provide gasoline purchases. Courtesy of Nebraska State Historical Society

and ranchers were issued a lower grade of gasoline for their tractors and equipment. Spare parts were a constant problem. Local machinists fabricated replacement parts to keep autos, trucks, tractors, and machinery operating.

During the war, the author's mother and sister in Altoona, Iowa, turned their yard into one big garden, harvesting vegetables for canning. They had a large corner room in the basement where these canned items were stored on shelves. They continued to can well into the 1950s, afraid that the Cold War in Korea would expand to another world war, along with the restart of rationing and food shortages.

The federal government constantly bombarded the American public that it was their patriotic duty to actively support the wartime economy by buying responsibly, but on the opposite side, posters advocated self sacrifice, conservation, and thrift and actually discouraged spending. Retailers countered by creating their own in store posters, urging customers to buy their products to prevent a return to the effects and life of the Great Depression. In response to prevent inflation from spending by workers with excess money, the Office of Economic Stabilization designed posters encouraging Americans not to spend their money freely, putting off purchases and not to buy goods on the black market. It took the famous photograph of Marines raising the American flag, on Mount Surabachi on Iwo Jima, to return feelings of patriotism and increase war bond sales. America was war weary and the reports of casualties from the Pacific were causing fear that an entire American generation would die in the Pacific.

We'll Have Lots to Eat This Winter Won't We mother? by Ale Parker, of the U.S. Officer of War Information.

August 16, 1945 *Schuyler Sun*.

The Schuyler Sun

War Ends; Japanese Surrender

With the passage of time since 1945—65 years, as the author wrote this account in 2010—the story of AAF efforts in Nebraska, along with war production, personal sacrifices, and more is more of a footnote to history than real events. Greater attention is given to the battles during the war than training and equipping for these battles. Wood frame buildings originally designed to last five to seven years during WWII numbered in the thousands, dwindling today to but a few. When the authror traveled through Nebraska from 1988-1991, many of these were in sad shape, with others gone, and more today are disappearing. He wanted to take photographs and record these facilities before they were completely gone. This is a tribute and a salute to the "Greatest Generation of Americans." The author served in the Air Force during the Cold War and today, and hopes this story will enforce the statement of military sacrifice of America's military today around the world and that *Freedom is not Free!*

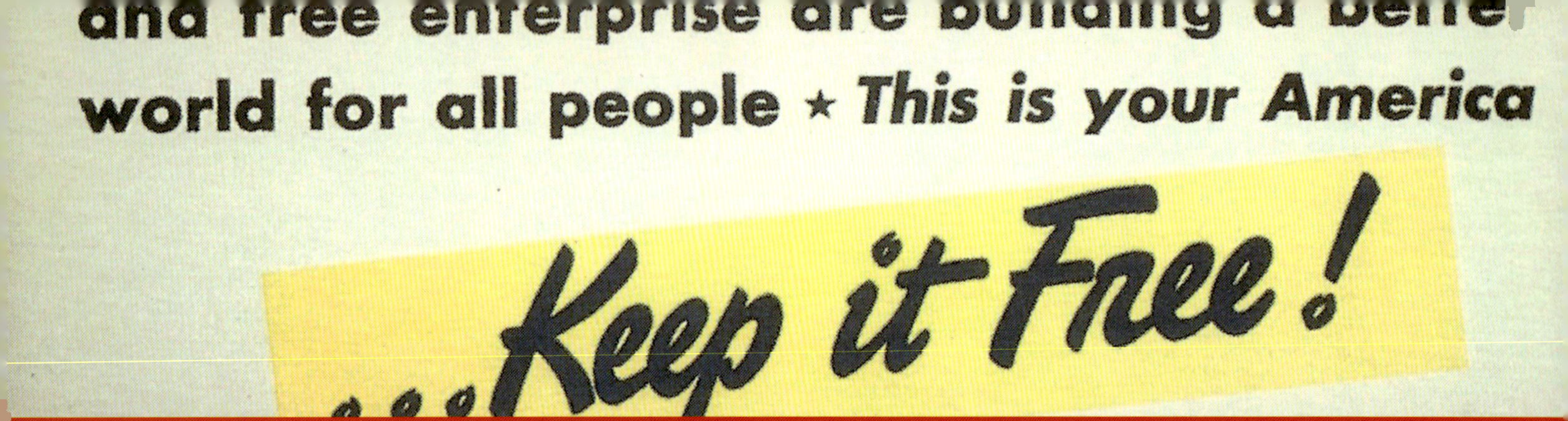

END NOTES

Introduction

1 Wesley Frank Craven and James Lea Cate, ed. *The Army Air Forces in World War II*, Volume six, *Men and Planes* (Washington, DC: Office of Air Force History, 1983), 600-607.

2 "What did you do in the war?" Exhibit, Nebraska State Historical Society, Lincoln, Nebraska, December 8, 1991.

3 Craven

4 *McCook Army Air Base* (McCook, Nebraska: McCook Army Air Base Historical Society.)

5 "Produce for victory, Posters on the American home front, 1941-1945," Washington, DC: Smithsonian Institution and State Humanities Council traveling display, South Dakota Air and Space Museum, Ellsworth Air Force Base, South Dakota.

6 "What did you do in the war?"

7 *POWs in Cheyenne County, 1943-1946*, Sidney High Historical Society, May 11, 1980. Lincoln, Nebraska: Nebraska State Historical Society.

8 Tom Bueker. Interview, Fort Robinson, Nebraska, Lieutenant Colonel George A. Larson, USAF, August 19, 1991.

9 Department of the U.S. Army, "Army Air Corps Fields," Omaha, Nebraska: Corps of Engineers, Omaha District to Lieutenant Colonel George A. Larson, USAF, May 16, 1991.

10 Craven (see end note 1), 456-457.

11 "What did you do in the war?"

12 Lorena Smith, Hastings, Nebraska to Lieutenant Colonel George A. Larson, USAF, June 1990.

13 Headquarters Second Air Force, "Emergency construction for Second Air Force accelerated program," Fort George Wright, Spokane, Washington.

14 Ibid

15 Lieutenant Colonel George A. Larson, USAF, "Steam Locomotive across the plains of Nebraska" *Mit der Dampflok durch die Ebenen von Nebraska, Nebraska-Nachrichten*, January 1992.

16 Department of the U.S. Army

17 "What did you do in the war?"

Chapter 1

18 Ainsworth Chamber of Commerce, "Middle of nowhere, welcome to Ainsworth, Nebraska," Ainsworth, Nebraska.

19 War Department, "Acquisition of Land," Washington, DC: Chief of Engineers, U.S. Army, Field No. 601.1, Ainsworth, Nebraska, September 14, 1942.

20 "Work on bomber field nicely started," The Ainsworth (NE) Star-Journal, Ainsworth, Nebraska, September 10, 1942.

21 "Ainsworth airfield important part of national war effort," Ainsworth (NE) Star-Journal, Ainsworth, Nebraska, June 23, 1983, 2H-3H.

22 "Satellite Field, Ainsworth, Nebraska, construction program," Headquarters Second Air Force, Office of the Commanding General, Fort George Wright, Washington, November 30, 1942.

23 "Progress of temporary construction, Second Air Force OTU station, Ainsworth, Nebraska," Washington, DC: Headquarters Second Air Force, August 19, 1942.

24 "Ainsworth airfield important part of national war effort." *Ainsworth (NE) Star-Journal.*

25 "Precision bombing and air-ground gunnery ranges for Ainsworth Field, Nebraska," Washington, DC: War Department, Office of the Chief of Engineers, Ainsworth, Nebraska, 2 November 1942.

26 "Camouflage instruction building, Ainsworth, Nebraska, airfield," Headquarters Second Air Force, Office of the Commanding General, Fort George Wright, Washington, 31 March 1943.

27 "Transmittal of request for new construction," Headquarters Second Air Force, Fort George Wright, Washington, 12 May 1943.

28 "Combat area hangars are manufactured in Omaha," *Sunday World-Herald Magazine*, Omaha, Nebraska, July 4, 1943, 4 C.
29 "Status of Army airfield, Ainsworth, Nebraska," Headquarters Army Airfield, Ainsworth, Nebraska, April 6, 1944.
30 "City takes over Ainsworth airfield today, October 24, 1946," Ainsworth (NE) Star-Journal, Ainsworth, Nebraska, June 23, 1983, 3H.
31 KBR News, Ainsworth, Nebraska, March 1989.
32 Ibid

Chapter 2
33 Lawrence H. Larson, "The Alliance Army Air Base case," Nebraska History, Fall 1986, 239.
34 Robert W. Lang, *Short Story, Smorgas Board* (Freeman, South Dakota: Pine Hill Press, 1986), 51-52.
35 Centennial Committee, "City of Alliance and Box Battle County (Nebraska)", Dallas, TX: Curtis Media Corporation, 1988, 28.
36 Larson, 240.
37 Rusty Reno, "Construction begins," Alliance (NE) Times-Herald, Alliance, Nebraska, June 25, 1976 (special historic issue), 1.
38 Sgt. Bill Davidson, AAF, "Alliance Air Base, training ground for airborne troops who get there first with the best punch," Alliance, Nebraska, Knights Museum.
39 "Major construction work has been going on for several weeks," Alliance (NE) Times-Herald, Alliance, Nebraska, June 1942, 1.
40 Centennial Committee
41 Ibid
42 "Nazi village in western Nebraska," Omaha Sunday-Herald, Omaha, Nebraska, June 6, 1943, 4cc.
43 Centennial Committee
44 George Brennan, "Short Bursts," Glider Museum News (Terrill, Texas: July/August 1991), 5.
45 *A brief history of the combat glider in World War II*, Yaki-Wall Company, 1990.
46 Milton Drake, *The Glider Gang: An Eyewitness History of World War II* (New York: J.B. Lippincott Company, 1977), 59.
47 Centennial Committee
48 Robert Breck to Lieutenant Colonel George A. Larson, USAF, October 29, 1991.
49 Douglas E. Smith to Lieutenant Colonel George A. Larson, USAF, July 17, 1991.
50 Smith
51 Frank L. Kehr to Lieutenant Colonel George A. Larson, USAF, June 18, 1991.
52 Roger L. Airgood, "Recollections of the first day at Alliance Army Air Base, June 12, 1943," to Lieutenant Colonel George A. Larson, June 12, 1991.
53 Robert C. Richards to Lieutenant Colonel George A. Larson, USAF, June 3, 1991.
54 Airgood
55 Mauer Mauer, *Aviation in the U.S. Army, 1919-1939* (Washington, DC: United States Air Force, 1987), 390-391.
56 Knights Museum
57 Airgood
58 Thomas L. Morris to Lieutenant Colonel George A. Larson, USAF, July 15, 1991.
59 440th Troop Carrier Association, "Long road to invasion," to Lieutenant Colonel George A. Larson, USAF, June 22, 1991.
60 Bill Humphrey to Lieutenant Colonel George A. Larson, USAF, September 9, 1991.
61 "Alliance base under command of 2nd Air Force on Sept 1st," Montgomery, Alabama: United States Air Force Historical Research Center, Maxwell Air Force Base, June 1990.
62 State Historic Preservation Office, Nebraska State Historical Society, Lincoln, Nebraska to Lieutenant Colonel George A. Larson, USAF, May 25, 1991.

Chapter 3
63 "Bruning Army Airfield," Lincoln, Nebraska: Nebraska State Historical Society, June 9, 2004.
64 Thayer County Historical Society, "The War Department tells how new bases like Bruning Army Air Base are built," from Missouri River Division of the United States Army Corps of Engineers (Kansas City, Missouri), printed in The Bruning Banner, November 12, 1942.
65 *Bruning Centennial History Book, 1887-1987*, Bruning, Nebraska: Thayer County Historical Society to Lieutenant Colonel George A. Larson, USAF, June 11, 1991.
66 Andy Raun, "History in our midst," The Hastings Tribune, Bruning, Nebraska: Thayer County Historical Society, July 20, 1998.
67 United States Air Force Historical Research Center, "262nd Army Air Force Base, for the period 18 March 1943 to August 1943," Montgomery, Alabama: Maxwell Air Force Base, February 1977.
68 United States Air Force Historical Research Center, "456th Bombardment Group, unit history, August 1943," Montgomery, Alabama: Maxwell Air Force Base, June 1991.
69 United States Air Force Historical Research Center, "456th Bombardment Group, unit history, September 1943," Montgomery, Alabama: Maxwell Air Force Base, June 1991.
70 United States Air Force Historical Research Center, "Base History, Bruning Army Air Force Base," Montgomery, Alabama: Maxwell Air Force Base, February 1977.
71 Ibid
72 Lieutenant Colonel George A. Larson, USAF (Ret.), "WWII high-altitude strategic bomber, the Consolidated B-24 Liberator," Military Technical Journal, April 1997, 14-15.
73 United States Air Force Historical Research Center, "Bruning Army Air Field, P-47 training, unit history," Montgomery, Alabama: Maxwell Air Force Base, February 1977.
74 United States Air Force Historical Research Center, "36th Fighter Group," Montgomery, Alabama: Maxwell Air Force Base, February 1977.
75 David Mondey, *The Concise Guide to American Aircraft of World War II* (Edison, New Jersey: Chartwell Books, Inc., 1994), 216-222.
76 United States Air Force Historical Research Center, "262nd Air Force Base Unit, Bruning Army Air Force Base, Unit History," Montgomery, Alabama: Maxwell Air Force Base, February 1977.

77 United States Air Force Historical Research Center, "262nd Air Force Base Unit, Bruning Army Air Forces, Base Unit History, May 1944," Montgomery, Alabama: Maxwell Air Force Base, February 1977.
78 United States Air Force Historical Research Center, "P-47 flight characteristics," Montgomery, Alabama: Maxwell Air Force Base, February 1977.
79 United States Air Force Historical Research Center, "262nd Air Force Base Unit, Bruning Army Air Forces Base, Unit History, September 1944," Montgomery, Alabama: Maxwell Air Force Base, February 1977.
80 United States Air Force Historical Research Center, "262nd Air Force Base Unit, Bruning Army Air forces Base, Unit History, March 1944," Montgomery, Alabama: Maxwell Air Force Base, February 1977.
81 United States Air Force Historical Research Center, "508th Fighter Group, Bruning Army Air Forces Base, Unit History," Montgomery, Alabama: Maxwell Air Force Base, February 1977.
82 United States Air Force Historical Research Center, "262nd Air Force Base Unit, Bruning Army Air Forces Base, Unit History, August 1944," Montgomery, Alabama: Maxwell Air Force Base, February 1977.
83 United States Air Force Historical Research Center, "262nd Air Force Base Unit, Bruning Air Force Base, Unit History, January 1945," Montgomery, Alabama: Maxwell Air Force Base, February 1977.
84 "Bruning Army Air Force Base," Bruning, Nebraska: Bruning City Library, June 1991.

Chapter 4
85 Lou Thole, "Historian and World War II aviation buff researched history of Fairmont Airfield," Nebraska Signal, July 6, 1989.
86 Lou Thole, "Fairmont Army Air Field, then and now," Friends Bulletin, Dayton, Ohio: Wright Patterson Air Force Base, Air Force Museum Foundation, Ohio, Spring 1989, 21.
87 "Construction work on satellite air base getting in full swing," Nebraska Signal, Geneva, Nebraska, September 24, 1942.
88 Fairmont Women's Club, *Fairmont Nebraska Centennial, 1873-1973*, Geneva, Nebraska, Geneva Signal, 1973, 5.
89 Thole
90 Fairmont Women's Club
91 United States Air Force Historical Research Center, "Fairmont Army Air Forces Base," Montgomery, Alabama: Maxwell Air Force Base, February 1977.
92 Fairmont Women's Club
93 Ibid
94 Thole
95 Mauer
96 451st Bombardment Group, "Fairmont/Geneva, Nebraska and the 451st Bombardment Group (H), a home coming," September 7, 1990.
97 451st Bombardment Group reunion, Fairmont, Nebraska, September 9, 1990.
98 United States Air Force Historical Research Center, "451st Bombardment Group, Unit History, Fairmont Army Air Field," Montgomery, Alabama: Maxwell Air Force Base, February 1977.
99 D. Sedgefield, *451st Bombardment Group* (Paducah, Kentucky: Turner Publishing, 1990), 16-17
100 "Fairmont/Geneva and the 451st Bombardment Group (H) a home coming."
101 United States Air Force Historical Research Center, "Fairmont Army Air Field," Montgomery, Alabama: Maxwell Air Force Base, February 1977.
102 Charles A. Harris to Lieutenant Colonel George A. Larson, USAF, November 26, 1991.
103 Beaz A. Aldi to Lieutenant Colonel George A. Larson, USAF, October 24, 1991.
104 United States Air Force Historical Research Center, "History of Fairmont Army Air Field, May 1944," Montgomery, Alabama: Maxwell Air Force Base, February 1977.
105 United States Air Force Historical Research Center, "History of Fairmont Army Air Field, June 1944," Montgomery, Alabama: Maxwell Air Force Base, February 1977.
106 Harris
107 Lieutenant Colonel George A. Larson, USAF, *Road to Tinian* (Dallas, Texas: Taylor Publishing, 1988), 37.
108 United States Air Force Historical Research Center, "History of Fairmont Army Air Field, July 1944," Montgomery, Alabama: Maxwell Air Force Base, February 1977.
109 Lawrence S. Slotsky to Lieutenant Colonel George A. Larson, USAF, October 1, 1991.
110 Ralph Schell, "Maintaining the B-29," 16th Bombardment Group, *Anthologies.*
111 Aldi
112 Schell
113 United States Air Force Historical Research Center, "History of Fairmont Army Air Field, September 1944," Montgomery, Alabama: Maxwell Air Force Base, February 1977.
114 United States Air Force Historical Research Center, "History of 16th Bombardment Group, October 1944," Montgomery, Alabama: Maxwell Air Force Base, February 1977.
115 United States Air Force Historical Research Center, "History of 16th Bombardment Group, December 1944," Montgomery, Alabama: Maxwell Air Force Base, February 1977.
116 Message, "B-29 modifications," from Williams CG 2AF Colorado Springs (171831Z) to CG 315th Wing, Peterson Army Air Field, Colorado Springs, Colorado. United States Air Force Historical Research Center, Montgomery, Alabama: Maxwell Air Force Base, February 1977.
117 United States Air Force Historical Research Center, "History of 16th Bombardment Group, January 1945," Montgomery, Alabama: Maxwell Air Force Base, February 1977.
118 United States Air Force Historical Research Center, "History of Fairmont Army Air Field, January 1945," Montgomery, Alabama: Maxwell Air Force Base, February 1977.
119 United States Air Force Historical Research Center, "History of Fairmont Army Air Field, February 1945," Montgomery, Alabama: Maxwell Air Force Base, February 1977.
120 United States Air Force Historical Research Center, "History of Fairmont Army Air Field, March 1945," Montgomery, Alabama: Maxwell Air Force Base, February 1977.
121 Thole
122 United States Air Force Historical Research Center, "History of Fairmont Army Air Field, April 1945," Montgomery, Alabama: Maxwell Air Force Base, February 1977.

123 Thole
124 United States Air Force Historical Research Center, "History of Fairmont Army Air Field, August 1945," Montgomery, Alabama: Maxwell Air Force Base, February 1977.
125 Thole

Chapter 5
126 Fairmont Women's Club
127 "History of the Glen L. Martin-Nebraska Company," Glen L. Martin Company Papers, M50366, State Archives, Nebraska State Historical Society (NSHS), Lincoln, Nebraska (M50366-NSHS).
128 Omaha-World Herald, December 25, 1940
129 M50366-NSHS
130 *History of Building D* (pamphlet 210-1), Offutt Air Force Base, Nebraska: Base Printing Office, April 15, 1988.
131 *LeMay*, xi.
132 Jerold Simmons, "Public leadership in a World War II boom town: Bellevue, Nebraska," Nebraska History, winter 1984, 485-488, 491-492, 495.
133 Papillion Times, Papillion, Nebraska, January 16, 1941.
134 Jacqueline McGlade, "The zoning of Fort Crook: urban expansionism vs county home rule," Nebraska History, Lincoln, Nebraska, spring 1983, 21-22, 30-32.
135 Nebraska History, 488 b& 491.
136 Omaha-World Herald, Omaha, Nebraska, March 3, 1941.
137 Omaha-World Herald, Omaha, Nebraska, December 5, 1955.
138 V. Kastens, "A survey of the employment situation in Omaha, Nebraska," Lincoln, Nebraska, State Employment Service, January 1941, 13.
139 Twenty-fourth Biennial Report of the Department of Roads and Irrigation to the Governor of Nebraska, 1941-1942, Volume 1, Lincoln, Nebraska, 239-240.
140 Ibid., 137 & 139.
141 The Unionist, Omaha, Nebraska, "Building D," February 7, 1941, 4.
142 Omaha-world Herald, October 26, 1941.
143 M50366-NSHS
144 Bill Gunston, *Illustrated Fighting Aircraft of World War II* (London: Salamander Books Limited, 2001), 420.
145 M50366-NSHS
146 Enzo Engellucci, *The Rand McNally Encyclopedia of Military Aircraft: 1914 to the Present* (New York: Galley Books, 1990), 289.
147 Deb O'Donnell, "Homefront heroines: women of the Glen L. Martin Nebraska Plant," M50366-NSHS.
148 *Lincoln Star*, April 29, 1943, 7:4.
149 Magazine of the Midlands, Omaha, Nebraska, Omaha-World Herald, March 1, 1981, 16.
150 *Building D*, 8.
151 "Information on Charles H. Day," The Martin Star, December 1942, 15.
152 Council Bluffs Nonpareil, September 19, 1982, 3A:1-8.
153 Omaha World-Herald, November 11, 1945, C14.
154 *Building D*, 8.
155 Columbus Daily Telegram, April 7, 1944, 2:4.
156 Columbus Daily Telegram, November 20, 1944.
157 The Martin Star, December 1942, 15.
158 *Building D*, 9.
159 Gilifillan
160 *LeMay*, 47.
161 Mary Rocka
162 Gilifillan
163 Ethric Brown, Red Oak, Iowa, Interview 10th annual reunion Martin-bomber plant workers, Council Bluffs, Iowa, Lieutenant Colonel George A. Larson, USAF, September 14, 1990.
164 Paul W. Tibbets, *Flight of the Enola Gay* (Reynolds, Ohio: Buckeye Aviation Book Company, 1989), 197.
165 Alywn T. Lloyd, *B-29 Superfortress* (Blue Ridge Summit, PA.), 11.
166 *Road to Tinian*, 38.
167 Vincent C. Jones, *U.S. Army in World War II, Special Studies, Manhattan: The Army and the Atomic Bomb* (Washington, DC: U.S. Government Printing Office, 1985), 522-523.
168 "Bomber plant remembered," *Lincoln Star*, October 8, 1982.
169 *Lincoln Star*, October 8, 1942, 14:1-3.
170 The Martin Star, December 1942.
171 Omaha World-Herald, November 11, 1945, C14.
172 Council Bluffs Nonpareil, September 19, 1982, 3A:1-8.
173 "Cafeteria worker," job specification, M50366-NSHS.
174 *Building D*, 8.
175 "The Glen L. Martin-Nebraska Company employment summary, entire facility as of January 5, 1945," M53066-NSHS.
176 The Martin Star, Baltimore, Maryland, November 1942, 8.
177 "Union negotiation exhibits," M50366-NSHS.
178 "Cooperative group insurance plan," M50366-NSHS.
179 "Work Simplification Engineering Department of Glen L. Martin Nebraska Company," M50366-NSHS.
180 Omaha-World Herald, September 30, 1945, C14.
181 Martin Star, March 1944, 12.
182 "Employee records for the Glen L. Martin-Nebraska Company," M50366-NSHS.
183 Falls City Journal, April 28, 1941, 1:5.
184 Omaha World-Herald, January 9, 1941.
185 Columbia Daily Telegram, November 20. 1944, 8:3.
186 Allen M. Winkler, *Home Front USA: America during World War II* (Illinois: Harlan Davidson, Inc., 1986), 50.
187 Omaha World-Herald, February 19, 1943, 1:4.
188 Martin Star, January 1943, 15.
189 Martin Marauder, August 29, 1943, 15.
190 Martin Marauder, September 1, 1944, 3.
191 "Employee distribution by labor grade, monthly breakdown, period ending February 20, 1945," Employment records for the Glen L. Martin-Nebraska Company, M50366-NSHS.
192 "Basic classifications, period ending February 14, 1945," Employment records for the Glen L. Martin-Nebraska Company, M50366-NSHS.
193 "Employee distribution."
194 "Information compiled from monthly labor turnover reports," M50366-NSHS.
195 Sunday World-Herald, April 1, 1945, 5C.
196 Carol Richards, "Rosie the riveter went home and raised daughters to work," Iowa City Press Citizen, Iowa City, Iowa, December 9, 1988, 7A.
197 Lieutenant Colonel George A. Larson, USAF (Ret.), "Sweet Eloise, B-29 on display at Atlanta, Friends Journal, United States Air Force Museum (today National Museum of the United States Air Force), Spring 1998, 29.

198 Omaha World Herald, August 14, 1943.
199 Martin Star, August 1943, 13.
200 *Building D*, 10.
201 Sunday World-Herald, June 19, 1955, 1A:17.
202 Building D, 11.

Chapter 6
203 *Mead Centennial, 1877-1977* (Mead, Nebraska: 1977), 48-49.
204 Historical Newsletter, "What did you do in the war: A commemoration of Nebraska's participation in World War II," Lincoln, Nebraska: Nebraska State Historical Society, volume 44, number 3, September 1991, 1.
205 *Mead Centennial*
206 www.meadnebraska, official home page.
207 "The Naval Ammunition Depot," Historical News, Hastings, Nebraska: Adams County Nebraska Historical Society, volumes 25 & 27, number 4.
208 "Sioux Army Depot," Lincoln, Nebraska: Nebraska State Historical Society, June 1990.
209 Lt. Col. George A. Larson, USAF (Ret.), "America's forgotten prisoner of war camps," Sea Classics, May 2003, volume 36, number 5, 63.
210 "POWs in Cheyenne County, 1943-46," Nebraska State Historical Society, Sidney High School Historical Society, May 11, 1980.
211 The Federal Engineer, "Damsites to missile sites: A history of the Omaha District of the U.S. Army Corps of Engineers," Omaha, Nebraska, U.S. Army Corps of Engineers.
212 "Cornhusker Ordnance Plant (Grand Island, Nebraska)," Lincoln, Nebraska: Nebraska State Historical Society, RG0825.
213 "Public health assessment, Cornhusker Army Ammunition Plant, Grand Island, Hall County, Nebraska," Atlanta, GA: Department of Health and Human Services, Agency for Toxic Substances and Disease Registry, August 1987.

Chapter 7
214 "History of Grand Island Army Air Base," Lincoln, Nebraska: Nebraska State Historical Society.
215 United States Army Corps of Engineers, "After action report, Grand Island satellite field, 15 January 1943," Montgomery, Alabama: United States Air Force Historical Research Center, Maxwell Air Force Base, December 1977.
216 Mauer Mauer, ed., *Air Force Combat Units of World War II* (Washington, DC: Office of Air Force History, 1983).
217 "History 6th Bombardment Group (V.H.), Army Air Base Grand Island, Nebraska, 1 June 1944 to 31 July 1944," Montgomery, Alabama: United States Air Force Historical Research Center, Maxwell Air Force Base, December 1977.
218 "History 6th Bombardment (V.H.), Army Air Base, Grand Island, Nebraska, 1 August 1944 to 31 August 1944," Montgomery, Alabama: United States Air Force Historical Research Center, Maxwell Air Force Base, December 1977.
219 "History of 502nd Bombardment Group (V.H.), for September 1944," Montgomery, Alabama: United States Air Force Historical Center, Maxwell Air Force Base, December 1977.

Chapter 8
220 "Boom transforms Harvard into bustling community," *Hastings Daily Tribune*, September 30, 1942, E.
221 *Harvard Nebraska, 100 years +2, Harvard, Nebraska: 1873-Centennial-1973* (Harvard, Nebraska: Harvard History Books Committee, 1973), 108.
222 Mauer
223 *Harvard, Nebraska, 100 years +2.*
224 "Gas alarm at Harvard," *Sunday World-Herald Magazine*, Omaha, Nebraska, July 4, 1943, 55(C).
225 "History of 447th Bomb Group (H)," Montgomery, Alabama: United States Air Force Historical Research Center, Maxwell Air Force Base, December 1977.
226 "History of the 484th Bombardment Group (H), 1 November 1943 to 30 November 1943," Montgomery, Alabama: United States Air Force Historical Research Center, Maxwell Air Force Base, December 1977.
227 "History of the 505th Bombardment Group (H), May 1944," Montgomery, Alabama: United States Air Force Historical Research Center, Maxwell Air Force Base, December 1977.
228 "History, 501st Bombardment Group (V.H.), December 1944," Montgomery, Alabama: United States Air Force Historical Research Center, Maxwell Air Force Base, December 1977.
229 "History, 501st Bombardment Group (V.H.), January 1945," Montgomery, Alabama: United States Air Force Historical Research Center, Maxwell Air Force Base, December 1977.
230 Ed Herring, *501st Bomb Group, Anthologies.*
231 "History, 501st Bombardment Group (V.H.), February 1945," Montgomery, Alabama: United States Air Force Historical Research Center, Maxwell Air Force Base, December 1977.
232 Glen L. Clark, "History of Swoose Squadron," *501st Bombardment Group, Anthologies.*
233 George Green, "Recollections," Montgomery, Alabama: United States Air Force Historical Research Center, Maxwell Air Force Base, December 1977.
234 Clark (see end note 232)
235 Mauer (see end note 216)
236 *Harvard, Nebraska, 100 Years +2.*

Chapter 9
237 Todd L. Petersen, "Kearney, Nebraska and the Kearney airfield in World War II," Nebraska History, Fall 1991, Lincoln, Nebraska: Nebraska State Historical Society.
238 "Contract for Kearny Project," *Hastings Daily Tribune*, Hastings, Nebraska, October 6, 1942.
239 "Alice Howell, "The Kearney Army Air Base, The Military," *Buffalo Tales*, Buffalo County Historical Society, April 1988, 1-4.
240 Ibid
241 Ibid
242 Gayla Parks, "Kearney Base's Cocoon Club saved lives," The Kearney Daily Hub, "Kearney Army Air Base Reunion, 1988, Supplement," June 1, 1988, 5.
243 "Kearney Army Air Base."
244 "Air Force Combat Units of World War II."
245 "History of the 100th Bombardment Group," Montgomery, Alabama: United States Air Force Historical Research Center, Maxwell Air Force Base, December 1977.

246 Gayla Parks, "Hollywood star gets same treatment at base," The Kearney Daily Hub, "Kearney Air Base reunion, 1988, Supplement," Kearney, Nebraska, June 1, 1988, 6.
247 "History of 100th Bombardment Group."
248 "Kearney Army Air Base."
249 Lieutenant Colonel George A. Larson, USAF (Ret.), "War Assets," Air Classics, May 1992, 6.
250 "Kearney Army Air Base."
251 "Base buildings still in use," The Kearney Daily Hub, "Kearney Army Air Base Reunion 1988, Supplement," Kearney Nebraska, June 1, 1988, 5.
252 "City's runways once again host B-17 bomber," The Kearney Daily Hub, "Kearney Air Base reunion, 1988, Supplement," Kearney, Nebraska, June 1, 1988, 2.

Chapter 10
253 Jake W. Spidle Jr., "Axis prisoners of war in the United States, 1942-1946: A bibliographical essay," Military Affairs, April 1975, 61.
254 Arnold D. Kramer, "German prisoners of war in the United States," Military Affairs, April 1976, 68.
255 Spidle, 63.
256 Arthur M. Kruse, "Custody of Prisoners of War in the United States," *Military Engineer*, February 1946, 70-71.
257 Kramer
258 "Custody of Prisoners of War in the United States."
259 "German Prisoners of War in the United States," 68-69.
260 "Custody of Prisoners of War in the United States."
261 "German Prisoners of War in the United States."
262 "Axis Prisoners of War in the United States."
263 Judith Gainsberg, *Stalag USA: The Remarkable Story of German POWS in America* (New York: Thomas Y. Cromwell Company, 1977), 93.
264 "Labor supply is major problem on the farms in the nation: set new rules to guide contract placement," *Harlan County Journal*, June 1, 1994, 1.
265 "Nebraska's POW camps," Lincoln, Nebraska: Nebraska State Historical Society, Archive Collection, June 1990.
266 Tom Buecher, "Fort Robinson internment camp," interview, Fort Robinson Museum, Lieutenant Colonel George A. Larson, USAF, July 25, 1991.
267 Jonathan Haring, "Prisoner of war camps in Nebraska during World War II," Hastings, Nebraska: Hastings College, 1989, 12, 16, 22.
268 "Nebraska's POW camps."
269 Haring
270 NSHS
271 Haring
272 NSHS
273 George C, Lewis and John Mauha, *History of Prisoner of War Utilization by the United States Army, 1776-1945* (Washington, DC: Department of the Army, 1955), 82.
274 Gainsberg, 25.
275 William Oberdieck, Nebraska City, Nebraska, interview with author, October 17, 1991.
276 Gainsberg, 27-40.
277 Oberdieck
278 "More Germans arrive at Camp Atlanta," *Harlan County Journal*, March 2, 1944, 1.
279 Kramer, 31.
280 Oberdieck
281 "Guard at local prison camp goes on rampage Monday night: many shots exchanged by guards and victim," Harlan County Alma Nebraska Journal, November 22, 1944, 1.
282 Oberdieck
283 Gainsberg, 31.
284 Oberdieck
285 *History of Cass County* (Dallas, Texas: Curtis Media Corporation, 1989), 41.
286 Oberdieck
287 John Underwood, interview, Sidney, Nebraska High School Historical Society, May 11, 1980.
288 Emmanuelle Campanella (Italian solider captured in North Africa and shipped to the United States), interview, Sidney, Nebraska High School Historical Society, May 11, 1980.
289 Bertrand Nebraska Herald, May 2, 1944.
290 Campanella

Chapter 11
291 "Lincoln Army Air Base," Montgomery, Alabama: United States Air Force Historical Research Center, Maxwell Air Force Base, December 1977.
292 The *Lincoln Star*, March 20, 1942, 1.
293 "Farm families must make hurried departure from land needed for new Lincoln air base," The *Lincoln Star*, April 12, 1942, 1.
294 The *Lincoln Star*, March 31, 1942, 1.
295 "City will build water line to municipal airport for Army air base," The *Lincoln Star*, April 6, 1942, 1.
296 "Lincoln air base project development," Lincoln, Nebraska: Lincoln Chamber of Commerce, May 1942.
297 "$242,885.00 offer on first group of 59 buildings at airport," The *Lincoln Star*, April 8, 1942, 1.
298 "Air base begins growing like a small city," The *Lincoln Star*, April 10, 1942, 8.
299 "Basloom and Ruagh Company, $963,700 low-bid on air base constriction," The *Lincoln Star*, April 14, 1942, 1.
300 "Air base hums with vast activity," The *Lincoln Star*, April 15, 1942, 1.
301 "Air Base may have 2,700 acres of land," The *Lincoln Star*, April 17, 1942, 1.
302 "Lincoln formally turns over airport to Uncle Sam," The *Lincoln Star*, April 21, 1942, 5.
303 The *Lincoln Star*, May 18, 1942, 1.
304 The *Lincoln Star*, May 19, 1942, 1.
305 "Four runways to cover 600 acres, OK'd," The *Lincoln Star*, May 23, 1942, 1.
306 The *Lincoln Star*.
307 "First trainees expected 1 July," The *Lincoln Star*, June 16, 1942, 1.
308 "Classes start at technical school now getting full under way," The *Lincoln Star*, July 19, 1942, 3B.
309 George W. O'Kelly to Lieutenant Colonel George A. Larson, USAF, November 6, 1991.
310 "30,000 fighter mechanics already trained at Lincoln," Sunday-World Herald Magazine, July 4, 1943, 26 (C).

311 "History of 489th Bombardment Group," Montgomery, Alabama: United States Air Force Historical Research Center, United States Air Force, Maxwell Air Force Base, December 1977.
312 "Lincoln Army Air Base."

Chapter 12
313 "Begin work on base at McCook," *Hastings Daily Tribune*, September 2, 1942, 1.
314 McCook Army Air Base Historical Society," *McCook Army Air Base*, McCook, Nebraska, 1991.
315 "Begin work on base at McCook."
316 McCook Army Air Base Historical Society
317 Mildred L. Zink, R.N., to Lieutenant Colonel George A. Larson, USAF, June 7, 1991.
318 Mauer
319 McCook Army Air Base Historical Society
320 "9th Bomb Group (H) Unit History, June 1944," Montgomery, Alabama: United States Air Force Historical Research Center, Maxwell Air Force Base, December 1944.
321 McCook Army Air Base Historical Society
322 Major Ralph L. Swann, USAF, "A unit history of the 315th Bomb Wing: 1944-1946," Air Command and Staff College, Montgomery, Alabama: United States Air Force Historical Research Center, Maxwell Air Force Base, United States Air Force.
323 Andrew Gordon, 331st Bomb Group, *Anthologies.*
324 Robert F. Griffin, 331st Bomb Group, *Anthologies.*
325 Larry McCarthy, 331st Bomb Group, *Anthologies.*
326 9th Bomb Group (H).
327 McCook Army Air Base Historical Society.
328 Harry S. Carl to Lieutenant Colonel George A. Larson, USAF, June 15, 1990.
329 "History of 331st Bombardment Group, Unit History, December 1944," Montgomery, Alabama: United States Air Force Historical Research Center, Maxwell Air Force Base, December 1977.
330 "History of 331st Bombardment Group, Unit History, January 1945," Montgomery, Alabama: United States Air Force Historical Research Center, Maxwell Air Force Base, December 1977.
331 "History of 331st Bombardment Group, Unit History, February 1945," Montgomery, Alabama: United States Air Force Historical Research Center, Maxwell Air Force Base, December 1977.
332 "History of 98th Bombardment Group, Unit History, June 1945," Montgomery, Alabama: United States Air Force Historical Research Center, Maxwell Air Force Base, December 1977.
333 "History of 98th Bombardment Group, Unit History, July 1945," Montgomery, Alabama: United States Air Force Historical Research Center, Maxwell Air Force Base, December 1977.
334 Tom Allan, "Vets spruce up old McCook Air Base," *Omaha World Herald*, September 25, 1990.

Chapter 13
335 "The Army trained canines of CBI," *CBI Roundup*, December 1959.
336 Lieutenant Colonel Eddy Bauer, *Illustrated World War II Encyclopedia* (New York: Orbis Publishing, 1978).
337 Glen M. Campbell to Lieutenant Colonel George A. Larson, USAF, October 24, 1991.
338 *135th U.S. Naval Construction Battalion Review.* (Private-undocumented-published document for the men and families of the 135th USNCB.)
339 T.P. Brewster to Lieutenant Colonel George A. Larson, USAF (Ret.), November 3, 1992.
340 Tom Buecker, "War dogs," *Nebraskaland*, December 1988.
341 Richard J. Zika to Lieutenant Colonel George A. Larson, USAF, November 2, 1991.
342 Richard J. Zika, "Dog days in the CBI," CBIVA Sound Off, Winter, 1991.
343 Zika to Lieutenant Colonel George A. Larson, USAF.
344 "Liberty ships," Washington, DC, Department of the Interior, National Parks Service, 1996.
345 Zika
346 B.K. Kennedy to Lieutenant Colonel George A. Larson, USAF (Ret.), October 10, 1991.
347 Fairfax Downey, "Serving the only God he knows," Blue Book Magazine, September 1947.
348 SSgt Carl M. Hutsell to Lieutenant Colonel George A. Larson, USAF (Ret.), November 15, 1992.
349 Bob Lischer to Lieutenant Colonel George A. Larson, USAF (Ret.), November 18, 1992.
350 Hutsell
351 Earl O. Cullum, "CBI War Dog Detachment," *CBI Roundup*, January 1990.
352 Rusty Mizner to Lieutenant Colonel George A. Larson, USAF (Ret.), November 15, 1992.
353 Hutsell
354 Zika, "Dog days in the CBI."
355 Campbell
356 Brewster
357 Fort Robinson Museum, Fort Robinson, Nebraska.

Chapter 14
358 "History of Scotts Bluff County Airport," Lincoln, Nebraska: Nebraska State Historical Society, December 1987.
359 Lieutenant Colonel George A. Larson, USAF (Ret.), "America's forgotten war camps," *Sea Classics*, May 2003, 62-65 & 74.
360 "History of Scotts Bluff County Airport."
361 Bernice Wilson, Goering, Nebraska to Lieutenant Colonel George A. Larson, USAF, May 21, 1991.
362 Lieutenant Colonel George A. Larson, USAF, "Nebraska's PW camps during World War II," research at Scotts Bluff and Sidney, Nebraska, August 1990.
363 "History of Scotts Bluff County Airport."
364 Lettie Morocco, "Typical bombing missions," *Sunday World Herald Magazine*, Omaha, Nebraska, July 4, 1943, 57.
365 "Heavy bombardment training program of the Second Air Force," Fort George, Washington: Headquarters Second Air Force, March 5, 1943.
366 "Uncompleted projects and minor additions necessary for OTU and RTU programs when the peak of production is reached," Fort George, Washington: Headquarters Second Air Force, January 18, 1943.

367 "Heavy bombardment training program of the Second Air Force."

Chapter 15

368 "History of Scribner Air Base and Detachment 2, 1st Aerospace Communication Group (AFCC)," Lincoln, Nebraska: Nebraska State Historical Society, June 1990.

369 *Scribner, Nebraska: 1871-Centennial-1971*, (Fremont, Nebraska: Nebraska Printing and Litho, 1971).

370 "History of Scribner Air Base."

371 Violet Pear Blumm, Fremont, Nebraska, interview, Lieutenant Colonel George A. Larson, USAF, August 15, 1991.

372 "History of Scribner Air Base."

373 Mauer

374 "History of Twenty-second Fighter Squadron, December 1943," Montgomery, Alabama: United States Air Force Historical Research Center, Maxwell Air Force Base, December 1977.

375 "Probe asked at Scribner," Omaha World Herald**,** June 4, 1944, 1.

376 "History of Scribner Air Base."

Chapter 16

377 Iowa Air National Guard, "History of Sioux City Air Base," Des Moines, Iowa.

Sources

135th U.S. Naval Construction Battalion Review. (Private-undocumented-published document for the men and families of the 135th USNCB.)

"$242,885.00 offer on first group of 59 buildings at airport." *The Lincoln Star*. Lincoln, Nebraska, April 8, 1942.

"30,000 fighter mechanics already trained at Lincoln." *Sunday World-Herald Magazine*. Omaha, Nebraska, July 4, 1943.

440th Troop Carrier Association. "Long road to invasion," to Lieutenant Colonel George A. Larson, USAF, September 9, 1991.

451st Bombardment Group. "Fairmont/Geneva, Nebraska and the 451st Bombardment Group (H), a home coming."

451st Bombardment Group. "451st Bombardment Group reunion, September 9, 1990." Fairmont, Nebraska.

A brief history of the combat glider in World War II. Yaki-Wall Company, 1990.

"Ainsworth airfield important part of national war effort." Ainsworth (NE) Star-Journal. Ainsworth, Nebraska, June 23, 1983.

Ainsworth Chamber of Commerce. "Middle of nowhere, welcome to Ainsworth, Nebraska." Ainsworth, Nebraska.

"Airbase hums with vast activity." *The Lincoln Star*. Lincoln, Nebraska, April 15, 1942.

Airgood, Roger L. "Recollection of the first day at Alliance Army Air Base, June 12, 1943." Letter to author, 15 June 1991.

Aldi, Beaz A. Letter to author, October 24, 1991.

Allan, Tom. "Vets spruce up old McCook Air Base." Omaha World-Herald. Omaha, Nebraska, September 25, 1990.

"Base buildings still in use." *The Kearny Daily Hub*. "Kearney Air Base Reunion, 1988, Supplement." Kearney, Nebraska, June 1, 1988.

"Basic classifications, period ending February 14, 1945." Lincoln, Nebraska: Glen L. Martin Company Papers, M50366. Lincoln, Nebraska: Nebraska State Historical Society Archives.

"Basloom and Raugh Company, $963,700 low-bid on air base construction." *The Lincoln Star*. Lincoln, Nebraska, April 14, 1942.

Bauer, Lieutenant Colonel Eddy. *Illustrated World War II Encyclopedia.* New York: Orbis Publishing, 1978.

"Begin work on base at McCook." *Hastings Daily Tribune*. Hastings, Nebraska, September 2, 1942.

Bertrand, *Nebraska Herald*. Bertrand, Nebraska, May 2, 1944.

Blumm, Violet Pear. Fremont, Nebraska. Letter to author, August 15, 1991.

"Boom transforms Harvard into bustling community." *Hastings Daily Tribune*, September 30, 1942.

"Bomber plant remembered." *Lincoln Star*. Lincoln, Nebraska, October 8, 1982.

Breck, Robert. Letter to author, October 29, 1991.

Brennan, George. "Short Bursts." *Glider Museum News*. Terrill, Texas: July/August 1991.

Brewster, T.P. Letter to Lieutenant Colonel George A. Larson, USAF (Ret.), November 3, 1992.

Brown, Ethric. Red Oak, Iowa. Interview, 10th annual reunion Omaha-Martin bomber plant workers, Council Bluffs, Iowa. Interview, Lieutenant Colonel George A. Larson, USAF, September 14, 1990.

"Bruning Army Airfield." Lincoln, Nebraska: Nebraska State Historical Society, June 9, 2004.

"Bruning Army Air Forces Base." Bruning, Nebraska: Bruning City Library, June 1991.

Bruning Centennial History Book, 1882-1982. Bruning, Nebraska: Thayer County Historical Society. Book to Lieutenant Colonel George A. Larson, USAF, June 11, 1991.

Buecker, Tom. Interview, Fort Robinson, Crawford, Nebraska, Lieutenant Colonel George A. Larson, USAF, July 25, 1991.

Buecker, Tom. Interview, Fort Robinson, Crawford, Nebraska, Lieutenant Colonel George A. Larson, USAF, August 19, 1991.

Buecker, Tom. "War dogs." *Nebraskaland*. Lincoln, Nebraska, December 1988. "Cafeteria worker, job specification." Lincoln, Nebraska: Glen L. Martin Company Papers, M50366. Lincoln, Nebraska: Nebraska State Historical Society Archives.

Camanella, Emmanuelle. Interview, Sidney, Nebraska High School Historical Society, May 11, 1980.

Campbell, Glen M. Letter to author, October 24, 1991.

Carl, Harry S. Letter to author, June 15, 1990.

Centennial Committee. *City of Alliance and Box Battle County (Nebraska)*. Dallas, Texas: Curtis Media Corporation, 1988.

"City's runways once again host B-17 bomber." The Kearney Daily Hub. "Kearney Air Base Reunion, 1988, Supplement." Kearney, Nebraska, June 1, 1988.

"Combat area hangars are manufactured in Omaha." *Sunday World-Herald Magazine*. Omaha, Nebraska, July 4, 1943.

"City takes over Ainsworth airfield today, October 24, 1946." Ainsworth (NE) Star-Journal. Ainsworth, Nebraska, June 23, 1983.

"City will build water line to municipal airport for Army airbase." *The Lincoln Star*. Lincoln, Nebraska, April 6, 1942.

Clark, Gen L. "History of Swoose Squadron." *501st Bombardment Group, Anthologies.*

"Classes start at technical school now getting full under way." *The Lincoln Star*. Lincoln, Nebraska, July 19, 1942.

Columbus Daily Telegram. Columbus, Ohio, November 11, 1944.

Columbus Daily Telegram. Columbus, Ohio, November 20, 1944.

"Construction work on satellite air base getting on full swing." The Nebraska Signal. Geneva, Nebraska, September 24, 1942.

"Contract for Kearney project." *Hastings Daily Tribune*. Hastings, Nebraska: October 6, 1942.

"Cornhusker Ordnance Plant, Grand Island, Nebraska." Lincoln, Nebraska: Nebraska State Historical Society.

Council Bluffs Nonpareil. Council Bluffs, Iowa, September 19, 1982.

Craven, Wesley Frank and James Lea Cate, Ed. *The Army Air Forces in World War II*. Volume 6. *Men and Planes.* Washington, DC: Office of Air Force History, 1983.

Cullum, Earl O. "CBI war dog detachment." *CBI Roundup*, January 1990.

"Damsites to missile sites: A history of the Omaha District of the United States Army Corps of Engineers." The Federal Engineer. Omaha, Nebraska: United States Army Corps of Engineers.

Davidson, Sgt, Bill (AAF). "Alliance Air Base, training ground for airborne troops who get there first with the best punch." Alliance, Nebraska: Knights Museum.

Department of the U.S. Army. "Army Air Corps Fields." Omaha, Nebraska: Corps of Engineers, Omaha District. Letter to author, May 16, 1991.

Downey, Fairfax. "Serving the only God he Knows." *Blue Book Magazine*, September 1947.

Drake, Milton. *The Glider Gang: An Eyewitness History of World War II*. New York: J.B. Lippincott Company, 1977.

"Employee distributing labor grade, monthly breakdown, period ending February 20, 1945." Employment record for Glen L. Martin-Nebraska Company. Lincoln, Nebraska: Glen L. Martin Company Papers, M50366. Lincoln, Nebraska: Nebraska State Historical Society Archives.

Engellucci, Enzo. *The Rand McNally Encyclopedia of Military Aircraft: 1914 to the Present.* New York: Galley Books, 1990.

Fairmont Women's Club. "Fairmont Nebraska Centennial, 1873-1973." Geneva Signal. Geneva, Nebraska, 1973.

"Farm families must make hurried departure from land for new Lincoln Air Base." *The Lincoln Star*. Lincoln, Nebraska, April 12, 1942.

"First trainees expected 1 July." *The Lincoln Star*. Lincoln, Nebraska, June 16, 1942.

Fort Robinson Museum. Crawford, Nebraska.

"Four runways to cover 600 acres, OK'd." *The Lincoln Star*. Lincoln, Nebraska, May 23, 1942.

Gainsberg, Judith. *Stalag U.S.A.: The Remarkable Story of German POWs in America.* New York: Thomas Y. Cromwell Company, 1977.

"Gas alarm at Harvard." *Sunday World-Herald Magazine*. Omaha, Nebraska, July 4, 1943.

Gordon, Andrew. *Anthologies.* 331st Bombardment Group.

Green, George. "Recollections." Montgomery, Alabama: United States Air Force Historical Research Center, Maxwell Air Force Base, December 1977.

Griffin, Robert. *Anthologies*. 331st Bombardment Group.

"Guard at local camp goes on rampage Monday night: many shots exchanged by guards and victim." *Harlan County Journal*. Alma, Nebraska, November 22, 1944.

Gunston, Bill. *Illustrated Fighting Aircraft of World War II.* London: Salamander Books Limited, 2001.

Harris, Charles A. Letter to author, November 26, 1991.

Harris, Jonathan. "Prisoners of war camps in Nebraska during World War II." Hastings, Nebraska: Hastings College, 1989.

Harvard Nebraska, 100 years +2, Harvard, Nebraska: 1873-Centennial-1973. Harvard, Nebraska: Harvard History Books Committee, 1973.

Herring, Ed. "501st Bombardment Group." *501st Bombardment Group, Anthologies.*

History of Cass County. Dallas, Texas: Curtis, Media Corporation, 1989.

"History of Grand Island Air Base." Lincoln, Nebraska: Nebraska State Historical Society.

"History of Scotts Bluff County Airport." Lincoln, Nebraska: Nebraska State Historical Society, December 1987.

"History of Scribner Air Base and Detachment 2, 1st Aerospace Communication Group (AFCC)." Lincoln: Nebraska: Nebraska State Historical Society, June 1980.

"History of the Glen L. Martin Company." Glen L. Martin Company Papers, M50366. Lincoln, Nebraska: Nebraska State Historical Society Archives.

Howell, Alice. "The Kearney Army Air Base, the military." *Buffalo Tales.* Kearney, Nebraska" Buffalo County Historical Society, April 1988.

Humphrey, Bill. Letter to author, September 9, 1991.

"Information compiled from monthly turnover reports." Lincoln, Nebraska: Glen L. Martin Company Papers, M50366. Lincoln, Nebraska: Nebraska State Historical Society Archives.

Iowa Air National Guard. "History of Sioux City Air Base." Des Moines, Iowa: Iowa Air National Guard.

Hutsell, SSgt. Carl M. Letter to Lieutenant Colonel George A. Larson, USAF (Ret.), November 15, 1992.

"Information of Charles H. Day." *The Martin Star*. Baltimore, Maryland, December 1942.

Jones, Vincent C. *U.S. Army in World War II. Special Studies, Manhattan: The Army and the Atomic Bomb.* Washington, DC: United States Government Printing Office, 1985.

Kastens, V. "A survey of the employment situation in Omaha, Nebraska." Lincoln, Nebraska: State Employment Service, January 1941.

KBR News. Ainsworth, Nebraska, March 1989.

Kehr, Frank L. Letter to author, June 3, 1991.

Kennedy, B.K. Letter to Lieutenant Colonel George A. Larson, USAF (Ret.), October 10, 1991.

Kramer, Arnold D. "German prisoners of war in the United States." Military Affairs, April 1976.

Kruse, Arthur M. "Custody of Prisoners of War in the United States." Military Engineer, February 1946.

"Labor supply is major problem on the farms in the nation: Set new rules to guide contract placement." *Harlan County Journal*. Alma, Nebraska, June 1, 1994.

Lang, Robert W. *Short Story, Smorgass Board*. Freeman, South Dakota: Pine Hill Press, 1986.

Larson, Lawrence H. "The Alliance Army Air Base case." Nebraska History, Fall 1986.

Larson, Lieutenant Colonel George A., USAF (Ret.). "America's forgotten prisoner of war camps." Sea Classics, May 2003, Volume 36, Number 5.

Larson, Lieutenant Colonel George A., USAF. "Nebraska's PW camps during World War II." Research at Scotts Bluff and Sidney, Nebraska libraries, August 1990.

Larson, Lieutenant Colonel George A., USAF. *Road to Tinian*. Dallas, Texas: Taylor Publishing, 1988.

Larson, Lieutenant Colonel George A., USAF. "Steam locomotives across the plains of Nebraska." *Mit der Dampflak durchdie von Ebenen von Nebraska. Nebraska-Nachrichten,* January 1992.

Larson, Lieutenant Colonel George A., USAF (Ret.). "Sweet Eloise, B-29 displayed at Atlanta, Georgia." Friends Journal. National Museum of the United States Air Force, Spring 1988.

Larson, Lieutenant Colonel George A., USAF (Ret.). "War assets." Military History, May 1992.

Larson, Lieutenant Colonel George A., USAF (Ret.). "WWII high-altitude strategic bomber, the Consolidated B-24 Liberator." Military Technical Journal, April 1997.

Lewis, George C., and John Mauha. *History of Prisoner of War Utilization by the United States, 1776-1945*. Washington, DC: Department of the Army, 1955.

"Lincoln formally turns over airport to Uncle Sam." *The Lincoln Star*. Lincoln, Nebraska, April 21, 1942.

Lischer, Bob. Letter to author, November 18, 1992.

Lloyd, Alywn T. *B-29 Superfortress*. Blue Ridge Summit, PA.

Magazine of the Midlands. Omaha, Nebraska: Omaha World-Herald, March 1, 1981.

"Major construction work has been going on for several weeks." *Alliance (NE) Times-Herald*. Alliance, Nebraska, June 1942.

Marco, Lettie. "Typical bombing missions." *Sunday World-Herald Magazine*. Omaha, Nebraska, July 4, 1943.

Mauer, Mauer. *Aviation in the U.S. Army, 1919-1939*. Washington, DC: United States Air Force, 1987.

McCarthy, Larry. *Anthologies*. 331st Bombardment Group.

McCook Army Air Base. McCook, Nebraska: McCook Air Base Historical Society.

McGlade, Jacqueline. "The zoning of Fort Crook: urban expansionism vs county home role." Nebraska History. Lincoln, Nebraska, Spring 1983.

Mead Centennial, 1877-1977. Mead, Nebraska, 1977.

Mizner, Rusty. Letter to the author, November 15, 1992.

Mondey, David. *The Concise Guide to American Aircraft of World War II*. Edison, New Jersey: Chartwell Books, Inc., 1994.

"More Germans arrive at Camp Atlanta." *Harlan County Journal*, March 2, 1944.

Morris, Thomas L. Letter to author, July 15, 1991.

"Nazi village in western Nebraska." *Sunday World-Herald Magazine*. Omaha, Nebraska, June 6, 1943.

Oberdieck, William. Nebraska City, Nebraska. Interview, Lieutenant Colonel George A. Larson, USAF. October 17, 1991.

O'Donnell, Del. "Home front heroines: women of the Glen L. Martin Nebraska plant." Lincoln, Nebraska: Nebraska State Historical Society.

O'Kelly, George W. Letter to author, November 6, 1991.

"Nebraska's POW camps." Lincoln, Nebraska: Nebraska State Historical Society, Archive Collections, June 1990.

Papillion Times. Papillion, Nebraska, January 16, 1941.

Parks, Gayla. "Kearney Base's Cocoon Club saved lives." The Kearney Daily Hub. "Kearney Air Base Reunion, 1988, Supplement." Kearney, Nebraska, June 1, 1988.

Parks, Gayla. "Hollywood star gets same treatment at base." The Kearney Daily Hub. "Kearney Air Base Reunion, 1988, Supplement." Kearney, Nebraska, June 1, 1988.

Petersen, Todd L. "Kearney, Nebraska and the Kearney airfield in World War II." Nebraska History, Fall 1991. Lincoln, Nebraska: Nebraska State Historical Society.

Photographs: Federal Aviation Administration. Washington, DC.

Photographs: Fort Robinson Museum. Crawford, Nebraska.

Photographs: Kearny Army Air Base Reunion Committee. Kearney, Nebraska.

Photographs: Knights Museum. Alliance, Nebraska.

Photographs: Larson, Lieutenant Colonel George A. Larson, USAF (Ret.)

Photographs: Lockheed Aircraft, Historian Office. Fort Worth, Texas.

Photographs: National Parks Service. Washington, DC.

Photographs: Nebraska State Historical Society. Lincoln, Nebraska.

Photographs: Silent Wings Museum. Lubbock, Texas.

Photographs: Strategic Air Command. Office of History. Offutt Air Force Base, Nebraska.

Photographs: Strategic Air Command Museum. Ashland, Nebraska.

Photographs: Union Pacific Railroad Museum. Omaha, Nebraska.

Photographs: United States Air Force Historical Research Center. Maxwell Air Force Base, Alabama.

Photographs: United States Geological Survey. Sioux Falls, South Dakota.

Photographs: WACO Museum. Battle Creek, Michigan.

Photographs: World War II Glider Symposium to Lieutenant Colonel George A. Larson, USAF (Ret.).

Photographs: 28th Bomb Wing, Office of Historian. Ellsworth Air Force Base, South Dakota.

"POWs in Cheyenne County, 1943-1946." Sidney, Nebraska High School Historical Society, May 11, 1980. Lincoln, Nebraska: Nebraska State Historical Society.

"Probe asked at Scribner." Omaha World-Herald. Omaha, Nebraska, June 4, 1944.

"Produce for victory. Posters on the American home front, 1941-1945." Washington, DC: Smithsonian Institution and States Humanity Council traveling display.

"Public health assessment, Cornhusker Army Ammunition Plant, Grand Island, Hall County, Nebraska." Atlanta, Georgia: Department of Health and Human Services, Agency for Toxic Substances and Disease Registry, August 1987.
Reno, Dusty. "Construction begins." Alliance (NE) Times-Herald. Alliance, Nebraska, June 25, 1976.
Richards, Carol. "Rosie the riveter went home and raised daughters to work." Iowa City Press Citizen. Iowa City, Iowa, December 9, 1988.
Richards, Robert C. Letter to author, June 3, 1991.
Schell, Ralph. "Maintaining the B-29." 16th Bombardment Group. *Anthologies*.
Scribner, Nebraska: 1871-Centennial-1971. Fremont, Nebraska: Nebraska Printing and Litho, 1971.
Second Air Force. "Emergency construction for Second Air Force accelerated program." Fort George Wright, Washington: Headquarters.
Second Air Force. "Heavy bombardment training program for Second Air Force." Fort George Wright, Washington: Headquarters, Second Air Force, March 5, 1943.
Second Air Force. "Satellite field, Ainsworth, Nebraska construction program." Fort George Wright, Washington: Headquarters, Office of the Commanding General, November 30, 1942.
Second Air Force. "Transmittal of Request for new construction." Fort George Wright, Washington: Headquarters, May 12, 1943.
Second Air Force. "Uncompleted projects and minor additions necessary for OTU and RTU programs when the peak of production is reached." Fort George Wright, Washington: Headquarters, January 18, 1943.
Sedgefield, D. *451st Bombardment Group*. Paducah, Kentucky: Turner Publishing, 1990.
Simmons, Jerald. "Public leadership in a World War II boom town: Bellevue, Nebraska." Nebraska History, Winter 1989.
Slotsky, Lawrence. Letter to author, October 1, 1991.
"Sioux Army Depot." Lincoln, Nebraska: Nebraska State Historical Society, June 1980.
Smith, Douglas E. Letter to author, July 17, 1991.
Smith, Lorena. Hastings, Nebraska. Letter to author, June 1990.
Spidle, Jr., Jake W. "Axis prisoners of war in the United States, 1942-1946: A bibliographical essay." Military Affairs, April 1970.
State Historic Preservation Office. Lincoln, Nebraska: Nebraska State Historical Society. Letter to author, May 25, 1991.
"Status of Army airfield, Ainsworth, Nebraska." Ainsworth, Nebraska: Headquarters, Army Air Field, Ainsworth, Nebraska, April 6, 1944.
Swann, Major Ralph l., USAF. "A unit history of the 315th Bomb Wing: 1944-1946." Air Command and Staff College. Montgomery, Alabama: United States Air Force Historical Research Center, Maxwell Air Force Base.
Thayer County Historical Society. "The War Department tells how new bases like Bruning Air Base are built." From the Missouri River Division, United States Army Corps of Engineers, Kansas City, Missouri. Bruning, Nebraska: The Bruning Banner, November 12, 1942.
"The Army trained canines of CBI." CBI Roundup, December 1959.
"The Glen L. Martin-Nebraska Company employment summery, the entire facility as of January 5, 1945." Lincoln, Nebraska: Glen L. Martin Company Papers, M50366. Lincoln, Nebraska: Nebraska State Historical\ Society Archives.
"The home front." Lincoln, Nebraska: Nebraska State Historical Society.
The Lincoln Star. Lincoln, Nebraska, May 18, 1942.
The Lincoln Star. Lincoln, Nebraska, May 19, 1942.
The Lincoln Star. Lincoln, Nebraska, March 20, 1942.
The Lincoln Star. Lincoln, Nebraska, March 31, 1942.
The Martin Star. Baltimore, Maryland, December 1942.
"The Naval Ammunition Depot." Historical News. Volumes 25 & 27, Number 4. Hastings, Nebraska: Adams County Nebraska Historical Society.
The Unionist. "Building D." The Unionist, February 7, 1941.
Thole, Lou. "Fairmont Army Air Field, Then and Now." Friends Bulletin. Dayton, Ohio: National Museum of the United States Air Force, Spring 1989.
Thole, Lou. "Historian of Fairmont Airfield." Nebraska Signal. Geneva, Nebraska, July 6, 1989.
Tibbets, Paul W. *Flight of the Enola Gay*. Reynolds, Ohio: Buckeye Aviation Book Company, 1989.
Twenty-fourth Biennial Report of the Department of Roads and Irrigation to the Governor of Nebraska, 1941-1942." Volume 1. Lincoln, Nebraska.
Underwood, John. Interview, Sidney, Nebraska High School Historical Society, May 11, 1990
Union Negotiation exhibits. Lincoln, Nebraska: Nebraska State Historical Society.
United States Air Force Historical Research Center. "Alliance base under command of 2nd Air Force on Sept. 1st." Montgomery, Alabama: Maxwell Air Force Base, June 1990.
United States Air Force Historical Research Center. "Bruning Army Air Field, P-47 training unit history." Montgomery, Alabama: Maxwell Air Force Base, February 1977.
United States Air Force Historical Research Center. "Fairmont Army Air Forces Base, April 1944." Montgomery, Alabama: Maxwell Air Force Base, February 1977.
United States Air Force Historical Research Center. "Fairmont Army Air Forces Base, May 1944." Montgomery, Alabama: Maxwell Air Force Base, February 1977.
United States Air Force Historical Research Center. "Fairmont Army Air Forces Base, June 1944." Montgomery, Alabama: Maxwell Air Force Base, February 1977.
United States Air Force Historical Research Center. "Fairmont Army Air Forces Base, July 1944." Montgomery, Alabama: Maxwell Air Force Base, February 1977.
United States Air Force Historical Research Center. "Fairmont Army Air Forces Base, September 1944." Montgomery, Alabama: Maxwell Air Force Base, February 1977.
United States Air Force Historical Research Center. "Fairmont Army Air Forces Base, January 1945." Montgomery, Alabama: Maxwell Air Force Base, February 1977.
United States Air Force Historical Research Center. "Fairmont Army Air Forces Base, February 1945." Montgomery, Alabama: Maxwell Air Force Base, February 1977.
United States Air Force Historical Research Center. "Fairmont Army Air Forces Base, March 1945." Montgomery, Alabama: Maxwell Air Force Base, February 1977.

United States Air Force Historical Research Center. "Fairmont Army Air Forces Base, April 1945." Montgomery, Alabama: Maxwell Air Force Base, February 1977.

United States Air Force Historical Research Center. "Lincoln Army Air Base." Montgomery, Alabama: Maxwell Air Force Base, December 1977,

United States Air Force Historical Research Center. "Message, B-29 modifications." From Williams CG 2AF Colorado Springs (171831Z) to CG 315th Wing. Montgomery, Alabama: Maxwell Air Force Base, December 1977.

United States Air Force Historical Research Center. "P-47 flight characteristics." Montgomery, Alabama: Maxwell Air Force Base, February 1977.

United States Air Force Historical Research Center. "Twenty-second Fighter Squadron, unit history, December 1943." Montgomery, Alabama: Maxwell Air Force Base, December 1977.

United States Air Force Historical Research Center. "6th Bombardment Group (H), unit history, Army Air Force Base Grand Island, Nebraska, 1 June 1944 to 3 July 1944." Montgomery, Alabama: Maxwell Air Force Base, December 1977.

United States Air Force Historical Research Center. "6th Bombardment Group (H), unit history, Army Air Force Base Grand Island, Nebraska, 1 August 1944 to 31 August 1944." Montgomery, Alabama: Maxwell Air Force Base, December 1977.

United States Air Force Historical Research Center. "9th Bombardment Group (H), unit history, June 1944." Montgomery, Alabama: Maxwell Air Force Base, December 1977.

United States Air Force Historical Research Center. "16th Bombardment Group (H), unit history, October 1944." Montgomery, Alabama: Maxwell Air Force Base, February 1977.

United States Air Force Historical Research Center. "16th Bombardment Group (H), unit history, December 1944." Montgomery, Alabama: Maxwell Air Force Base, February 1977.

United States Air Force Historical Research Center. "16th Bombardment Group (H), unit history, January 1945." Montgomery, Alabama: Maxwell Air Force Base, February 1977.

United States Air Force Historical Research Center. "36th Fighter Group, unit history." Montgomery, Alabama: Maxwell Air Force Base, February 1977.

United States Air Force Historical Research Center. "98th Bombardment Group (H), unit history, June 1945." Montgomery, Alabama: Maxwell Air Force Base, December 1977.

United States Air Force Historical Research Center. "98th Bombardment Group (H), unit history, July 1945." Montgomery, Alabama: Maxwell Air Force Base, December 1977.

United States Air Force Historical Research Center. "100th Bombardment Group H), unit history." Montgomery, Alabama: Maxwell Air Force Base, December 1977.

United States Air Force Historical Research Center. "262nd Army Air Force Base, unit history, for the period 18 March 1943 to August 1943." Montgomery, Alabama: Maxwell Air Force Base, February 1977.

United States Air Force Historical Research Center. "262nd Army Air Force Base. unit history, March 1944." Montgomery, Alabama: Maxwell Air Force Base, February 1977.

United States Air Force Historical Research Center. "262nd Army Air Force Base. unit history, April 1944." Montgomery, Alabama: Maxwell Air Force Base, February 1977.

United States Air Force Historical Research Center. "262nd Army Air Force Base. unit history, May 1944." Montgomery, Alabama: Maxwell Air Force Base, February 1977.

United States Air Force Historical Research Center. "262nd Army Air Force Base, unit history, September 1944." Montgomery, Alabama: Maxwell Air Force Base, February 1977.

United States Air Force Historical Research Center. "262nd Army Air Force Base, unit history, December 1944." Montgomery, Alabama: Maxwell Air Force Base, February 1977.

United States Air Force Historical Research Center. "262nd Army Air Force Base, unit history, January 1945." Montgomery, Alabama: Maxwell Air Force Base, February 1977.

United States Air Force Historical Research Center. "331st Bombardment Group (H), unit history, December 1944." Montgomery, Alabama: Maxwell Air Force Base, December 1977.

United States Air Force Historical Research Center. "331st Bombardment Group (H), unit history, January 1945." Montgomery, Alabama: Maxwell Air Force Base, December 1977.

United States Air Force Historical Research Center. "331st Bombardment Group (H), unit history, February 1945." Montgomery, Alabama: Maxwell Air Force Base, December 1977.

United States Air Force Historical Research Center. "447th Bombardment Group (H), unit history." Montgomery, Alabama: Maxwell Air Force Base, December 1977.

United States Air Force Historical Research Center. "451st Bombardment Group (H), unit history, Fairmont Army Air Field." Montgomery, Alabama: Maxwell Air Force Base, February 1977.

United States Air Force Historical Research Center. "456th Bombardment Group (H), unit history, September 1943." Montgomery, Alabama: Maxwell Air Force Base, February 1977.

United States Air Force Historical Research Center. "489th Bombardment Group (H), unit history. Montgomery, Alabama: Maxwell Air Force Base, December 1977.

United States Air Force Historical Research Center, "501st Bombardment Group (V.H.), unit history, December 1944." Montgomery, Alabama: Maxwell Air Force Base, December 1977.

United States Air Force Historical Research Center, "501st Bombardment Group (V.H.), unit history, January 1945." Montgomery, Alabama: Maxwell Air Force Base, December 1977.

United States Air Force Historical Research Center, "501st Bombardment Group (V.H.), unit history, February 1945." Montgomery, Alabama: Maxwell Air Force Base, December 1977.

United States Air Force Historical Research Center. "502nd Bombardment Group (V.H.), unit history for September 1944." Montgomery, Alabama: Maxwell Air Force Base, December 1977.

United States Air Force Historical Research Center. "505th Bombardment Group (H), unit history, May 1944." Montgomery, Alabama: Maxwell Air Force Base, December 1977.

United States Air Force Historical Research Center. "508th Fighter group, Bruning Army Air Forces Base, unit history." Montgomery, Alabama: Maxwell Air Force Base, February 1977.

United States Army Corps of Engineers. "After action report, Grand Island satellite field, 15 January 1943." Montgomery, Alabama: United States Air Force Historical Research Center, Maxwell Air Force Base, December 1977.

War Department. "Acquisition of land." Washington, DC: Chief of Engineers, U.S. Army, Field No. 601.1, Ainsworth, Nebraska, September 14, 1942.

War Department. "Precision bombing and air-ground gunnery ranges for Ainsworth Field, Nebraska." Washington, DC: Office of the Chief of Engineers, Ainsworth, Nebraska, November 2, 1942.

"What did you do in the war: A commemoration of Nebraska's participation In World War II" Historical Newsletter. Volume 44, Number 3, September 1991. Lincoln, Nebraska: Nebraska State Historical Society, December 8, 1991.

"What did you do in the war?" Lincoln, Nebraska: Exhibit, Nebraska State Historical Society, December 8, 1991.

Wilson, Bernice Goering, Nebraska. Letter to author, May 21, 1991.

Winkler, Allen M. *Homefront USA: America during World War II.* Illinois: Harlan Davidson, Inc., 1986. "Work on bomber field nicely started." The Ainsworth (NE) Star-Journal. Ainsworth, Nebraska, September 10, 1942.

Work Simplification Department of the Glen L. Martin-Nebraska Company. Lincoln, Nebraska: Glen L. Martin Company Papers, M50366. Lincoln, Nebraska: Nebraska State Historical Society Archives.

www.meadnebraska.officalhomepage

Zika, Richard J. Letter to author, November 2, 1991.

Zink, Mildred L., R.N. Letter to author, June 7, 1991.

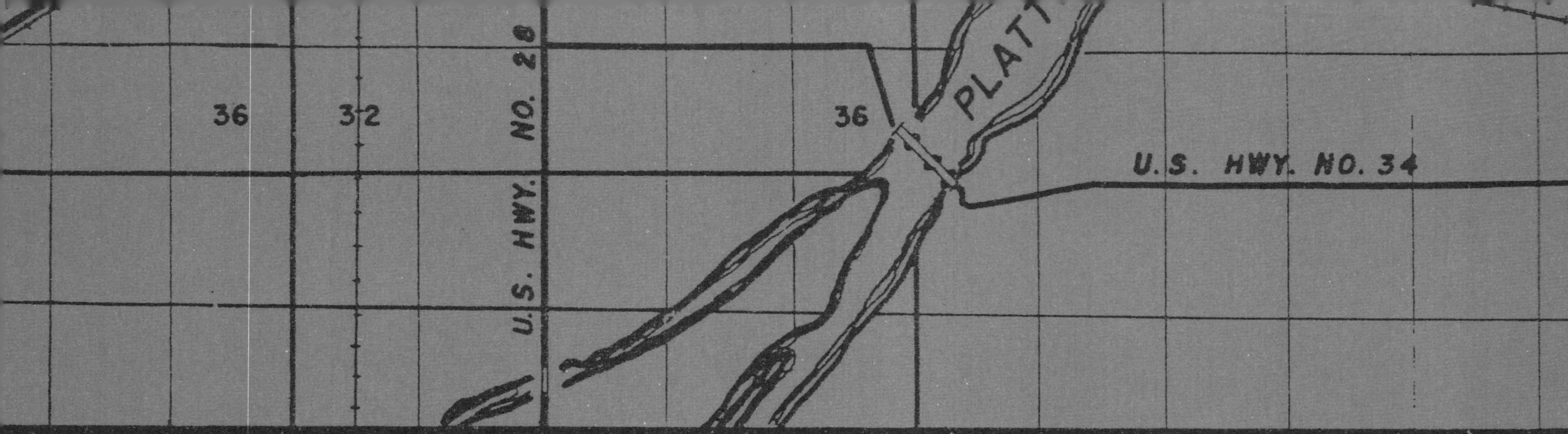

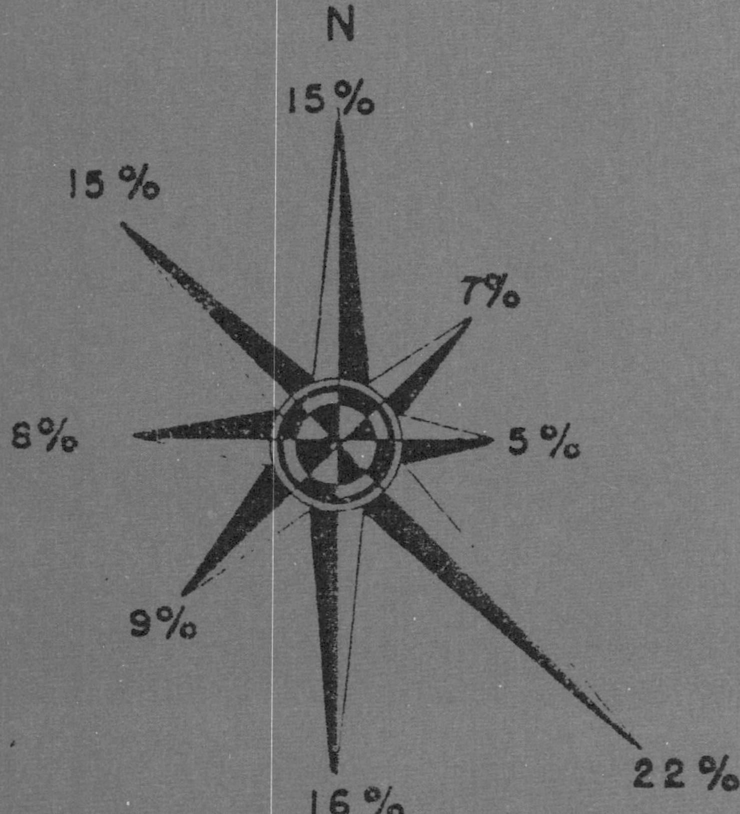

WIND ROSE

GRAND ISLAND AIRFIELD

HALL COUNTY, NEBRASKA

VICINITY MAP

ALTITUDE 1840' MSL

21

HQS. 2ND AIR FORCE, ENGR

RESTRICTED